KANT'S

Critique of Pure Reason

KANT'S
Critique of Pure Reason

BY

T. D. WELDON

FELLOW OF MAGDALEN COLLEGE
OXFORD

SECOND EDITION

OXFORD
AT THE CLARENDON PRESS
1958

Oxford University Press, Amen House, London E.C.4

GLASGOW NEW YORK TORONTO MELBOURNE WELLINGTON
BOMBAY CALCUTTA MADRAS KARACHI KUALA LUMPUR
CAPE TOWN IBADAN NAIROBI ACCRA

FIRST EDITION 1945

PRINTED IN GREAT BRITAIN

PREFACE TO THE SECOND EDITION

THE first edition of this book was finished in a hurry, under conditions not ideal for philosophical reflection, in the summer of 1940. When I returned to more or less normal life in 1944, I had forgotten too much about Kant to be capable of more than a very superficial revision of what I had previously written about him. Later on, a succession of lectures, classes, and tutorials convinced me that a fairly comprehensive rewriting was needed if the book was to do the job of explaining how the Critical Philosophy is related to live philosophical issues. In particular the summary of Kant's central argument in Part II needed far more explanatory comment than I had given it.

Bearing in mind Kant's well-known reference to the Abbé Terrasson, I have regretfully made the book a good deal longer and therefore more expensive than it was. I have not, as far as I know, changed my view as to what Kant's main aims were in writing the *Critique* or as to the arguments on which he rested his case; but I am not the best judge of this.

T. D. W.

Oxford

1957

PREFACE TO THE FIRST EDITION

THE aim of philosophers is always to understand and to interpret the achievements of scientific and other specialists in different fields. This does not mean that the philosopher should tell the scientist how to be a good scientist or the politician how to be a good politician. It would indeed be both foolish and presumptuous to inform the physicist that a particular view about the nature of space or matter cannot be correct because it has awkward metaphysical implications. Such a contention would be intelligible only if metaphysics possessed a peculiar subject-matter of its own about which it could make discoveries without reference to what occurs in other departments of knowledge. It has no such subject-matter, but its function is none the less important. It must supplement the work of the specialist not by undermining or destroying his hypotheses, a pursuit which is both unwarranted and unprofitable, but by thinking out the general view of the universe and of man's place in it which those hypotheses, if verified, must entail. Kant's claim to be a great philosopher rests on the uncommon insight and perseverance with which he devoted himself to this task.

It is not my intention in this book to add yet another to the imposing list of commentaries on the *Critique of Pure Reason* as a whole or in part which have appeared during the last twenty years. Those of Professor Paton[1] and Professor de Vleeschauwer[2] in particular are essential to any serious student of Kant, and I have learned a great deal from them. My own purpose, however, is more limited. It is to provide an introduction to Kant's Critical Philosophy and especially to draw attention to an aspect of his thought which seems to me in danger of being overlooked because of the thoroughness with which the *Critique* as a contribution to modern epistemology has been analysed and documented. It is not always remembered that since Kant was thinking and writing in 1781 and not in 1940, the material with which he was concerned differed in many important respects from that with which we are now confronted. The views of Descartes, Leibniz, and

[1] *Kant's Metaphysic of Experience* (George Allen & Unwin, 1936).

[2] *La Déduction transcendentale dans l'œuvre de Kant* (Paris, 1934).

Newton, not those of Einstein, Heisenberg, and Schrödinger, provided his problems. Hence if we are to understand and appreciate him we must begin by recalling, at least in outline, the physical and philosophical beliefs of his contemporaries and predecessors; for it is to the particular difficulties which these encounter rather than to what are vaguely called general philosophical problems that the Critical Philosophy owes its origin and development.

This is perhaps obvious, and I may be accused of merely repeating what requires no confirmation. I submit, however, that even if the importance of historical factors in determining Kant's thought is commonly admitted, their practical effect on both the method and teaching of the *Critique* itself is to a great extent overlooked. For Kant's attitude towards contemporary thought, and in particular contemporary science, is not a matter which concerns only his general approach to and treatment of metaphysics. The whole structure and detailed argument of the *Transcendental Analytic* is to a great extent determined by it. I have therefore two objects in view. The first is to help the student who is approaching Kant for the first time to realize the actual questions in which Kant was interested and the answers to them which the *Critique* puts forward. This is the purpose of Parts I and II which will, I hope, be intelligible to readers who have no previous acquaintance with Kant's writings. Part III is more detailed and presupposes familiarity with the text of the *Critique of Pure Reason* itself. It does not establish completely my view of the scope and method of the *Analytic*, but I believe that it does indicate a line of approach which is likely to be profitable and which has received too little attention hitherto.

One result of the addiction of Kant's fellow-countrymen to world wars has been that this book has taken as long to produce as did the *Critique of Pure Reason* itself. This, unfortunately, is the only respect in which the two works are comparable with one another.

T. D. W.

Oxford

1944

CONTENTS

PART III. INNER SENSE AND TRANSCENDENTAL SYNTHESIS

ABBREVIATIONS

Critique	=	*Kritik der reinen Vernunft.*
A	=	1st edition.
B	=	2nd edition.
K.P.V.	=	*Kritik der praktischen Vernunft.*
K.U.	=	*Kritik der Urteilskraft.*
Proleg.	=	*Prolegomena.*
G.	=	*Grundlegung zur Metaphysik der Sitten.*
M.A.N.	=	*Metaphysische Anfangsgründe der Naturwissenschaft.*
Ak.	=	*Akademieausgabe.*

Translations from the *Critique* are mainly from Prof. Kemp Smith's version which is now generally used by British students. I have sometimes altered them to avoid what seem to me misleading implications.

PART I

PRE-CRITICAL

I

EUROPEAN INFLUENCES

THE NEW WAY OF IDEAS

§ 1

PHILOSOPHERS have usually led uneventful lives, and in this respect at least Kant was a typical philosopher. There is no reason to suppose that his experiences, except in the strictly intellectual sphere, were of the slightest interest or importance; and if they were, we shall certainly never know it, since his biographers could discover nothing but the most meagre trivialities to record of him. Even his reading would seem to have been copious rather than exciting. Nevertheless, it would be a mistake to suppose that, like so many of his contemporaries, he was a mere pedant resenting 'enthusiasm' in all its forms; on the contrary, he thought highly of it,[1] though, apart from some isolated passages such as his tribute to Newton and Rousseau,[2] his writing showed little sign of this.[3]

No earlier philosopher stands to him as Plato did to Aristotle, and although the views of Leibniz were those which most influenced him, it would be incorrect to suppose that he was at all clearly aware of this himself. For one of the few surprising facts about his development is his reliance on second-rate disciples rather than on immediate contact with important philosophical works.[4] The result of this is that the precise problems which he

[1] *Versuch über die Krankheiten des Kopfes*, Ak. ii. 267.

[2] Hartenstein, *Kants Werke*, viii. 624 and 630.

[3] The story of his Scottish ancestry (Ak. xii. 206) is unsupported, as such stories often are (Ak. xiii. 462).

[4] His summaries of the Leibnizian position, both in the *Amphiboly of the Concepts of Reflection* (B 326–46) and in *Fortschritte der Metaphysik seit Leibniz und Wolff*, Hartenstein, viii. 519 ff., are both superficial.

was trying to solve are not easy to discover, and indeed are not discoverable without greater attention than is usually given to his work and intellectual environment at Königsberg. And that is why the belief that his philosophy, though very important, is extremely obscure and difficult to understand is widely held and is only partially justified. All serious philosophy is difficult. It consists of concentrated thought about problems which are not obviously relevant to practical life and are for that reason alone unfamiliar and hard to appreciate without considerable practice. This, however, may be at least partially concealed by the literary skill of the philosopher, though the wisdom of such concealment is open to doubt. It is so easy not to see the difficulties of Hume. But certainly Kant is uncompromising. He makes no attempt to conceal either from his reader or from himself the necessarily arduous character of the work on which he is engaged, and deliberately rejects the temptation to make it appear any more simple than it is.[5] This attitude may be misguided, but it is not culpable.

The charge against Kant, however, is not that he is difficult, but that the difficulty is superfluous and that what he had to say might have been, and therefore ought to have been, expressed in more simple and lucid terms. I believe that this charge cannot be sustained, and that those who make it fail to distinguish between two quite different inquiries, namely (1) 'What precisely were the questions which Kant was trying to answer and what was his answer to them?' and (2) 'Are Kant's answers to his questions relevant to the questions which I am trying to answer for myself?' These are both sensible, but what is not sensible is to ask 'Did Kant solve the problem of causality?' for this implies that there exist for philosophy, as there do for arithmetic, problems which have no historical context and are therefore capable of being asked and answered in the twentieth century in precisely the same terms as they might have been asked and answered by a competent calculator three hundred years before. If Kant ever set himself to calculate the square root of two to ten places of decimals, he either got the answer right or he did not, and whether he did or not, he might be properly criticized now for the clumsiness of the method which he employed. But to suppose that there is a 'problem of causality' or 'problem of the interrelation of mind and

[5] A xviii.

body' which presents itself unaltered to succeeding generations of human beings is mere moonshine. The verbal form of the question may be identical, but that is all. It is therefore neither fair nor useful to analyse the work of Kant or any other philosopher into (*a*) the eternal problems to which he was trying to find an answer, and (*b*) the historically conditioned and irrelevant form in which his answer is presented. We cannot discard the latter and retain the former, for the former have no existence. They are merely our own favourite difficulties pretending to universal and timeless relevance.

Consequently the work of any great philosopher is doubly hard to understand. His problems were intrinsically difficult, or he would not have bothered to write about them; and, in addition, we cannot even understand what they were without thoroughly grasping the process through which he went in order to formulate them as he did. If we do not take this trouble we wrongly charge him with obscurity, that is with incompetence as a philosopher, when the fault is our own.

That Kant was sometimes obscure as well as difficult I certainly do not deny, but I hold that much of what is frequently regarded as his obscurity is in fact nothing of the kind but is simply the natural and indeed the only way in which he could put what he wanted to say. I also think it unlikely that anyone will agree with me who does not approach his work historically and consider it as essentially the outcome of a development which took place over the whole of western Europe for two hundred years before the composition of the *Critique* as well as of Kant's own earlier philosophical training and outlook. It is indeed in the nature and working out of the system of Descartes that the problems of the *Critique* have their origin, and the solutions which Kant puts forward are such as would naturally occur only to one who had grown up intellectually in the rather one-sided outlook which dominated Europe in the seventeenth and eighteenth centuries.

For the history of philosophy from Descartes to Kant has a unity of its own, even though it must be admitted that any division of the history of philosophy into 'periods' involves some degree of false abstraction. This unity depends mainly on the almost universal acceptance by educated people of the claims of the new method of mathematical physics to interpret the universe and explain man's place in it. The extent of this acceptance can hardly be exaggerated, and was perhaps attributable not merely to the obvious success of the method in practice but also to the absence of any serious competitor. Evolutionary biology had not yet arisen to give an even ruder shock than the physics of Galileo had done to accepted theological presuppositions.

The relative compactness of the period is further emphasized by the personalities of Descartes and Kant themselves. Each of them commenced serious study as a physicist rather than as a philosopher in the modern sense, and each of them was driven by the necessity of his own thought to come to terms with the philosophical problems from which physics can never escape. There is a striking similarity between Descartes's somewhat apologetic assertion[6] that everyone ought to go through the process of rigorous doubting and reassurance once in his life and Kant's contention[7] that there is no metaphysical problem to which the answer is not provided in the *Critique*; and the thought which underlies these pronouncements runs through the whole period. Substantially it is that the future lies with natural philosophy and above all with mathematical physics. Metaphysics is indeed of vital importance since it is the foundation on which the whole superstructure must rest, but just because of this it is of comparatively modest dimensions[8] and can be mastered once and for all when clearly stated and attentively examined. It is difficult since it involves a high level of abstraction, but those who find this an obstacle should remember, as Kant is careful to remind them, that it is by no means necessary for them to study it.[9]

§ 2

Although there are no philosophical 'problems' which lie about like uncompleted crossword puzzles set by God to baffle successive generations of professional philosophers, it may fairly be held that there is at least a family likeness between the questions to which men of European culture have thought it worth while to look for answers during the last two thousand years. These may very roughly be grouped as questions concerned with God, the self, and the physical universe. But the emphasis which has been laid

[6] Descartes, *Prin.*, pt. i, § 1; cf. *Med.* I ad init. and *Regulae*, VIII.
[7] A xiii.
[8] A xx; B 23.
[9] *Proleg. Preface*, Ak. iv. 263.

on one or another of these topics has varied very considerably. Throughout the Middle Ages the third had naturally occupied a very subordinate place indeed, and it was in restoring it to a position comparable in importance to that claimed by the other two that the philosophical revolution of Descartes ultimately consisted. So thoroughly, however, did he and his contemporaries do their work that the general prima-facie view of the universe held by the educated inquirer as a preliminary to detailed investigation into metaphysics, psychology, or physics changed hardly at all for a period of two hundred years. Indeed we may go further and say that even now it has not changed beyond recognition, and that the uncritical view of the educated man today is far more closely akin to that of Descartes than the Cartesian view itself was to the Scholastic position which it superseded.

Certainly biology has made a great difference and has led to the reconsideration if not to the actual reintroduction of those substantial forms and occult qualities to which the philosophers of the seventeenth and eighteenth centuries professed such uncompromising hostility; and certainly, too, this further development has seriously impaired the admirable simplicity of the Cartesian system. None the less, a great deal of it remains in principle unchallenged.

The general notion of the physical universe propounded by Descartes and his successors was atomic. This did not imply in the seventeenth century, any more than it does now, the conception of an enormously large number of minute inelastic billiard balls perpetually colliding with one another and creating the objects which we perceive by their endless rearrangements. Indeed no such view could have been put forward as a completed picture without meeting the criticism that it involved accepting an Epicurean materialism which was theologically indefensible. Nevertheless, it is not unfair to say that the first rough draft which had to be worked over and improved upon before it could be finally offered to the public was something on these lines. At least it was universally agreed that there are minute parts of matter which physically affect our sense organs and by so doing convey to us something of the character of the material world, and further that all the bodies which together make up that physical universe behave in accordance with absolutely rigid mechanical laws which are capable of being discovered by the human mind.

The discovery of these laws was held to occur partly as the result of the operation of pure thought quite independently of any acquaintance with phenomena, but partly also as a result of observation. The ultimate aim of all investigation was to substitute precise mathematical formulae for the qualitative conceptions of the Schoolmen. In the first flush of their enthusiasm for this revolutionary way of studying nature investigators saw no reason why there should be any limit to its applicability. Mechanics,[10] optics, and astronomy were easily shown to yield results of overwhelming interest when attacked by the new method; medicine, anatomy, and physiology offered a further field; and it seemed possible that even chemistry might some day be brought within the sphere of rational knowledge. These, however, were early aspirations. By the end of the eighteenth century doubts were already prevalent as to the extent to which mechanical explanations could go; and it was Hume's sceptical inquiry as to whether, in the last resort, they could honestly be said to explain anything at all which woke Kant from his dogmatic slumbers and gave the *Critique* its central theme.

The self or soul was conceived as essentially distinct from the material world, though standing in a vital and more or less unintelligible relation to it. In so far as its operations of thinking, perceiving, and willing did not admit of direct quantitative assessment, they were not very promising material for the new method, and it must be admitted that, on the Continent in particular, the mind tended to be of interest rather as the machinery by which the new knowledge could be acquired than as an object of study in itself. To a more limited extent the same may be said of God. Admittedly no considerable philosopher was an avowed atheist, but, on the other hand, the philosophical importance of the Deity depended very largely on the extent to which the problem of the interaction of mind and body was allowed by any particular philosopher to become a major issue. From a metaphysical standpoint, which was regarded as entirely distinct from that of revealed religion, God was conceived as a *deus in machina*. His function was to bridge the gaps and occasionally also to provide the motive power of the entire contrivance. Thus the universe was openly conceived as a gigantic piece of machinery, comprehensible in principle though not necessarily in detail to the human mind. It

[10] Cf. Boyce Gibson, *Philosophy of Descartes*, p. 186.

was certainly the work or at least the expression of God and bore clearly on it the marks of its divine origin. The more theological philosophers were never weary of drawing attention to the exquisite skill displayed in its workmanship, though they were not always equally ready to acknowledge its apparent defects—for indeed it was for a long time uncertain whether it was more in keeping with theology to regard the machine as so perfect that, once created, it required no further attention, which for practical purposes would make God philosophically irrelevant, or to regard it as perpetually in need of his support, which would reflect somewhat on his mechanical competence.

§ 3

This summary of a general point of view or attitude towards reality needs development and specification in terms of the actual views maintained by some of Kant's more important predecessors. Before we proceed to this task, however, it is well to consider the main issues to which the view, however generally formulated, is bound to give rise. Of these the first and enormously the most important is the problem of interaction. For if once we grant (and it is absolutely vital to the success of the mechanical method that we should grant) the distinction in kind between what happens in the soul or conscious self and what happens in the material world, we are bound to ask how it is even conceivable that the one should have any connexion with the other at all. Matter, in order to be mathematically determinable, is conceived as just extended, mobile stuff devoid of any perceptible qualities except those with which geometry is competent to deal. Mind, on the other hand, is conceived as necessarily immaterial and non-extended. How, then, can mind by its willing impart motion to matter or matter by its impact produce perceptions in mind? Even the intervention of God as a prime mover to set matter in motion is prima facie inconceivable, since God, too, is necessarily immaterial. This leads to a second serious though less apparent difficulty, namely what account, if any, can we offer of the status of sensation?

The mechanist conception is bound to distinguish sharply the sensible qualitative characteristics of material things from their true or essential characteristics which are purely quantitative. This naturally suggests the conclusion that sensibility is a tiresome and irrelevant intruder which does nothing but interfere with the orderly process by which mind comes to know its proper object, but here the other main tenet of the view stands in the way. For experiment as well as mathematical calculation is necessary to give us knowledge, and without observation of results which is unavoidably sensuous in character, experiment is unlikely to be of any great assistance. Sensation is very troublesome, and Kant, like his predecessors, found great difficulty in including it in his final scheme of things.

Finally there is a problem of a different and more obvious kind, namely that of human free will. For if the material universe is really a machine controlled by eternal and unalterable laws of whose existence and nature we can be as certain as we are of the validity of elementary arithmetic, it is not easy to see how either the freedom of man to determine his own action or the omnipotence of God in relation to the self and the world can any longer be maintained.

§ 4

The result of any attempt to classify the influences which have operated in the formation of the completed system of a philosopher is inevitably arbitrary. There is, indeed, the best of evidence for the conclusion that in this as in other matters men are bad judges in their own causes, and it frequently happens that the most obvious influence is missed altogether simply because it is so obvious. In the case of Kant there is a special reason for making the attempt, because the philosophers with whose works he was most closely acquainted were not those whose works have continued to be generally read by students of philosophy. The latter, however, are often mistakenly regarded as the principal source of his inspiration. The plain truth is rather that no trace is discoverable in Kant's works of anything which we should now regard as a detailed knowledge of the actual writings of any of the four philosophers with whom we are first concerned, namely Descartes, Leibniz, Locke, and Hume. This is not intended to suggest that he had no direct acquaintance with their works, though it would of course be rash to assume that he had anything like the same degree of access to them as the modern student takes for granted. This is not really surprising, since the works of Descartes and

Leibniz were simply not available to him in anything like complete collected form, and it is highly improbable that he was able to read English sufficiently well to enable him to study Locke or Hume in the original. Consequently his knowledge of Hume did not include any acquaintance with the *Treatise*.

But though Kant's acquaintance with what we now tend to regard as the primary sources of his philosophical inspiration was general rather than detailed, his minute study of the eighteenth-century German philosophy in which he was himself educated and on which he lectured throughout his active academic life is unquestionable. The metaphysical works of Wolff and Baumgarten and the *Vernunftlehre* of Meier were his daily bread—indeed he must have known them by heart. It is true that even these authors are mentioned but little by name in his major works, but this should not lead us to forget that their opinions were always and inevitably his starting-point. On many vital issues he disagreed with and refuted them, but what is more important is that where he did agree with them he was fatally liable to suppose that no serious difficulty existed. If, therefore, we are to achieve any real insight into what Kant took for granted (which is a considerable part of his view), it is in Baumgarten, Wolff, and Meier that we are most likely to discover it rather than in the leading works of the first-class philosophers. It might, indeed, be argued that there were many other and better German philosophers in the eighteenth century with whom Kant was acquainted and who exercised a considerable influence on his thought. Moses Mendelssohn, Tetens, and Lambert, to name only three, were in a far higher class than the tedious Baumgarten. This is true, but not to the point. The justification for dealing in detail with the views of these obsolete philosophers is mainly that they were so inferior that hardly any trace of them now remains and that, to English readers in particular, their doctrines are entirely unknown. There is nothing in the English thought of the eighteenth century which corresponds to them at all, and indeed their only claim to resurrection is the influence which they exercised on the development of Kant.

Some explanation may seem to be required for the omission from all consideration of the views of Spinoza and Berkeley. This is not wholly due to considerations of space. As regards the former, his works had little direct influence in Germany till they were brought into prominence by the Lessing–Jacobi controversy in the 1780's, and there is no reason for supposing that Kant had submitted them to any careful study. As regards Berkeley it is true that Kant mentions him both in the *Critique* and the *Prolegomena*, but always as a typical rather than an actual philosopher. He is 'the good Berkeley'[11] who, as a result of his failure to apprehend the true nature of space, became a hopeless idealist and 'reduced bodies to mere illusions'. This does not suggest that Kant had ever read, let alone carefully studied, Berkeley's view. Most probably he was acquainted with it only through the extremely misleading account given in Beattie's *Essay on Truth*,[12] with which he was certainly familiar.[13]

DESCARTES

§ 1

The central doctrine of the Cartesian philosophy is that physics, under which is included the whole of what we now call natural science, must be mathematical in its method if it is to achieve true and valuable results. In his attempt to prove this doctrine Descartes is led to formulate those views of God, the self, the material world, and the connexion or lack of it between them, for which he is now chiefly remembered.

But before we examine his view a caution is necessary which applies, though with somewhat less force, to all his successors with whom we shall be concerned. It must always be borne in mind that neither Descartes nor any other human being began philosophizing in a void. On the contrary, he was well versed in one of the most influential systems which has ever been worked out, namely that of St. Thomas Aquinas with which he found himself in complete disagreement on a number of major issues. Philosophy, however, is not merely a matter of views; for we cannot even reach a view without going through a process of more or less complex thinking. This thinking is conceptual in character, and the conclusions which it reaches are largely determined by its initial assumptions. Those assumptions, as Kant was the first to emphasize, are implied by the very nature of our thinking,

[11] B 71.

[12] James Beattie, *An Essay on the Nature and Immutability of Truth*, 1771, pt. ii, chap. ii.

[13] Ak. iv. 259.

but since the discovery of them involves an exhaustive inquiry into the foundations of our logical procedure, their existence tends to pass unobserved. In the philosophical thinking of Aquinas there were in particular two such assumptions on which his whole system ultimately rested, namely the notions of substance and essence. The mechanistic philosophers of the seventeenth and eighteenth centuries all more or less unconsciously retained these notions, and attempted to found on them an entirely different system.[14] Their doing so is simply another instance of the tendency, already noticed in Kant, to retain uncritically those elements in a received system which are not openly at variance with newer methods of thought, but it was of far-reaching importance in determining the development of their various doctrines.

Descartes, then, accepted without question the traditional view that everything which exists can be analysed into substance and essence, which between them constitute its reality, and that in addition to being these, it may be found to possess certain more or less accidental properties and relations known as modes. His revolution lay in an entirely different conception of what in fact were the substances, essences, and modes of things. St. Thomas had maintained that substance, or that which truly exists in its own right and which needs nothing further to support it in existence, such as a tree or a table as contrasted with a colour or a relation, was a union of form with matter. Thus the true reality of any particular thing was the embodiment in it of a form or species, and knowledge consisted in the apprehension by the mind of that species. To enable it to do this the mind was endowed with the power of making actual or explicit the nature of the species immediately apprehended in sense perception, and the method of science became primarily an analysis of sense experience with a view to discovering what elements in the perception of an object belonged to its species, that is, constituted its real essence, and what were merely accidents or modes. Thus it might be discovered that the species man involves as part of its essence the possession of reason, whereas the possession of red hair is merely an accident to it. It is a natural corollary of this view that there is to be found in nature only a limited number of substantial forms, and that these have been unalterably determined by the divine will.

It is erroneous to regard this theory as primitive or unsatisfac-

[14] Cf. Boyce Gibson, op. cit., p. 164.

tory in itself, since many of its leading features though exorcized by the physicists have subsequently been reintroduced under thin disguises by the biologists of the nineteenth and twentieth centuries. Nevertheless when held in an obscurantist spirit it was liable seriously to interfere with the freedom of investigation on purely mathematical lines, and it must be admitted that the Church, in the early seventeenth century in particular, was naturally rather doubtful as to how far such investigation could be allowed to go without becoming a menace to revealed theology with which the view of Aquinas was inextricably intertwined.

§ 2

We are now in a position to consider the extent and also the limitations of the change in the traditional philosophy which Cartesianism produced, and the most convenient point from which to set out is the problem of perception in relation to knowledge. Aquinas and his followers maintained that the data of perception, when abstracted and refined by the intellect, were in fact knowledge. Hence for them sensibility was an essential element in the process of coming to know the real. In this respect Cartesianism is from the very start unalterably opposed to the traditional view in maintaining that the data of perception provide us with a false and not a true representation of real things. Indeed, no other position was logically tenable by the new philosophy, for if knowledge of the real must in the end be mathematical, it follows that the real, in so far as it is knowable, must be susceptible of mathematical treatment. The data of the special senses, however, colours, sounds, &c., do not directly admit of such treatment, and consequently they cannot as such be objects of scientific knowledge at all. They are intelligible only in so far as we regard them as the effects or perhaps the concomitants in consciousness of something of an entirely different nature from themselves which can be treated mathematically and therefore can establish a prima-facie claim to be regarded as independently real. This conclusion was entirely in harmony with the results of the gradually evolving science of optics as well as with the physiological theory of perception, and it led naturally to the further notion that the physically real was nothing but material particles in motion, and that these particles by their impact on the sense organs produced somehow in consciousness the immediate data of sense.

This leads to a further drastic revision of the traditional system, since it is no longer possible to regard the reality of an object as being bound up with the presence in it of a particular sensible form. On the contrary, its reality must now be looked for in the material particles of which it is composed, and as all bodies, *qua* mathematically cognizable, must be held to consist of material particles, it follows that the question to be answered if we are to determine what substance is becomes simply: what is the essential characteristic of matter? This is only half the problem. For what is postulated is not merely that things can be known by mathematical reasoning, but also that there are beings capable of reasoning mathematically about them.

This method of formulation suggests immediately the existence of a non-material substance or mind entirely distinct from the material substance or matter which in scientific investigation it is attempting to know, and this is what Descartes in fact maintained; but, having gone so far, he fell back without a struggle into the view which he was criticizing. He rejected substantial forms and thereby immensely simplified the general conception of the universe; but he accepted the view that every independent real or substantial thing must have a real essence which makes it what it is, and that this essence is somehow differentiated into ways or modes of existence. For the innumerable kinds of scholastic substance he substitutes two only, namely material and immaterial. Each of these is held to possess only a single essential characteristic: immaterial substance is conscious, material substance is extended, and these essences are further specified into modes, e.g. willing, perceiving, figure.

From this position two vital consequences followed. In the first place all the properties of body were so unequivocally distinct from those of mind that any interaction between the two different kinds of substance was by definition inconceivable; and in the second, mind or thinking substance was, also by definition, more immediately knowable than body. But the knowability of body was precisely what Descartes wanted to assert, and indeed his whole metaphysics from first to last is aimed at demonstrating it.

There can, however, be no empirical demonstration, since that in body which is knowable, namely the relations and motions of minute particles, is simply not an object of sense at all. Hence the proof must be *a priori*. The immediate certainty of my own existence is held to be a ground for demonstrating the existence of God, and when this has been done the veracity which belongs necessarily to God precludes me from doubting the validity of the mathematical method. Here again it may be noted that Descartes was quite prepared to accept rather easily the methods and demonstrations of the Schools provided that they were not inconsistent with what he held to be the truth. There is not the slightest ground for charging him with hypocrisy in this respect, nor can it be plausibly argued that the introduction of God into the system was a mere evasion to satisfy contemporary theological prejudice. All the evidence goes to show that Descartes was throughout his life a perfectly sincere Catholic, and although it is true that his physical theory is quite tenable independently of his proofs of God's existence, this point is in itself irrelevant. What is clear is that, apart from his theological excursus, his physics would wholly have lacked metaphysical support and have remained merely a tentative hypothesis, and this was precisely what he wanted to avoid.

§ 3

The working out of this essentially simple metaphysical view requires some further consideration. We have to start with material and immaterial substance and with God who creates both and somehow holds them together in spite of their irreconcilable diversity. Material substance has one essential property and one only, namely that of extension, and the implications of this doctrine are of considerable importance and interest. In the first place, matter must be held to be wholly inert, its only necessary attribute is extension and it cannot therefore be held to contain in itself any active power whatever. Secondly, there can be no void or empty space, since as extension is the essence of matter there can be no extension which is immaterial any more than there can be anything material which is not extended; and from this it follows that there can be no limits or bounds to extended substance, since that which bounded it could be conceived only as empty space which *ex hypothesi* has no existence. Thirdly, motion does not belong to the essence of matter; but neither is it consistent with the new physics to treat it as a mere accident or mode of matter, though Descartes himself sometimes makes this mistake; therefore motion must be regarded as simply an ultimate fact introduced into the material universe by the miraculous agency of God. And lastly, the conception of extension as the sole essence of material things implies that all divisions within extension are in the end illusory. They are what Descartes described as *entia rationis*, and are to be regarded as mere modes or accidental determinations of a single indivisible extended substance.

As contrasted with material substance thinking substance is conceived as pluralistic. There is a multiplicity of finite and mutually independent thinking substances known as selves. Each of these has consciousness as its essence, and, again in contrast to material substance, is non-extended and active. Its modes are thinking and willing, which belong to it in its own right, and also sensing, which arises in a manner which to us must remain completely mysterious from its union with the body of which, again in accordance with the traditional view to which in this connexion Descartes sees no particular objection, it is actually the substantial form.

As before mentioned the self is naturally better known than body ever can be, not in the sense that we can formulate a greater number of indubitable propositions about it, for this is not the case, but in the sense that its actual existence cannot logically be called into question whereas that of the body and of extended substance can be. In other words the idea of extension which I reason about in physics might be produced in my consciousness by God (as Berkeley subsequently held that it was) without there being at the same time a real extended substance to correspond to it, but the line of thought which culminates in the formulation of the *cogito* satisfies us that no similar possibility exists in relation to myself.

The place filled by God in the system needs no further exposition. Apart from his functions of guaranteeing the validity of my physical knowledge, introducing motion into the otherwise inert mass of extended substance, and miraculously combining mind and body into a single whole, he is conceived strictly on the traditional model (as omnipotent, omniscient, &c.). But it must always be emphasized that the performance by him of those functions is absolutely vital to the existence of Descartes's metaphysical system.

§ 4

Cartesianism alters radically the purpose as well as the method of philosophical inquiry. Metaphysics is no longer to be conceived as a straightforward extension of physics concerned with being in general as distinct from being of a particular kind, nor is it merely the handmaiden of theology. Its aim is rather to mediate between the two studies and to show that their fundamental propositions, far from being inconsistent with one another, are mutually supporting elements in the whole system of the universe. To do this successfully, however, it must show that there is some intelligible connexion between the world of physics and that of theology, and in this respect it must be admitted that the metaphysics of Descartes is far from successful. It shows no link whatever between the notion of extended substance and that of particular bodies, nor in the end did its originator believe that it could do so; and it does not establish anything but an alleged miracle to mediate between God's creative activity and the causal efficacy of those particular bodies. What it does achieve is the inauguration of a distinction which, though it might have been unwelcome to the author himself, is of the utmost importance in the subsequent development of physical and metaphysical thought. For what emerges clearly from his whole view is that the new physics differs from the old in asking rather how things happen than why they happen. Its aim is to discover the laws of the physical world, and it is not interested in the secret or hidden powers of nature except in so far as they cease to be either secret or hidden and become mere exemplifications of a universal law. Theology, on the other hand, was and must remain interested in the 'why?', and consequently there remains between physics and theology a gap which metaphysics must attempt to fill. Physics investigates how bodies affect one another, but is not required to explain why they should; theology can explain why there is extended substance (God created it) but cannot explain how it becomes differentiated into particular bodies or particles. But in these circumstances to say that God introduced motion as such into extended substance as such is no explanation of anything. Extension as a whole obviously does not move, and to argue that God communicated specific motions to specific parts of extension is simply to beg the whole question and to leave the divergent views as far apart as ever.

Similarly the two-substance or mind-body dualism which is so basic to the entire Cartesian system makes the question 'What is the relation between physical and psychological events?' logically insoluble. There just cannot be any such relation, though Descartes and his successors were perfectly well aware that, in some sense, there is. Hence a further miracle has to be postulated to 'explain' it.

Finally there is the problem of sense perception. The basis of the whole Cartesian position is that mathematics alone can give us genuine knowledge, and that it can do so in virtue of the clearness and distinctness of the notions which it employs and of the necessary relations which subsist between them. But sense perception never possesses clearness and distinction of this order, and if we use it as a basis for demonstration we tend to fall into error. Yet it has to be admitted that we do and must start from perception in our physical inquiries and that even geometry requires some sensuous apprehension as its starting-point. Here again Descartes gives no help to the solution of the problem of how the cognitive faculty which belongs to the self can be brought into connexion with the facts of empirical or *a priori* cognition. Metaphysically he is committed to the view that nothing but what I clearly and distinctly perceive is certainly true, but as an actual scientific investigator he must make use of sense perception. Hence he tends to adopt the view (contrary again to traditional metaphysics) that all clear and distinct ideas are innate in the mind, that is, are miraculously imparted to it at its creation by God, and that sensibility does no more than furnish the occasion for their becoming explicit. This, too, is unhelpful; though it is interesting to observe that a like distinction between sensibility and understanding had formerly led Plato to a precisely similar declaration of philosophical bankruptcy.

LEIBNIZ

§ 1

The position of Leibniz both in physics and in metaphysics is a development of the views of Descartes, though it involves no essential modification of the general seventeenth-century outlook.

Metaphysical speculation is regarded, though not explicitly, as reconciling the method and discoveries of physics with revealed theological truth to their mutual advantage. For Leibniz, like Descartes, was not content to regard physics as a purely hypothetical science concerned merely to demonstrate empirically how things happen, he believed that the more ultimate question why they happen must be both asked and answered if science was to be secure in its possessions.

Hence his physics must be based immediately on metaphysics and ultimately on revelation. It must be admitted that Leibniz in common with all pre-Kantian thinkers frequently failed to draw any clear distinction between physical and metaphysical conceptions and that this failure is extremely detrimental to the intelligibility of his views. It is clear, however, that his first doubts as to the capacity of either Cartesianism or any form of physical atomism to provide a satisfactory account of reality arose from metaphysical rather than experimental considerations. Briefly, he was convinced that the physical world must consist of substances, and by substances he meant things which possess an intrinsic and not merely a conventional unity.

Obviously we may choose to regard an army, a heap of stones, or a collection of postage stamps as 'one', but there is at least a good prima-facie case for maintaining that such unity as they possess is the product of an arbitrary decision on the part of an observer rather than a characteristic of the things themselves. A particular man or animal seems at least to be a unity in a different and more important sense.

Now if this distinction is borne in mind it becomes clear that neither Cartesianism nor atomism can consistently admit that the physical universe contains or consists of substances, for both are committed to the view that it is essentially spatial. Space, however, has two characteristics which are incompatible with the existence in it of real substances. In the first place it is divisible without limit, and in the second its parts are all completely indifferent to one another. They can be interchanged without the slightest difference being made to the whole. Hence it seems clear that any whole which is spatial must be simply an aggregate or conventional unit, and consequently that Descartes must be mistaken in maintaining both that the physical world is substantial and that its essence is extension; strictly speaking, the phrase *res extensa* involves a contradiction unless *res* means merely 'what is regarded by custom or convention as one thing'. But Descartes certainly did not mean that.

This *a-priori* criticism is emphasized by experimental evidence. For, if the Cartesian theory is correct, it follows that material things, since they have no essential property other than extension, must be wholly inert and immobile. Motion must be introduced into the system entirely *ab extra*, by a miracle, and when it is so introduced, the quantity of it will necessarily remain unchanged. It is essential for Descartes to hold that in a physical system the quantity of motion is constant.

It is easy to show that this assumption is inadequate to give a complete account of the facts, and on purely empirical grounds it is found necessary to maintain that *vis viva*, not motion, is what is conserved.[15] Hence, if Descartes's view is to be maintained, the interference of the *deus ex machina* cannot be restricted to the mere introduction of a quantity of motion into an extended mass, but would have to be continuous and complicated in character; and since *miracula non sunt multiplicanda praeter necessitatem*, it is urgent to provide an account of the nature of things which will explain the conservation of *vis viva* on rational grounds.

Thus the problem of Leibniz may be formulated in the question, 'What account can we offer of the universe which will avoid (*a*) the metaphysical, (*b*) the physical problems to which Cartesianism gives rise?' His answer lies in the doctrine which he offers of the unit of substance or monad. We have already seen that if this is to be a real and not merely a fictitious unit, it must be conceived as non-spatial, and that if it is to serve as a satisfactory basis for physics it must be conceived as active. The question is whether we can conceive anything which satisfies these conditions, and the answer is at once given if we turn for a moment away from the physical universe and consider the character of the self. For here we have at once an entity not extended in space (though admittedly connected somehow with a body which is), and active both in thinking and willing. It may therefore be profitable to consider the possibility of conceiving the whole universe, not as a mass of

[15] Cf. *Leibniz. Mathematische Schriften*, Gerhardt, vi. 117 ff.; Latta, *Leibniz*, pp. 89–93; Leibniz, *Discourse on Metaphysics*, English translation, Lucas & Brint, pp. xxiii–xxv.

extended inert matter, but as consisting wholly of substances analogous to what we call our selves.

At this point caution is necessary. It might be supposed that what Leibniz wanted to do was to improve the Cartesian system simply by eliminating *res extensa* and filling the universe entirely with *res cogitantes*. This is partly true, but it should be noticed that the monads of Leibniz differ from the selves of Descartes in a vital respect. They are active indeed, but not wholly active. In fact, what is suggested is that the Cartesian view is vitiated by a double error. It maintains on the one hand that matter is bare extension and therefore wholly inactive, and on the other that mind is pure thought and therefore wholly active. From this arises the complete dualism of the two substances and the enigmatic position of sense perception which cannot properly belong to either. As against this, what Leibniz wishes to maintain is that the self is active in thinking and willing, but only in so far as its thought is clear and distinct. Confused thought, and the willing which depends on it, are passivity, and sense perception is confused and obscure thought.

Thus by reflection on the self we are led to suppose that the monad or substantial unit of which it is to be the type includes both activity and passivity within itself. These are named by Leibniz *entelechy* and *materia prima* respectively, and it is to be observed that neither of them, considered in abstraction from the other, has any real existence. Leibniz's criticism of Descartes's philosophy is that it is based on two abstractions, bare mind and bare extension, instead of on a concrete view of the nature of substance.

But suppose it is granted that instances of monads are to be found in selves, can it plausibly be maintained that the physical universe consists of them and not of things essentially extended?

At this point Leibniz fell a victim to inadequate knowledge of facts, and his mistake certainly adds to the initial plausibility of his view, though the discovery of it does not actually refute him. He certainly believed that any particle of matter, however minute, could be found to contain microscopic organisms and that therefore the belief of the plain man in the existence of completely inorganic matter was a mere mistake, due simply to confused perception. This view, though it lends colour to the suggestion that the physical universe may consist of entities analogous to selves, does not by any means escape difficulty, for even microbes occupy space and therefore are not strictly monadic in character. Hence a further complication must be introduced.

The monad consists of *entelechy* and *materia prima*. It is non-spatial and must therefore be regarded as an object of thought. It cannot be imagined. Some account, however, must be offered of the bodies which we do perceive by sense and imagination, and to do this Leibniz introduces the notion of *materia secunda*. What this involves may be best understood by further reference to the Leibnizian doctrine of the self, and to the two distinct senses in which he holds that the soul may be said to 'have a body'. The first of these has already been mentioned. Strictly speaking I am a simple substance differentiated into *entelechy* and *materia prima*, activity and passivity; but this monad, which is myself, is related in a specially intimate way to what is called my body, and it is this body which is a physical object subject to physical laws. But we have already seen that this body properly considered is not bare *res extensa*. If it were, it would be a mere aggregate, a false abstraction indistinguishable from *materia prima*. It must rather be held to consist of an infinite number of minute living things each of which on investigation will be revealed as a monad (*entelechy* and *materia prima*) related to a body. Body is thus simply the unanalysed residuum of our perception. It is called *materia secunda*, and, in the last analysis, it is an abstraction. More accurately it is what Leibniz calls phenomenon or appearance, not mere illusion, but rather reality confusedly perceived (*phaenomenon bene fundatum*).

Hence Leibniz's complete account of an individual man runs somewhat as follows:

1. Inasmuch as he is an actual and not merely a conventional unit, he must be conceived as a monad.
2. This monad is related to an infinite number of other monads which it 'dominates' and which together make up the physical body.
3. The relation of dominant and subordinate may occur over again among the monads constituting the body, since it does so by definition wherever we have a genuine unity or whole which is not merely an aggregate.

§ 2

On the face of it this view gives rise to two questions. In the first place, we are told that the essence of monads is not extension but activity. But of what kind is the activity? Evidently it cannot be conceived as *vis viva* in the physical sense, since this necessarily involves the characteristics of velocity and mass which cannot be attributed to monad as such at all. Secondly, in view of this criticism, how can Leibniz hold that his theory is capable of developing or of contributing to the physical theory of Cartesianism at all? It certainly seems that, as metaphysics, his doctrine avoids the Cartesian dualism of mind and matter by maintaining that both are in the end false abstractions, and that both are involved in any actual substance; but if this is achieved only at the expense of making all physical speculation barren, it might fairly be held that he was merely a reactionary attempting to smuggle back into philosophy under a new terminology the substantial forms of the Schoolmen which Descartes claimed to have disposed of for ever in the interest of clear and distinct thinking.

Further, it may be argued that, metaphysically considered, the Leibnizian position is far from satisfactory, since no account has yet been given, except in highly metaphorical terms, of the relations which hold between monads themselves; for 'dominance' and 'subordination' are unhelpful and in any case tell us nothing of the way in which selves are related (*a*) to one another, (*b*) to those monadic or aggregational wholes which are not strictly selves, and which are generally called animals and physical things.

Obviously the character of the monad requires further elucidation if it is to be a satisfactory basis for either physical or metaphysical theory, and this elucidation is most easily understood if it is first approached from the physical side.

We have seen that, according to Leibniz, all actual physical things are constituted solely of monads, and these monads, though infinite in number, could never fill the smallest space since they are by definition non-spatial. Furthermore, we know that physical things are not merely spatial since physical science is constrained to regard them as somehow active or possessed of *vis viva*. One is therefore tempted to suppose Leibniz to have maintained that the *vis viva* of physical things arises from the presence in them of monads in the sense in which currants are present in a cake or fish in a pond. This is mistaken—even though Leibniz himself sometimes used language which is capable of such an interpretation; for it is obvious that from this point of view monads must be the foundation of bodies and not elements in them.[16] Bodies are *phaenomena bene fundata,* and the monadic structure of the real world provides only the metaphysical basis of the physical or mechanical laws in accordance with which all phenomena must be explained. All physical laws involve space, time, substance, and causality, but all these are, for Leibniz, relations involving sense or imagination. No world which includes them can be real as such or in itself, but they may well be actual characteristics of a real world obscurely or imperfectly apprehended. These relations cannot hold between genuine substances, but are not therefore to be relegated to a world of mere illusion. They are valid of phenomena, and phenomena are grounded in monads.

It is clear that if this is to be more than a pious hope, some account must be given of the relations between monads to which relations between phenomena correspond or which they obscurely represent, and also some explanation of the notion of correspondence or representation. To take the second point first, it can hardly be questioned that 'representation' is in the end the fundamental conception of the Leibnizian philosophy; though opinions differ as to whether we should regard the introduction of it as a stroke of genius or a philosophical disaster. As it is a conception common to Leibniz and his successors, including especially Kant, it is examined more thoroughly at a later stage and no more than a general indication of its meaning is given at this point. It is, however, essential to recognize from the outset that while a representation is not conceived as a simple copy or mirror-image of its original, there is a discoverable and point-for-point relation between what is represented and the representation of it. Thus on an empirical level, a curve would be said to represent the equation which it expresses, and more obviously the impression of a seal on a piece of wax would be a representation of the seal. An important aspect of the doctrine and one which perhaps historically was responsible for the Leibnizian concentration on it is its bearing on causality; for if, in accordance with the scholastic view, there can be nothing in the effect which was not previously in the cause,

[16] Leibniz, *Metaphysische Abhandlung*, 1686, § 18.

any effect can properly be regarded as the representation or resemblance of its cause. It was most important for Leibniz to maintain that this was a permissible mode of expression.

§ 3

The application of this view both on the empirical and on the metaphysical level must now be considered. Empirically Leibniz maintains that every physical particle can be held to represent the whole universe from a particular point of view, and it is obvious that he must hold this as soon as his terminology is understood. For since the material universe consists of particles endowed with *vis viva* and in thoroughgoing causal connexion with one another, no change can occur in any of them without the whole being, however slightly, altered thereby; and this in Leibnizian language is simply to maintain that every other particle, in so far as it is affected by the alteration of the first, represents in itself the body which has caused that alteration. Now the empirical world as a whole represents the metaphysical world as a whole, but here a difficulty arises, for monads are conceived as substances on strict Cartesian lines. Each of them is entirely self-supporting and possessed of a determinate essence of its own (it is simply a unit of *vis viva*). Substances, however, cannot interact with one another at all, for by so doing they would lose their substantial independence; and yet Leibniz is convinced that every monad must be held to represent the metaphysical world of monads just as every particle represents the physical world of particles. Clearly a miracle is called for, and it is duly forthcoming. There is no interaction between monads, we learn. They really have no windows, but each of them simply unfolds in accordance with its own internal necessity. God, however, in the act of creating them ensured that these unfoldings should be harmonious and consistent with one another. Hence every one *de facto* does represent the whole universe of them, but this representation is to be attributed not to any interaction but to the divinely pre-established harmony.

From this it follows that space, time, and causality cannot be conditions of monads themselves, but only of the physical particles which are representations of them; space is in monads, not monads in space. The explanation, or at least what Leibniz believed to be the explanation, of this paradox is contained in his conception of the nature of the self. Here again, as in respect of the ultimate metaphysical nature of the material world, he is led to a considerable divergence from the Cartesian point of view, though he agrees with it on the central point that the soul must be conceived as a substance. It is not, however, to be thought of as wholly different in kind from the monads which are the basis of physical things, but rather as connected with them by a series of infinite gradations.[17]

The monad which is the self in fact represents the universe just as any other monad does, but we must realize that monads throughout the universe are distinguishable from one another simply by the intensity of their representational capacity. The lowest order, that of inorganic nature, has a very confused and obscure representational capacity, but as we rise higher in the scale we eventually reach the levels of conscious representation (perception) and pure self-conscious thought (apperception). Thus within ourselves we can discover an infinite range of representations varying from the extreme confusion and obscurity of mere sensation to the absolute clearness and distinctness of pure intellectual activity.

Now space, time, and causality clearly belong to our sensuous awareness of things, and therefore must be regarded as occurring at a relatively obscure level of perception. A divine intelligence which apprehended monads as monads would represent them with absolute clarity as distinct substantial entities and therefore as neither spatial, temporal, nor causal in character.

§ 4

The weakness of the Cartesian system as a whole lay in its total inability to reconcile the substantial or independent existence of a plurality of observable phenomena with their undeniable interrelatedness to one another. The solution of Leibniz lies in his acceptance of relations between phenomena as a fact. From this he draws two momentous conclusions, namely that the objects of the senses, just because they are really related, cannot in the end be regarded as real, and that the real is therefore accessible not to sensibility but to understanding. This suggests a distinction between the intelligible and sensible worlds such as Kant later drew

[17] There is a close connexion between Leibniz's philosophical position and his mathematical investigations, especially into the differential calculus.

in the *Dissertation*, but this was not the line which Leibniz followed. As we have seen, he chose to regard the transition from sense to understanding as a continuous one involving only an infinite number of degrees of clearness in representation, thereby apparently bridging another of the gaps in the system of Descartes, for whom thought and sense had necessarily been different in kind and not merely in degree.

But even if this procedure is allowed to be sound in principle it can hardly be denied that the problem of substantial interrelation is shelved by it rather than solved, since the conception of a universe of monads, each entirely self-subsistent and all bound together by nothing but the pre-established harmony ordained by God's creative act is, to say the least of it, extremely difficult to accept. This, however, is neither the only difficulty nor the most serious which the view involves, for when carefully considered it is found inevitably to cast a doubt on the central contention on which the whole of the new philosophy of nature rests, namely the doctrine that the material universe is real and is through and through intelligible on mathematical principles. For if space, time, and causality are all relational forms valid only of obscure perceptions and bound to dissolve away with the coming of true intellectual insight into the nature of the real, we are bound to ask in what sense geometry and physics can be regarded as giving us knowledge of the real at all; but the idea that geometry and physics are not strictly valid of reality was essentially incompatible with the whole outlook of seventeenth-century philosophy, and Leibniz himself naturally draws no attention to this aspect of his doctrine. Another acute problem of the same general character arises in respect of causality, in that the interaction of physical particles with one another is, like the space in which it happens, appearance only. To say that these are all *phaenomena bene fundata*, as Leibniz tends to do, is really no answer but a mere evasion, and ultimately he is bound either to face the question 'Why, strictly speaking, does anything happen at all?' or to show that it is unaskable.

It is at this point that Leibniz's theory of logic is invoked to bear out his physical and metaphysical views. As a physicist he considers that the total effect is necessarily identical with the total cause and that within the physical universe *vis viva* is always conserved. This in itself is a purely physical notion and is a natural consequence of his substitution of *vis viva* for motion in the Cartesian doctrine of conservation.[18] The consequence of it, however, is that, physically speaking, when once we know the effect we can discover the cause simply by a process of analysis, since in the end they are identical with one another. This physical identity between effect and cause can lead us to the metaphysical (or rather logical) notion on which it depends or which it represents. In logical inference as in physical causation we are dealing with a process of necessary connexion in which a consequent is held to follow from certain antecedent conditions, and here again we may take it that the consequent and the antecedent are in the end identical with one another. Hence Leibniz maintains that in every true proposition *praedicatum inest subjecto*,[19] the predicate is contained in the subject, and that consequently all valid inference is explicitly analytical in character and involves simply the discovery of what is actually contained in the original subject. On these principles it follows that the supreme principle of all valid thinking is the principle of identity, and it should be found that the whole universe can be deduced analytically from the notion of substance. This is the view which Spinoza had actually attempted to develop without any very notable success. Leibniz, however, was no Spinozist, and attempted a less heroic and more complex solution. Realizing that the principle of identity in itself is inadequate to account for the concrete diversity either of the universe of substantial monads or of the physical universe which represents it, he simply introduces a second metaphysical principle, namely that of sufficient reason to produce that diversity. Identity, he argues, is necessarily the criterion of possibility, since that which involves contradiction cannot be real. But of the infinite number of possible universes of which this principle would admit, one and one only is actual. God, we must suppose, elected to actualize this of all the possibles for the sufficient reason that it was the best of them all. Thus the diversity of the monadic world depends on God's will; its logical coherence on his intellect. The 'why' of the real world is solved by a miraculous intervention, but the solution of it has an important repercussion in the phenomenal sphere, for the real world is now not conceived as merely mechanical but also as essentially purposive in character. Its function is to realize the maximum of good, and it was actually

[18] Leibniz, op. cit., § 17.

[19] Leibniz, op. cit., § 8.

created in preference to all other possible universes in order that the maximum amount of good might thereby be realized. The only possible answer to a 'why' question of this kind is a purposive answer, someone intended it. That is why Descartes had excluded such questions from natural philosophy.

Hence even in the phenomenal world according to Leibniz we shall be mistaken if we look only for efficient causes. Our account will be true, but it will be incomplete, since the phenomenal world represents, however obscurely, the essentially purposive character of the real monadic universe. Thus another of Descartes's cherished beliefs is thrown overboard.

Yet even these weighty concessions are inadequate to cover the gulf between physics and revelation which Cartesianism had opened. For at the end the problem remains, and even the helpful notion of representation can do no more than conceal it temporarily, 'How can we effect a transition from the particular laws which physics formulates to the real universe intelligible to pure reason?' The existence of this as a problem is ultimately concealed from Leibniz by the fatal facility with which he transfers himself from the world of physics to that of monads without observing that he has done so; in fact the term 'monad' is a snare to him in much the same way as terms like 'complex' and 'repression', which have both a physical and a psychical meaning, are to the modern psycho-analyst.

This, though it is, as Kant was ultimately to demonstrate, the true problem with which the Cartesian philosophy and its successors are faced, is not the point of the Leibnizian system which his immediate followers in Germany found most difficult; indeed they never noticed its existence. They were concerned with the obvious theological problems to which the notion of substantial monads in a pre-established harmony necessarily gives rise.

LOCKE

§ 1

It is somewhat unfortunate for Locke's reputation as a philosopher that he is frequently thought of as part of a kind of apostolic succession which begins hopefully with Descartes and ends triumphantly with Kant. It is thereby suggested that his aim was similar to if not identical with that of Leibniz and Spinoza, and it soon becomes obvious that, in so far as it was, he notably failed to achieve it. This is to judge him in entirely the wrong light. He was acquainted with the views of Descartes and of the Cartesians, and appears to have studied at any rate the *Meditations* and the *Discourse* with some care;[20] but he certainly did not regard himself as in any way carrying on or completing the metaphysical theories which Descartes had initiated.[21] On the contrary his purpose was as far as possible to avoid metaphysical complications, which he thought were rather tedious and a waste of time, and confine himself to more practical investigations into the origin and extent of human knowledge. In the nature of the case it was not possible for him to carry out this purpose without straying into metaphysics, and he seems to have recognized very imperfectly the extent to which his theory of knowledge entailed a metaphysical doctrine; nevertheless, he is entitled to be judged mainly by his success or failure in what he was explicitly attempting rather than by his unwilling intrusions into a sphere which did not interest him. All that can usefully be maintained as to the connexion between Descartes and Locke is that they are often found to be in the same area of thought, but that, when this happens, it is to be attributed to accident rather than design, since their philosophical problems and methods have no intrinsic connexions with one another. Locke takes for granted in principle practically the whole of what Descartes believed himself to have established as to the general character of the external world, and is interested simply in the question how we come to know that world, assuming that it is really there to be known. He admits, indeed, the bare possibility of its non-existence, but regards this doubt as purely academic and of no philosophical importance. Similarly, he accepts quite uncritically, as Descartes himself had done, the traditional metaphysic of substance, essence, and mode, though he raises important difficulties as to what items in the real world should properly be classed under these headings, and much of the incompleteness and obscurity of his position is attributable to the fact that those categories, in the form in which he accepted them, were themselves unsuitable and inadequate for his purpose.

As contrasted with Descartes, Locke is interested in maintaining two fundamental logical truths. The first is that we have

[20] Gibson, *Locke's Theory of Knowledge*, p. 184.
[21] Op. cit., p. 205.

genuine knowledge only of relations, never of things themselves or substances; the second is that analytical propositions are always 'trivial' whereas synthetic propositions are 'instructive'.

His position is most easily understood if we regard him as inspecting the world from outside as God or an angel might do. He seems to take it for granted that a being so situated would observe a mechanical system of minute physical particles moving in accordance with determinate laws and imparting motion to one another by impact, though they possess no active power of initiating motion themselves. He was not particularly interested in this part of the processes of nature, since his own scientific interests were almost wholly confined to medical and biological studies. He believed further that the material particles which by their combinations make up the physical world would be seen by a competent supernatural observer to have a capacity of cohering with one another so as to form macroscopic 'bodies', but that to the human mind the nature of this power was wholly inexplicable. There were also in the universe minds or selves which, though immaterial, were nevertheless in spatial relations to one another, and were also closely connected with bodies, but this union, too, was unintelligible to us, though it might and presumably would not be so to an intelligence of a sufficiently higher order of penetration. Locke wrote (in his *Examination of Malebranche*):

> What I have said here, I think sufficient to make intelligible, how by material rays of light visible species may be brought into the eye, ... but when by this means an image is made on the retina, how we see it I conceive no more than when I am told that we see it in God.... Impressions made on the retina by rays of light, I think I understand: and motions thence conveyed to the brain may be conceived, and that these produce ideas in the mind, I am persuaded, but in a manner to me incomprehensible. This I can resolve only into the good pleasure of God, whose ways are past finding out.

Taking all this incuriously for granted, as he was perfectly entitled to do, the question which he put to himself was roughly as follows. Granted that the universe, seen from outside, is like that, how do we, who are situated inside it, come to know that it is? His aim is thus primarily psychological, and he desired to be what Kant subsequently asserted that he was, the physiologist of the human understanding.

§ 2

Locke's method of attack is simple and straightforward. He is convinced on empirical grounds that the mind can have no content before it which can be the object of its thinking activity unless that content is conveyed to it by the senses. Hence it cannot have, as the Cartesians had generally supposed, innate principles in the sense of intelligible propositions, implicitly present in it from birth, which can become explicit on the occasion of a sensible stimulus; *a fortiori* no such principles can be available for contemplation without any such stimulus. This precludes any answer to his main question on Cartesian lines. On the other hand, the mind is in possession of an innate or natural capacity for acquiring knowledge by means of the contents, or ideas, which come to it through the senses, and it is precisely that capacity which Locke proposes to investigate.

These ideas of sense fall into two classes. Some of them are presented to the mind as a result of the operation of the minute particles of matter on the sense organs of the body; others as a consequence of the mind's introspective attention to its own operations. This distinction between 'sensation' and 'reflection' is implicit in the distinction between thinking and extended substance, and is the natural assumption of all philosophies which set out from that position. As regards the second class, the data of inward sense, Locke is not really much interested in them, since at first sight they have nothing to do with the problem of how we come to know the real world. The first class, which is for him more immediately important, is subdivided into ideas of primary qualities on the one hand and secondary qualities on the other. The former are ideas of the metrical properties (solidity, motion, &c.) and are held to be actual resemblances of the things which cause them; the latter (colour, &c.) are also the effects of the operation of things on the senses, but bear no resemblance to their causes.

Now when we consider the essentially dependent character of these qualities we are led to posit the existence of substances, material and immaterial, in which they inhere, or which support them, but of these substances themselves we have only a very confused and inadequate idea. They can be known only as 'something, I know not what' whose sole function discoverable by us is just a capacity to be qualified by the primary and secondary qualities whose ideas we do apprehend.

Consideration of the contents of our consciousness next shows us that we apprehend immediately not merely simple ideas of the qualities of substance but also modes, or combinations of those simples, so that our idea of a piece of gold contains in it the simple ideas yellow, hard, &c.; and in addition to this we find in ourselves a faculty of combining ideas into modes spontaneously, so that we can frame to ourselves the idea of a chimera, even though no such complex of simple ideas has ever been presented to us by sense. Finally, the mind is found to have a power of abstracting which enables it to form general ideas from either simple ideas or ideas of modes.

This completes the modest catalogue of the kinds of furniture which are constantly being conveyed by the senses into the empty room of the mind's consciousness. Locke has next to consider the uses to which the mind can put them when they arrive. Knowledge, he holds, is nothing more than the discovery of the connexion or repugnancy of our ideas with one another, and such union or incompatibility is discovered immediately by an unanalysable act of intuitive inspection. The existence and infallibility of this intuitive certainty can no more be questioned than can the existence of ideas themselves or of the self which has them, and Locke had little patience with sceptics who questioned it or metaphysicians who attempted to derive it from more ultimate general principles.

Starting from this assumption, he had no difficulty in demonstrating that we can have knowledge in respect of our general ideas. For these are entirely our own creations and we know exactly what is included in them. I can have no doubt as to what ideas are necessarily implied by or excluded from my idea of a chimera since I myself have defined a chimera as possessing certain specific characteristics, and have therefore only to attend to my own definition in order to know whether a further determination follows from it or is repugnant to it. Such knowledge, however, though in some cases it is not merely certain but extremely valuable, does not necessarily apply to real existences. We can be certain that it does so only in cases where the definition or nominal essence is identical with the actual construction of the thing, that is with its real essence, as in geometry. Locke's most fundamental contention is that we can in fact achieve such certainty in respect of modes, but never in respect of substances. Thus, if I choose to define gold as hard, yellow, malleable, and soluble in *aqua regia*, I can know what further ideas are implied in my idea and what are excluded by it, and this enables me to say whether the particular piece of matter which I am considering falls under my general idea of gold or not. But to achieve knowledge of the internal structure of this piece of matter itself would involve a knowledge not of nominal but of real essence, and that I am totally unable to achieve. Even if I were endowed with superhuman powers of observation and could actually see the movements of these insensible particles which are the real piece of matter (as distinct from my present inadequate idea of it), I should not be much farther on, for I should know only the 'how' of nature, not the 'why'. I should perceive that, as a matter of fact, a piece of matter constituted in a certain way has a certain effect on a body constituted as mine is; but I should still not know the reason why it produced that effect rather than a different one, since no repugnancy of ideas would be involved in the latter supposition.

This is unquestionably a limitation to the extent of our knowledge, but, as Locke holds, it is of no great practical importance, since we are able to know all that is necessary for our ultimate salvation. For this inevitable ignorance as to the nature and even, for the avowed sceptic, as to the existence of substance is qualified at two vital points. We possess an intuitive certainty of our own existence and a demonstrative knowledge of the existence of God, though it must be conceded that we have no clear idea of either his essence or our own. This would indeed be fatal if knowledge presupposed, as the Cartesians imagined, the existence in us of clear and distinct ideas of substances and their real essences, but Locke believes himself to have demonstrated that no such presupposition is required in order to account for the kind of knowledge which we possess. For to him it is certain that we can apprehend necessary connexions between our ideas even in cases where the ideas related are not adequately known to us.

§ 3

Locke's new way of ideas constitutes an innovation in philosophy different in character though comparable in importance to the Cartesian introduction of mathematical principles of reasoning. What he asserts is in effect that knowledge ought not simply to be taken for granted, but that a serious philosopher should conduct an investigation, largely psychological in character, into the way in which it comes about, with a view to determining its nature and extent.

He is a critical philosopher, neither dogmatic nor sceptical, and his influence on the course of philosophical thinking both in logic and morals cannot be overestimated. Although his direct influence on Kant was probably not considerable, the whole empirical school in Germany culminating in Tetens derived its views directly from him.

In spite of his wide divergence from Descartes in many important respects, it is useful to consider the affinities as well as the disagreements of the two, since we can thereby set Locke's position in a clearer light. We have already seen that he accepted without question the general categorical scheme of substance, essence, and mode which Descartes himself had taken over from his predecessors. It is, however, noticeable that Locke is by no means consistent in his application of it. Sometimes it seems as if the real essence, for example, of a piece of gold simply is the number, texture, and motion of its insensible parts; while at others, more consistently with his general view, it is found in the 'something, I know not what', or substance, which is numerable, figured, and mobile. Either doctrine is reconcilable with his undoubted view that the piece of gold has a real essence whose nature we are incompetent to discover, though in the former case the incompetence would really depend only on the inadequacy of our perceptual mechanism and scientific instruments, whereas in the latter it would be inherent in the nature of things.

Locke agrees with Descartes in holding that substantial forms can be of no service whatever towards an account of real essences, but he does so for an entirely different reason. Descartes had maintained that substantial forms, because they were capable of immediate apprehension by sense, could not serve as a basis for mathematical calculations about the nature of the real, whereas it was their non-empirical character which rendered them objectionable to Locke. To admit substantial forms of which we can have knowledge would be, as he quite correctly observed, to credit ourselves with an *a priori* cognition of real essences which was precisely what he held that we never do and never can obtain. It is really in support of this contention that he rejects even the Cartesian substitute for substantial forms, namely innate ideas. As we have seen, he actually restricts knowledge to the intuitive apprehension of connexion and repugnance between ideas, whether the latter are received through the senses or framed by the mind itself, and consequently he is committed to the view that all our knowledge is on a single level. In that it all depends on the exertion of a power of apprehending inherent in the mind, we can maintain, if we want to, that the whole of it is innate; but since the mind cannot from its own resources produce ideas, except by composition of those which it has already received from the senses, Locke prefers to say that none of it is.

And so in the last resort the existence of material things independent of the mind must be allowed to admit of nothing more than an empirical proof, and this, although it can give us an infinitely great degree of probability, is still not in the strictest sense demonstrative. As contrasted with this we have the intuitive awareness of the existence of ourselves which enables us in the strict sense to demonstrate the existence of God. But although on this point Locke is to some extent in agreement with Descartes in that both believed that the existence of myself is more certain than the existence of material things (though Descartes believed that, granted God's existence, his veracity would provide us with a true demonstration of those things), Locke continues to maintain that the true nature of God, the self, and material things can never be discovered by us.

HUME

§ 1

Hume sets out with the same general assumptions as Locke as to the existence of a material world and the physiological origin of our sense experience of independent objects, but as he rejects Locke's rationalist procedure in respect of substance and cause, he comes ultimately to doubt the admissibility of these assumptions and to maintain a completely sceptical attitude towards the possibility of our gaining any rational certainty concerning matter of fact and existence. In his own words: ''Tis evident, that all reasonings from causes or effects terminate in conclusions, concerning matter of fact; that is, concerning the existence of objects or of their qualities. 'Tis also evident, that the idea of existence is nothing different from the idea of any object.'[22] Locke had believed without question that the existence of qualities was in itself an adequate ground for presuming the existence of a substance to which those qualities belonged, and that the occurrence of anything was in itself a proof of the existence of something else of an unspecified character on which it followed necessarily as an effect. What Hume does is to restate Locke's doctrine of ideas in such a way as to rob both these beliefs of their plausibility.

Actually he concentrates his attention mainly on the second of them, and, in the *Enquiry* more than in the *Treatise*, takes as his main theme the problem of how we can claim to apprehend any necessary connexion between events which are temporally related, that is, the problem of the validity of the causal axiom. But in spite of this, Kant was probably mistaken in supposing that Hume had failed to grasp the possibility of generalizing his scepticism concerning the truth of this axiom so as to cover the whole problem of our knowledge of necessary connexions between distinct existences. It seems more likely that the failure of the *Treatise*, which Kant had not read and which is sceptical over a much wider front than the *Enquiry*, led Hume to hope for better success if he directed his attention to a single major issue.

His development from Locke is to be found in his attempt to analyse further Locke's term 'idea', and in the conclusions which follow necessarily from his restatement of it. Locke's use had been extremely wide, covering as it did whatever is present to the mind when it thinks, so that the data of sense, memory, imagination, and thought are all indifferently described as 'ideas present to the mind'.

Hume, on the contrary, opens by drawing a sharp distinction between ideas properly so called and impressions. The latter, which are for him the only genuine data which the mind has to work upon, are simply the immediate data of inner or outer sense, pains, colours, sounds, &c. Corresponding to these are ideas, which are quite literally faint copies of them which the mind preserves and makes use of in memory, imagination, and reasoning. Thus all simple ideas must somehow be reduced to copies of impressions, and complex ideas are considered as nothing but aggregates of

[22] *Treatise*, I. III. vii.

simple ideas which may or may not have been copied from complex impressions, since Hume agrees with Locke in granting the mind a power to frame complex ideas to which no actual impression corresponds.

Such a view involves a limitation of our knowledge far more drastic than Locke had contemplated or would have accepted had it been proposed to him, as appears when we consider its bearing on the question of relations. Locke had gone no further than to maintain that our ideas of these must be founded on or traceable to the simple ideas of sense; whereas Hume, demanding as he does that ideas should be admitted as legitimate only when they can produce a birth certificate showing from what impression they have been derived, is limited to the relations of resemblance, contrariety, and spatio-temporal order. His very formulation makes it impossible to give any but a sceptical answer to his own question, since the phrase 'impression of necessary connexion' is not merely meaningless but self-contradictory. An impression is by definition just a *de facto* occurrence to which the idea of necessity, except as regards its origin, which is not here in question, is, in Locke's terminology, repugnant.

Clearly, then, Hume is badly placed for explaining how we come even to suspect the existence of any world independent of our own fleeting impressions, or any continuous self to apprehend those impressions. He cannot appeal, as Locke had done, to the notion of substance to help him out, for substance is easily seen to be an illegitimate idea. We cannot offer any impression from which it is copied to support its claim to be entertained. Nor does causality, to which he might have appealed as Berkeley did to save him from complete subjectivism, fare any better. Hume quickly disposes of Locke's attempt to derive it from the impression of power or effort in myself; and the possibility of a rationalist proof, which Locke had also accepted, is shown to have no more validity here than in the case of substance. It might therefore be anticipated that nothing could emerge from Hume's initial assumption but a completely sceptical conclusion in which nothing could be accepted but a temporal stream of events in which no order, necessity, or objectivity could ever be discovered.

Against this conclusion Hume has two lines of defence. He first develops the doctrine of the association of ideas which Locke had already introduced. On the strength of this he avoids doubting that the future will resemble the past, although if pressed he can offer no better ground for our expectation that it will do so than 'a kind of pre-established harmony'. By this, however, he must not be held to mean anything so profound as Leibniz had previously done. Hume's view is that we find out by simple introspection sufficient of the working of our minds to realize that when a given impression (fire) has been followed in a past by another impression (heat) the recurrence of the former will in fact be followed by a 'lively idea' or expectation of the latter; and this expectation will be strengthened proportionately to the frequency of the recurrence and the absence of contrary instances. Assuming, then, that there really is regularity in nature, we shall be justified in our expectations, provided that we classify our impressions with appropriate care, and the result will be precisely as if we genuinely apprehended that regularity in terms of necessary connexion which in fact we are wholly incompetent to do.

What Hume does is to postulate causality, deny that we can have knowledge of it, and offer as a reasonably efficient substitute for such knowledge our admitted tendency to expect regularity in nature. If we could know that such a regularity or affinity of phenomena is actual, our causal inferences would rest, as in his view they do not, on reason instead of on custom or habit.

To account for our belief in the existence of an independent world he advances, in addition to the association theory, an original and highly ingenious doctrine of imagination[23] which has much in common with Kant's subjective deduction of the categories.

§ 2

Hume's advance on Locke may now be summarily stated. His chief contribution, and it was entirely original and completely justified, was to draw attention to the absence of any demonstration of the legitimacy of the categories of substance and cause. As we have seen, Descartes, Leibniz, and Locke, widely as they disagreed on many points, agreed that reality must consist of substances characterized by essences differentiated into modes, and must somehow contain causal relations within itself. Hume does not actually deny that this may be the case, but he does ask what grounds, other than habit, we have for saying that it must be so.

[23] Hume, *Treatise*, I. II. '*Of scepticism with regard to the senses.*'

He is the first philosopher to raise explicitly the question 'How can knowledge of real existence be reached by pure reason alone?' and to point out that the assumption of the applicability of the category of cause in particular to real existence without any proof involves the begging of this vital question. In pursuance of this line of thought he discriminates more sharply than Locke had done between propositions which assert merely necessary connexions between ideas (including those of proportion, quantity, and number) and those which claim to penetrate farther into matter of fact. The former he allows to pass unchallenged, though he should properly have asked whether anything but tautological or trivial propositions could really be discovered by the use of them. Had he done so, as Kant noted,[24] he must have concluded that geometry was in as precarious a position as the causal axiom. In fact he did sometimes, though by no means always or in his maturer work, hold that it was, but for a different reason. But as regards real existence, he entirely disowned Locke's admittedly limited and tentative claims to discover necessary connexions in it by means of ideas.

His great merit is that he makes evident once and for all the danger of extreme subjectivism to which any consistent empiricism is exposed.[25] This is what Kant derived from Hume and what instigated him to attempt a systematic deduction of those fundamental categories which are so involved in all our thinking that we hardly are conscious of the ontological presuppositions which they appear to involve.

CONCLUSION

It is convenient for some purposes to classify the philosophers whose work I have briefly considered so far as Rationalists and Empiricists, and I shall use this classification when it suits. If the view of Berkeley is grouped with those of Locke and Hume, and is Spinoza joins Descartes, Leibniz, and the Wolff–Leibniz succession, we have convenient pigeon-holes into which pre-Kantian philosophers can be sorted out, and Kant himself can be treated as a kind of philosophical arbitrator or conciliator in their dispute.

This procedure, however, misrepresents the development of thought in the seventeenth and eighteenth centuries. It is correct up to a point, but it leads to over-emphasis of the matters on which

[24] B 20.

[25] *Enquiry*, § xii, pt. i.

pre-Kantian thinkers disagreed with one another and to relative disregard of those on which they were substantially united.

All were acutely conscious of the intellectual need to do something about the new way of gaining knowledge about matter of fact which was revealed by the application of mathematics and, to a much smaller degree, by experimental methods of inquiry. These had somehow to be reconciled with the claims of metaphysics and theology. It is helpful now to look at the whole proceeding as a sustained attempt to solve a logical problem, and to say that what really troubled Descartes and his successors was in the end linguistic. They had to cope with the unsuitability of the categories of substance, essence, and mode in which pre-Cartesian discussions had been conducted, to inquiries in which relations and not substances were accepted as the most important constituents in the real world. To put it differently, they were more or less systematically disinfecting the category words of physics, especially 'cause'.

Two aims can be distinguished here. The first is the original Cartesian desire to depersonalize 'cause' completely as far as material substance is concerned, and to hold that, in this department, 'why?' simply did not occur. Everything that could be said at all could be said in the language of matter and motion, and the 'quantity of motion' in the universe was constant.

The Leibnizian opposition, while not challenging the mechanical assumption in principle, held that 'purpose' still had an important job to do, but they were far from clear as to the way in which the qualified rehabilitation of 'why?' questions could be achieved.

The attempt to clarify 'cause' was naturally accompanied by a growing recognition that 'causal' and 'logical' necessitation also needed attention. The distinction between them was mainly Hume's contribution.

To say, however, that what the pre-Kantians were really doing was to hammer out a usable language in which to talk about physics without begging the question against theology and metaphysics is to over-simplify the issues involved. It is helpful as a starting-point but, like all such generalizations, it becomes a hindrance if taken too seriously. Pre-Kantian philosophers only occasionally recognized that the source of their troubles was mainly or wholly linguistic.

II

LOCAL INFLUENCES

WOLFF (1679–1754)

ALTHOUGH Wolff was certainly not a great philosopher,[1] his rather voluminous works are nothing like as dull as is sometimes supposed. His aim was to systematize and render intelligible the views of Leibniz, and it cannot be denied that up to a point he was immensely successful in doing so, but his greater service lay in making German for the first time a philosophical language. The demand for his works was extremely heavy and led him to republish in Latin with a view, as he says himself, to making them internationally accessible. Admittedly his version of Leibniz is far from being satisfactory, since it leaves out altogether much of what now seems to be of the greatest importance. The distinction between the physical and the metaphysical is for him practically non-existent, and by deriving the principle of ground and consequent from that of contradiction he establishes a hard-and-fast rationalism in respect of the world of nature which Leibniz himself would certainly have rejected. Against this, however, there are two important facts to be remembered. The first is that in the almost complete absence of published works by Leibniz, Wolff's insight into the system which he was expounding must have depended very largely on personal intercourse with its originator; the second, and more important, is that he openly regarded philosophy as being essentially concerned with morals and only secondarily with metaphysics. In this he was in full agreement with the great writers of the German *Aufklärung*, and also with the view of Kant himself.

It is not necessary to deal further with his doctrines, as they are faithfully reproduced except in very minor details by his pupil Baumgarten, from whom Kant seems in the main to have derived them.

[1] Kant, however, described Wolff as 'the greatest of the dogmatic philosophers'. B xxxvi.

BAUMGARTEN (1714–62)

§ 1

It is unlikely that any philosopher has ever produced a more unutterably tedious work on metaphysics than Baumgarten's *Metaphysica*;[2] or combined so successfully the pedantry of a dying scholasticism with the illusory clearness of a pseudo-geometrical demonstration. Indeed the *Metaphysica* might well be taken as the type of that method of exposition which had made the term 'systematic philosophy' one of abuse in England and France before the end of the eighteenth century. In spite of its defects, however, it enjoyed considerable success and appears to have been the standard exposition of the Wolff–Leibniz metaphysical position available for the use of university students. The fact that Kant consistently employed it as a textbook is at least an indication that nothing substantially better was available, for, although he was officially bound to use some book as distinct from merely stating his own views, it does not appear that the Prussian authorities cared what particular author he chose to expound. Thus when Kant talks of the dogmatism of his predecessors in metaphysics, it is reasonable to suppose that Baumgarten was the author whom he had primarily in mind. It is fortunately unnecessary to consider Baumgarten's position in detail here, and all that will be attempted is a brief outline of the scope of his work with a rather more detailed account of those parts of it which are of interest as elucidating the relation between Leibniz and Kant. In fairness to the author it must be stated that Baumgarten himself was under no illusions as to his own stature as a philosopher. He regards his own book quite explicitly as an exposition of the Wolff–Leibniz view, and lays no claim to originality in respect of the position which he occupies or the arguments by which it is supported. Actually his position does differ materially from that of Leibniz, but it is doubtful whether Baumgarten knew this or whether he could be blamed for not doing so. The first (very incomplete) collected edition of Leibniz's philosophical works did not appear till 1765, and practically the whole of his writings were till then buried in more or less private correspondence (with Clarke, Bayle, &c.) and in the back numbers of the Leipzig *Acta*

[2] Kant considered Baumgarten an admirable analytical thinker. B 35.

Eruditorum.[3] In fact, the 'Wolff–Leibniz view' is really Leibniz as interpreted by Wolff, and Baumgarten is a popularization which reduces further the Leibnizian element in it. It is especially noticeable that no hint is to be found in the *Metaphysica* that the position which is being stated has any connexion with either mathematics or experimental physics. All that survives is the inadequate summary contained in the *Monadology.*

§ 2

Baumgarten's *Metaphysica* (1739) consists of exactly one thousand sections, and any doubt as to whether this number is dictated by the nature of the subject of by the author's passion for tidiness is settled by the fact that its subdivisions are also constrained to occupy round numbers of sections. It is written in a kind of Latin and consists of four parts dealing respectively with Ontology, Cosmology, Psychology, and Theology. The first is strictly speaking propaedeutic. It is concerned with those truths which are valid of all reality, whereas the remainder are restricted, at least by implication, to the universe in which we actually exist. This ontological section opens with a number of logical and metaphysical assumptions which, if they are accepted, lead inevitably to Wolff's interpretation of Leibniz's *Monadology*. The only important divergence from Leibniz lies in the explicit reduction of the principle of causality to that of logical entailment which begins in § 14[4] and § 21 and is completed in § 307. The ground of anything is that from which we can understand why it is. That which contains the ground of anything is its *principium,* the *principium* of existence is a cause. It is also maintained that nothing but a substance can strictly be a cause, since nothing but substance can ultimately be a ground, for by definition substance alone is intelligible in itself (*in et per se*) and requires nothing beyond itself to explain its nature. The nature or essence of a substance is its internal possibility,[5] and to this essence existence is superadded as a further determination (*complementum*).[6] A unit (*Unum, Eins*) is that whose determinations are inseparable, and

[3] The Dutens Collected Works (Geneva, 1768) was very incomplete, and not available to Baumgarten.

[4] Meier's *Vernunftlehre* and Baumgarten's *Metaphysica* are reprinted in Ak. xv, xvi, and xvii.

[5] § 40.

[6] § 55.

a transcendental unit (*wesentliches Eins*) is that whose parts are intrinsically inseparable; consequently anything which possesses existence merely as a mode and not as a determination intrinsic to its essence is contingent.[7] That which can exist only as a determination of something else is not a substance but an accident, and accidents which appear to be independent existences are *phaenomena substantiata*.[8]

Now there must be some ground for the inherence of accidents in a substance, and this ground is defined as force (*vis*); but force itself cannot be an accident since it is the ground of their inherence, therefore it must be the substance itself.[9] In other words, substance must itself be regarded as the ground of the inherence of accidents in itself, and in so far as force is loosely ascribed to entities which are in fact accidents, this is only in so far as those accidents are regarded as *phaenomena substantiata*.[10] Now change is an accident which inheres in particular substances, therefore it must be grounded either in the substance in which it occurs or in some other substance. If it is the former, the substance is said to be active, if the latter, passive.[11]

This argument leads to the distinction which is vital to the whole of Baumgarten's position, namely that between *influxus realis* and *influxus idealis*. 'Si passio illius substantiae, in quam altera influit, simul est ipsius actio, passio et influxus dicuntur ideales. Si vero passio non est patientis actio, passio et influxus dicuntur reales.'[12] This enables him immediately to distinguish between spontaneity and receptivity, the former being *facultas* (*potentia activa, Vermögen*) and the latter *potentia passiva* (*Fähigkeit, Empfänglichkeit*) from which is derived the definition of *vis viva* (*lebendige Kraft*) and *vis mortua* (*todte Kraft*). 'Granted the existence of a faculty and a capacity, action and passion do not necessarily occur. But they do occur if we also grant the existence of force as the determination (*complementum*) of the faculty to action, i.e. that which is added to the faculty to produce action. Thus a specific amount of existent force either is or is not sufficient to produce a given action; the former is a living, the latter a dead stimulation to action.'[13]

At this point Baumgarten leaves the notions of force and action

[7] § 134. [8] § 193. [9] § 198.
[10] § 201. [11] § 210. [12] § 212.
[13] § 220.

to be taken up again later, and proceeds to an account of monads or simple substances.[14] Here he merely repeats the doctrine of the *Monadology*. Monads are simple, and therefore no composites are strictly substances but only *phaenomena substantiata*. Hence no individual monad can occupy space, though a whole which consists of monads (*totum monadum*) which is a composite and therefore really a *phaenomenon substantiatum*, can do so. Furthermore, such a *substantiatum* is conceived as exercising force (though only in the loose sense before considered) either in producing motion in other *substantiata* (*vis motrix*) or in resisting such motion (*vis inertiae*). Any extended thing (*substantiatum*) which possesses *vis inertiae* alone, i.e. which is purely passive, is *materia prima*: one which possesses also *vis motrix* is a physical body (*materia secunda*).[15]

The ontological section closes with an account of cause of which the fundamental point, namely the identification of cause with ground, has already been mentioned. It is further developed by the statements that any effect is qualitatively like and quantitatively identical with its cause.[16]

§ 3

The Cosmological section which follows is no more than a restatement of the conclusions reached in the Ontological section so as to give them reference not merely to things in general but to a physical universe; and as the ontological definitions have been carefully drawn so as to yield exactly the required conclusions, it is not surprising that little is added to what has gone before except the appearance of rigid geometrical demonstration. We are reminded that the universe as a whole has a contingent existence only, since the existence of each of its parts taken separately is contingent.[17] This is not a very good argument, but it serves to show how little Baumgarten ever succeeded in distinguishing between the implications of the relation of whole to part and those of the relation of universal to particular. The elaboration of the doctrine of monads as applied to the physical world is more interesting. The monads which make up the universe, since they are actual entities existing independently of one another, must be

[14] §§ 230–42.
[15] §§ 294–6.
[16] §§ 329, 331.
[17] § 361.

either simultaneous or successive, or both. Thus each of them has position.[18] They must not, however, be envisaged as bare mathematical points having no property except position, nor must adjacent monads be thought to touch or coincide with one another. But since each of them is impenetrable, a plurality of them coexisting is extended or occupies space. They should be described as physical points to distinguish them from mathematical points which are mere abstractions.[19]

Now the monads which constitute a world must be completely interconnected, since otherwise they would not form a world at all. Hence they must all stand to one another in relations of ground or consequent, and as a ground can be known from its consequent, every monad mirrors or reflects the whole of the universe of which it is a member.[20] Differences in the clearness of this representation make possible the differentiation between soul monads on the one hand and bare or physical monads on the other. Between the former of these exists a nexus which may be called *pneumaticus* and they form together a *mundus intellectualis, moralis, regnum gratiae*.[21] The latter, too, are never merely passive (since they are by definition active substances) so that *materia prima* or bare *res extensa* is an abstraction, and every part of matter should properly be regarded as *materia secunda* possessed of *vis motrix* and never absolutely at rest, for rest, like *res extensa*, is an abstraction.[22] Thus *vis inertiae* is simply the force in one body which opposes motion or the actualization of *vis motrix* in another.

As regards the constituent parts of body, it follows from the preceding arguments that the ultimate elements are monads and are therefore immaterial. There are in fact no atoms in the sense of indivisible yet extended particles. There are, however, minute physical bodies (*corpuscula*) which are imperceptible to sense and must therefore be distinguished from such phenomena as admit of being sensuously apprehended;[23] and, though he does not say so quite explicitly, Baumgarten appears to have supposed that knowledge of such *corpuscula* and their behaviour was to be preferred to sense acquaintance with macroscopic phenomena just because it was non-sensuous and therefore free from the confusedness to which he believed the latter necessarily subject.

[18] § 397. [19] § 399. [20] § 400.
[21] § 403. [22] § 417. [23] § 425.

Having thus distinguished between monads and *corpuscula*, he can at once maintain that the latter, *qua* occupying space, are divisible without limit, while still holding to the existence of the former as simple, non-spatial, and indivisible substances.[24]

Baumgarten next turns to the final question whether the relation between bodies is to be considered as one of *influxus physicus* or 'pre-established harmony', and, as a result of his earlier definitions, is easily able to prove that it must be the latter. For the admission of *influxus physicus* involves him in maintaining that when body A acts on body B, B is purely passive. In Baumgarten's terminology, *influit A in B realiter*. This, however, he has already shown to be impossible since bodies are 'really' composite wholes of non-spatial monads, and monads are necessarily active since force belongs to their essence. Hence the *influxus* of A into B must be ideal, not real. Thus if we denote their states before and after the impact, A_1 A_2 and B_1 B_2 respectively, on the *influxus physicus* view it follows that B_2 is the consequence simply of A_1 (since B is purely passive). Baumgarten, on the other hand, conceives it indifferently as the product either of A_1 or of B_1, since both are active, and it could be inferred from the nature of either of them that at that particular juncture in the history of the universe it would behave in just that way and also that the other would behave as in fact it has done. The true statement of the case is therefore that A has received a new mode or determination x and B has received a new determination y; Ax could be inferred from A by anyone who really understood A's essential character, and, since it is part of A's character to reflect the whole universe (including B), By could also be inferred from A by a perfect intelligence.

This conclusion is to Baumgarten doubly satisfactory. In the first place it eliminates from the universe the conception of bare *res extensa*, inert corporeal substance, which can never properly speaking be regarded as the productive cause of anything, and in the second it is completely consistent with the Leibnizian conception of this as the best of possible worlds. For Baumgarten argues that, since 'best' means 'containing the maximum of compossible reality', a world in which both A and B are wholly responsible for, i.e. the ground of, a given result must be more real and therefore

[24] § 428.

better than a world in which A alone is the ground of it while B remains entirely passive.[25]

§ 4

The third section of the *Metaphysica*, although it is entitled *Psychologia Empirica*, has in fact little we should now consider empirical about it except the title. It is based throughout on the metaphysical view which has preceded it and relies on observation only for the establishment of matter of fact such as that there are five special senses and that we do remember, imagine, &c. The nature or essence of these activities is then formulated entirely *a priori*.

The central point of the view is the doctrine of pre-established harmony. The soul is a monad, the body is a composite whole of monads, and consequently any occurrence in the former may be explained either in terms of itself or in terms of the body, and each of these explanations is complete and self-contained.[26] Further, the soul *qua* monad, though it does not occupy space, has position in space,[27] which accounts for the fact that it represents some events in the universe more clearly than others. More precisely, its 'location' in the body constrains it to observe the universe as reflected by the monads which constitute that body, but this reflection inasmuch as it is sensuous is always to a great extent confused. As distinct from this outer sense (*sensus externus*) there is also an inner sense (*sensus internus, conscientia strictius dicta*) by which the soul represents its own state to itself;[28] but no further account of this faculty or of its alleged representational character is offered. Sensibility strictly so-called, however, constitutes only a part of the lower or more confused representational part of the soul. To it must be added the capacity to apprehend immediately identity and diversity in the content represented, memory in so far as it is sensuous and not intellectual, imagination and immediate judgement of value as well as an instinctive expectation that the future will resemble the past.[29] All these activities involve the obscure awareness of connexion, and the faculty which they together constitute is therefore described as *Facultas cognoscitiva inferior* or *analogon rationis*. It is in fact an

[25] §§ 451, 459. [26] § 768. [27] § 745.
[28] § 535.
[29] § 640 and cf. Kant's note on it. Ak. xv. 38.

imperfect or obscure version of that clear apprehension of necessary connexion which only pure reason can give, but none the less it is apprehension of connexion,[30] and therefore may fairly be described in this way.

As regards the nature and activity of the superior intellectual faculty little is said, since the treatment of it properly belongs to logic and not to psychology, but Baumgarten makes it evident that the only apprehension of connexion which can properly be regarded as clear is that which occurs in syllogistic reasoning.[31] He does not in fact state that the distinction between sensibility and understanding is one of degree and not of kind, and indeed he seems often to assume that the latter is the case, but certainly he never openly professes this view and could not have done so without damaging the coherence of his entire system.

The work concludes with 300 sections on morals and theology with which it is unnecessary to deal here, though they were not unimportant in determining Kant's approach to these subjects.

MEIER (1718–77)

§ 1

Meier's *Auszug aus der Vernunftlehre* (1752), which is an abridgement of the same author's *Vernunftlehre* published at the same time, is a far less exhausting work than Baumgarten's *Metaphysica*. Judged by modern standards its contents are a curious mixture. The core of it (rather less than a third of the whole) is an exposition of the principles of Aristotelian or formal logic, but this is enclosed in what may be described as a prolonged discourse on method in general, a kind of plain man's guide to correct thinking and exposition in all branches of knowledge. It cannot be denied that parts of this read very oddly today, and the sections which deal with the character of a learned man and his methods of expressing himself in speech and on paper are vaguely reminiscent of Aristotle's account of the μεγαλόψυχος. Nevertheless, the work as a whole is quite a good exposition of the kind of sensible and undogmatic empiricism adopted by Locke, to whom Meier was heavily indebted. The *Vernunftlehre* is usually described as eclectic philosophy, in that it qualifies its empiricism

[30] § 544.

[31] § 642.

with a number of obvious rationalist assumptions as Locke himself had previously done.[32] Certainly these assumptions if pressed are quite inconsistent with the basic empiricism of the book as a whole, but Meier, like Locke, was not given to making difficulties for himself unnecessarily, and there is a strangely modern ring about his contention that no knowledge worthy of the name could be altogether devoid of practical value.[33] Yet, though he would probably have agreed with Locke and Hume that metaphysical speculation is in itself useless and rather boring, he yields to no one in his admiration for systematic procedure in all philosophical as distinct from historical investigation. In his own way he is just as tidy as Baumgarten, and far more superficial, but it is a different kind of tidiness. Obviously it gave him great pleasure to put labels on things and classify them neatly in pigeon-holes, but he did not insist that the number of pigeon-holes should be an exact multiple of 100. The *Auszug* has 563 sections.

Three aspects of Meier's work deserve consideration, namely his views on Logic, on Psychology, and on Architectonic or system-building in general, since in each of these his influence on Kant was considerable and in the last two at any rate it was decidedly bad. As regards the Logic little needs to be said since in principle it is strictly in accordance with the traditional view. But it is hardly doubtful that when Kant talks of *General* as distinct from *Transcendental Logic* he has Meier more or less definitely in mind. It is noteworthy that the table of judgements[34] to which Kant relates his categories, and which he has often been accused of making up to suit his own convenience, is taken almost verbally from Meier;[35] and also that Meier himself, in spite of his empiricism, remained convinced that the deductive syllogism was the only satisfactory method of demonstration, though he admitted its defects as a method of discovery.

§ 2

Meier's psychological theory is so much an integral part of his view that it cannot be treated in abstraction from the remainder. It is especially prominent in relation to his account of the origin

[32] *Einleitung*, § 2.

[33] §§ 216–19.

[34] Meier is not the only contemporary logician to whom Kant was indebted for this table. See de Vleeschauwer, op. cit. i. 244 ff.

[35] §§ 301–5.

of our judgements about things and of the manner in which we employ those judgements to obtain demonstrative knowledge. His general position is roughly as follows. Ideas (*Vorstellungen*) are the sole contents of the mind, and are explicitly described as pictures of things,[36] which exist independently of our representation of them. This usage covers a fatal ambiguity which seems not to have occurred either to Meier himself or to Kant who reproduced it. For *Vorstellung* comes thereby to be used as equivalent both to Locke's 'idea' and to Leibniz's *repraesentatio*, in spite of the fundamental distinction which really separates the two notions. Locke maintained that ideas (of sensation) were related to their objects either simply as effects to causes (in which case they were essentially unlike their objects) or else (in the case of primary qualities only) both as effects to causes and as copies to originals. But in so far as they were copies at all, they were exact copies. Leibniz, on the other hand, held that ideas were neither exact copies of nor totally different from their originals, since for him the relation was rather that of ectype to archetype than that of copy to original. Meier attempts to combine these views, but only succeeds in vacillating between them, using each when it suits him to avoid the unpleasant implications of the other.

He next proceeds to define a cognition (*Erkenntniss, cognitio*) as being either an aggregate of representations or the act by which a representation of a thing is produced, cognition and representation being regarded as interchangeable terms.[37] They are in fact equivalent to what Hume understood by a complex impression. The next step is to distinguish between a representation (or cognition) and its object, but although Meier asserts the existence of such a distinction,[38] he would have found it difficult if not impossible to say wherein it consisted. Indeed, he was apparently quite unaware, as even Berkeley was not, of the inevitable subjectivism of any consistent copying theory unless it is helped out by an explicit doctrine of innate ideas. In practice he simply follows the method of Hume in treating 'complex impression' and 'object' as synonymous terms without considering the implications of so doing.

The next problem is the consideration of the different kinds of content or representation which the mind is capable of employing in its operations, and it is here that Meier's attempted compromise

[36] § 10. [37] § 11. [38] § 12.

between Locke and Leibniz is most evident. He holds, with the former, that in the end the mind has no materials save those provided by the senses, though his attitude towards such truths as the principle of contradiction and the causal axiom is really inconsistent with this doctrine, and with the latter that different kinds of awareness (sensation, perception, thought) differ from one another only in degree, that is, only as more or less clear and distinct representations. As regards the latter distinction he is a straightforward Leibnizian. A representation is clear when it is such as to enable me to distinguish the object of it from other objects. It is distinct when in addition the relations of its own constituent parts (*Mannigfaltige*) to one another are distinctly apprehended.[39] Now the lowest level at which clear representation can occur is that of sensation (*Empfindung*), which is defined as the representation of a present thing, and in so far as such representation is clear, it constitutes experience (*Erfahrung*).[40] Such experience is either mediate or immediate, the former being 'whatever is derivable by a short proof from what is immediate'. Thus, that I think is an immediate experience, but that I possess a faculty of thinking is a mediate experience.

We next come to *conceptus* (*Begriff*), a term which does not admit of translation without misrepresentation. It is defined[41] as 'a representation of a thing in a being which possesses the faculty of thinking. Hence all our representations are *Begriffe*.' Furthermore,[42] 'there are as many kinds of *Begriffe* as there are different ways of cognizing (philosophical, aesthetic, plain man, &c.)'. This, on the face of it, is a very puzzling view. It becomes less so when we remember that for Meier different levels of apprehension differ only in degree. On this view it is impossible for him to draw any logical distinction between sensation and thought except by specifying, as he naturally makes no attempt to do, the precise degree of clearness which is the border-line between them. Hence he is reduced to introducing the term *Begriff*, which he has to use in its sense of 'concept' to make his logical theory plausible, and immediately pointing out that strictly speaking it is merely a synonym for *Vorstellung* or for the *Inbegriff der Vorstellungen* which is interchangeable with it. Having thus salved his conscience, he proceeds to inquire into the formation of *Begriffe*,

[39] § 14.
[40] § 201.
[41] § 249.
[42] § 250.

and lays it down[43] that this can occur in three ways, namely by 'experience, abstraction, or arbitrary connexion'. Thus *Begriff* is employed to cover (*a*) my 'idea' of the particular motion of a particular body, (*b*) my general or abstract 'idea' of motion, (*c*) hypotheses which I form to explain (*b*) by connecting it at will with other abstract 'ideas', e.g. gravitation.

Now (*b*) may be explained as originating from (*a*), which is immediately apprehended by sensation, and clearly apprehended as by the application of the method of observation and experiment. We must analyse what is given to sense (i) by the help of instruments (microscopes, &c.), (ii) by physical dissection, (iii) by attention to its origination and the source thereof, (iv) by observing it in different environments so as to pick out what is essential to it.[44] By this method we achieve an empirical conception (*Erfahrungsbegriff*) of the particular with which we are dealing 'and this conception is true and certain. It represents to us the object as it is constituted, since otherwise we should be inhabitants of another universe.'[45] This actually is the nearest Meier ever gets to recognizing and disposing of the subjective idealism which haunts his psychological view.

Now from this *Erfahrungsbegriff* (*a*) we can proceed to the general idea (*b*). This is done by 'contrasting the agreeing conceptions of different things and representing distinctly to ourselves those marks which they possess in common'.[46] The method of framing hypotheses requires no special comment.

It is clear that in admitting the above processes Meier is going well beyond the limits of strict empiricism. He is taking for granted what Kant subsequently termed the 'affinity of phenomena', that is, the possession by things or aggregations of particular sensa, of determinate common properties which admit of isolation and abstraction. He does this without explanation or apology, since he is convinced that a thing possesses characteristics (*Merkmale, notae*)[47] which are differentiated in the traditional way into attributes, properties, and modes and that the sum of its necessary characteristics is its essence. Furthermore he maintains without hesitation that this essence, which, in Lockean terms, he holds to be a real and not merely a nominal essence, can be discovered by the empirical method described above.

[43] § 254. [44] § 257. [45] § 258.
[46] § 259. [47] § 121.

He is therefore in no difficulty as to whether the method of logical analysis can give us knowledge of real existence, since he has quietly begged the whole question and is free to proceed at once to expound his logic on traditional lines. For if it is obvious, as he thinks it is,

(1) that the universe consists of things having essences, modes, and relations of which the first are necessary and the others contingent;
(2) that we can discover those essences experimentally;
(3) that cause and logical ground are identical[48] (which he also held in accordance with the tenets of the Wolff–Leibniz view), and that the effect is 'contained in' its cause,

then none of the metaphysical problems of Hume and Kant need ever arise.

CONCLUSION

The works of Baumgarten and Meier are not exhilarating, and if the study of them led only to the satisfaction of antiquarian curiosity it could hardly be justified. There are, however, two substantial reasons for including them in any introduction to Kant's *Critique*. In the first place their terminology and manner of exposition influenced the form of his work to a greater extent than is generally recognized. Indeed, it is not too much to say that all Kant's leading conceptions, such as appearances, representations, and inner sense, and much of his greatly abused architectonic are clearly foreshadowed in the two works which we have just considered. It is impossible to do more than indicate this in a brief survey, and I certainly do not suggest that the content of Kant's mature thought is to any considerable extent anticipated by philosophers who never even recognized the existence of the problems which the *Critique* claims to solve. What we can discover from them concerns Kant's terminology and his presentation; but these are far from being unimportant or free from controversy. In the second place, the mere fact that Kant deliberately chose these books as the basis of his lectures on Metaphysics and Logic and retained them for many years is informative. We are apt to forget that German, unlike French and English, was far from possessing a reasonably developed philosophical termi-

[48] § 15.

nology by the middle of the eighteenth century. Its technical vocabulary consisted of terms translated from other languages and employed without any great attempt at precision. We recognize that words such as 'idea' and 'concept' are of uncertain meaning in the British empiricists, but it is frequently assumed that their German equivalents in the writings of Kant must admit of unambiguous definition. The most cursory reading of Baumgarten and Meier, who were after all standard authors, not philosophical outcasts, will show how little justification there can be for this assumption.

I have not considered here the work of the psychologist, Tetens. His contribution is of a different and more substantial character, but it is especially relevant to Kant's doctrine of inner sense and is best treated in this connexion.[49]

[49] For the influence of other contemporaries, especially Lambert, on Kant's logical development, see de Vleeschauwer, op. cit., vol. i, chap. iii, § C.

III

KANT'S EARLY WORKS

§ I

BEFORE 1766

So far we have considered the specifically philosophical thought by which Kant's development was conditioned, though to do this it has been essential to go beyond what is now considered as purely philosophical subject-matter and to pay some attention to speculations which belong rather to the department of physical and even biological science. In addition it is clear without further argument that the theological implications of metaphysical and scientific theories were of far greater moment in the seventeenth and eighteenth centuries than they are now. In fact it is a convenient over-simplification to consider Kant's development as dominated by the metaphysical view of Wolff and his successors on the one hand and by the physical theories of Newton on the other, since in this connexion it is impracticable to abstract from the difficulties of rationalism in the sphere of physics or the alleged materialist consequences of the Newtonian conception of space. The philosopher was still considered as the spectator of all time and all existence, and a glance at the titles of Wolff's works will show how seriously he felt his responsibility to live up to this reputation. Hence Kant's problem should not be regarded in modern terms as an attempt to harmonize science with theology, but rather as an attempt to reconcile two complete philosophies each of which had scientific as well as theological implications.

Empiricism and rationalism, however, were not the only influences to which he was subjected. Throughout his life he was to a considerable extent controlled by his respect for the religious doctrines of Pietism. These were a reaction against the intolerant dogmatism of rationalist theologians and aimed, as such reactions do, at basing religion on the private convictions of the individual rather than on the authoritative pronouncements of an organized Church or philosophical school. Pietism, therefore, was wholly opposed to the Wolffian conception of a rational theology, mathematically demonstrable and as such completely objective and impersonal in character. It was a religion of the heart rather than the head, and attached importance to the performance of moral acts and to the possession of a good will rather than to the elaboration and acceptance of a logically coherent philosophical system. Its efficacy depended, as that of non-rational religions is bound to do, entirely on the personal qualities of its adherents, and it must be admitted that many Pietists on obtaining posts of authority were at least as tyrannical and dogmatic as their dogmatic opponents. Kant, however, was on the whole fortunate in his experiences of the manifestations of Pietism, and appears to have seen its effects at their best in the persons of his parents, for whom his admiration seems to have been justified. To this influence, as well as to his own common sense, is to be attributed his constant persuasion that no view, especially in morals, which runs counter to the plain man's convictions or is too complicated for his intelligence can in the end be satisfactory.

It is therefore fair to say that while Kant was educated both at school and at the university of Königsberg in accordance with the tenets of Wolff and his successors, his acceptance of their system was seriously prejudiced at the start. The two teachers chiefly responsible for this were Schultz and Knutzen.[1] The former was the leading theological authority in Königsberg as well as being Rektor of the Collegium Fredericianum where Kant received his early education; he succeeded in combining the virtues of Pietism with a general adherence to the views of Wolff whose pupil he had been. The latter was a physicist who propagated and defended the Newtonian theory against rationalist criticism, and was responsible for the predominantly physical character of Kant's earlier works.

§ 2

Kant's development from his first essay on the *Correct Method of Calculating the Active Force of Bodies* published in 1747 to the first edition of the *Critique* in 1781 is on the whole straightforward and can be briefly summarized. He set out primarily as a rationalist philosopher, though with some doubts as to the perfection of that system especially as regards physical investigations,

[1] See Benno Erdmann, *Martin Knutzen und seine Zeit*, Leipzig, 1876.

and until about 1760 he maintained this attitude, though his doubt increased continually as time went on. There ensued a period from 1760 to 1769 in which his difficulties grew so rapidly as almost to overwhelm his conviction and in which his sympathy with the empiricist case almost amounts to conversion. Whether or not he read Hume's *Enquiry* before or during this period is uncertain. The fact that he subsequently attributed to the author of it his awakening from a dogmatic slumber suggests that he had, but the manner in which he formulated and attempted to deal with his problems provides on the whole better evidence that he had not. On the other hand, he almost certainly did read the *Nouveaux Essais* of Leibniz, which were published in 1765, and it is reasonable to suppose that this study was largely responsible for his subsequent refusal to accept empiricism as a satisfactory philosophy. At any rate the year 1769, as he says, 'brought him great light', and it may be assumed that the nature of that light is shown by his *Dissertation* published in 1770. Its teaching is that the empiricist and rationalist philosophies are not strictly irreconcilable with one another, but that their conflict is the result of a misunderstanding of the nature of the objects with which mathematics and philosophy respectively have to deal. The complete elaboration of this doctrine is given in the *Critique of Pure Reason* (1781); and the *Critiques of Practical Reason* and *Judgement* published respectively in 1788 and 1790.

It is hardly necessary to point out that for Kant himself the process of evolution was nothing like as simple as this, and that this division of his thought into periods is largely arbitrary. None the less he did regard 1769 as a crucial date in the growth of his view, and in this it is generally agreed that he was perfectly correct. His publications before that date will be considered only in so far as they seem to throw light on his subsequent treatment of the problems which he finally regarded as being fundamental. Only two of them require anything like detailed discussion, namely *Dreams of a Spirit Seer* published in 1766 and *The Ground of the Distinction between different Regions in Space* (1768). The importance of these works lies in the fact that they show Kant's maximum concessions to the claims of scepticism and make clear the necessity which he then felt either to abandon rationalism completely or to adopt an entirely new and revolutionary standpoint from which it could be still maintained without prejudice to those empiricist doctrines which he could not refuse to accept. The difficulties whose consideration gradually forced him into this position are in the end all reducible to two, namely the problem of the status of the principle of sufficient reason and the problem of the nature of space. The history of his pre-Critical thought is best understood in terms of these.

§ 3

As a natural consequence of his rationalist training Kant's attitude towards the principle of sufficient reason was very different from that of the British empiricists. Locke and Hume regarded it as obvious that a distinction existed between our capacity to apprehend relations of ideas and relations of real existence, with the result that for both of them the hardest of philosophical questions was how the transition from one kind of knowledge to the other could be effected. The problem was for Leibniz only secondary and for his successors virtually non-existent. To them it was evident that our perception of the relations of matter of fact was nothing but a more or less obscure representation of the relations between conceptions which the mind by common consent could apprehend clearly and distinctly, and thus it came about that Kant's problem in relation to the principle of sufficient reason was formulated as the outcome of an accumulation of apparently minor difficulties and was not articulated as a whole until later in his career. This unsatisfactory method of approach was rendered much easier by Baumgarten's 'simplification' of Leibniz, whereby the principle of sufficient reason was regarded as derivative and demonstrable by means of the principle of contradiction, since this derivation tended to distract attention from the notion of ground and consequent itself and concentrate it on the difficulties to which that notion as so derived inevitably gave rise in the interpretation of phenomena. For the immediate consequence of such a derivation is to obliterate the distinction between the physical and the metaphysical and to make the self-contained monad itself an element in the physical world, as Wolff and Baumgarten had done. The implication was that actual physical bodies were connected with one another only as members of a pre-established harmony, and this view, which was clearly inconsistent with the Newtonian doctrine of attraction, gave rise to the prolonged dispute on the issue of pre-established harmony versus *influxus physicus* which was the dominant issue between physicists in Kant's early years. It is worth observing that Knutzen, as opposed to Baumgarten, was an ardent Newtonian and supported the theory of *influxus physicus*.

Kant's first examination of the principle of sufficient reason occurs in the *Nova Dilucidatio*,[2] in which he insists on the importance of the distinction between logical and real or causal necessitation. The *ratio essendi* of anything, which is its *ratio antecedenter determinans*, is not to be confused with its *ratio cognoscendi* or *ratio consequenter determinans*, so that sequences in the real world in accordance with the law of cause and effect involve a different relation from that which holds between ideas in an inferential process. Although Kant does not here develop this thought, it evidently remained very much in his mind, and applications of it are made to different aspects of the rationalist view in most of his subsequent works.

The first of these which is of importance here deals with the classical doctrine of the *Four Syllogistic Figures* (1762). From one point of view this essay represents an extreme rationalist position, since what Kant wishes to maintain is that the nerve of all demonstration is the *dictum de omni et nullo*, and that consequently the only truly valid syllogistic mode is *Barbara* (the first mode of the first figure).[3] But just because of his uncompromising stand in this, he is driven to admit that a great many propositions which we actually hold to be true do not admit of such demonstration. Indeed, all judgements involving concepts whose agreement or repugnancy is immediately obvious without the interposition of any third concept as a middle term are indemonstrable judgements, and human knowledge contains many such judgements. Here again Kant does not inquire whether the causal axiom itself is an indemonstrable judgement, but the line of investigation which he has commenced is clearly a dangerous one for an orthodox rationalist to pursue very far.

Kant does pursue it, though without any apparent recognition of the conclusion to which it inevitably leads, in his *Essay on the Introduction of Negative Magnitudes into Philosophy* (1763). The purpose of this work is to draw attention to a matter of some

[2] *Principiorum primorum cognitionis metaphysicae nova dilucidatio* (1755).
[3] Cf. B 141.

interest about which rationalist metaphysics is inadequate to provide an account consistent with that offered by physical science. Metaphysics maintains that opposition can be clearly apprehended only in its logical signification, in which contrary predicates simply annihilate one another. But, as Kant rightly points out, this is not what takes place in the case of real opposition, for instance in a collision between bodies, for here the consequence is a resultant of their previous motions. The point itself is of no great importance, but the use which Kant makes of it is instructive. All he wishes to maintain is that metaphysics must take account of such real oppositions and include the notion of negative quantities which are used to express them as notions of realities and not merely privations. He does not notice that he himself has now rendered such inclusion impossible by showing, (1) that causal sequences are distinct from inferential sequences, (2) that inferential sequences are strictly valid only when they can be demonstrated by means of the *dictum*, (3) that physical truths cannot be so demonstrated since the real opposition which many of them involve is entirely different from logical negation. But instead of criticizing rationalism for its failure to provide any logical basis for scientific method at all, he merely urges it to use the notion of negative magnitudes to help its own investigations. The conclusion of the essay shows that Kant is on the verge of formulating his real difficulty in an adequate way. Here he returns from the special question of logical and real opposition to the wider one of the contrast between logical and real connexion in general. The whole passage[4] is too long to quote, but the gist of it is that a causal connexion is never really rendered intelligible by the only account which rationalism can offer of it; for in a valid inferential process, conceived in the very narrow way in which Kant insists that it ought to be, the concept of the predicate in the conclusion is regarded as being actually part of and therefore contained in the concept of the subject. All that inference does is to make the fact that it is so contained explicit by exhibiting the relation of both concepts to a third concept which is the middle term. But it is quite clear that the causal sequences which as scientists we are concerned to study are not at all like this, for the motion of a body A which is the effect of the impact on it of another body B is not 'contained in' the motion of B but is

[4] Ak. ii. 201–4.

something quite distinct from it which can never be discovered by analysis of it. But if, as seems to be the case, effects are not discoverable by analysis of their causes, how on rationalist principles are they to be discovered at all?

At this stage the conclusion of Hume that they are not discoverable, but can only be guessed at, is inevitable unless the situation can be saved by a complete revolution in Wolffian metaphysics.

§ 4

Kant's growing dissatisfaction with the rationalist account of causality was accompanied by his gradual recognition that a rather similar problem existed as regards space. In the first instance this, too, appealed to him simply as a minor difficulty within the system and not as a weakness inherent in it owing to its fundamental assumptions. He first encountered the problem in the form of the antinomy or conflict between the infinite divisibility of space itself and the alleged indivisibility of the ultimate constituents of matter. In his *Monadologia Physica* (1756) he attempted to solve this problem by the very modern suggestion that particles, since their essence is held by Leibnizian physics to consist in the possession of *vis viva*, need not be conceived as occupying space but should be thought of simply as having position in it. This would be consistent with their having the only important space-occupying quality of impenetrability, since if a particle simply is force radiating from a mathematical point, the resistance offered to any other particle will increase to infinity as that point is approached. This conception of matter as occupying space 'intensively' Kant continued to hold, and the section in the *Critique* entitled *Anticipations of Perception* is actually based on it. But whether or not such an account was satisfactory from the point of view of natural philosophy, it could hardly if pressed be made consistent with orthodox Wolffian physics, since it attributed to space a reality in relation to monads which is scarcely to be reconciled with the notion of space as simply a confused perception.

The real difficulty, however, is not formulated till 1764. In that year Kant produced his unsuccessful prize essay on *The Relative Clearness of the Fundamental Principles of Mathematics as contrasted with those of Morality and Religion.* Mathematics, he there argues, proceeds by drawing conclusions about the implications of concepts which exist only in so far as certain figures have been constructed. It can never be in doubt whether these concepts correspond to the facts or not. But the purpose of moral philosophy is to make precise a concept which is given, though in a confused manner. Mathematics in fact proceeds synthetically by constructing figures, whereas philosophy in general proceeds analytically by the clarification of concepts. This contrast is further emphasized when we reflect that mathematics deals with its universal terms by means of concrete symbols whose content is objective and invariable (lines, figures, &c.), whereas philosophy must work with words, which are notoriously indeterminate and variable in their import. It follows that ultimate unanalysable notions and indemonstrable propositions are few in mathematics but extremely numerous in philosophy, whose starting-point must be true propositions immediately apprehended about the object, not arbitrary definitions. The proper procedure of philosophy is simply to accept as true propositions derived from experience whose truth we cannot doubt even though they lack the kind of demonstration which mathematics owing to its entirely different procedure is able to provide.

The importance of this essay lies not merely in the extremely empiricist attitude which it advocates in moral and religious philosophy, as well as physical science; from the point of view of Kant's final doctrine it is noteworthy as containing his first explicit recognition of the essentially intuitional or perceptual character of geometry. For having now clearly recognized that the actual perception of lines and figures is essential to geometrical demonstration, he can no longer maintain both that geometry is valid of the world of real objects and that the space in which geometrical constructions are made is simply a confused perception. The position adopted in the essay could only be maintained as long as he thought it self-evident that the space of which I am aware in perception is identical with the objective space in which things exist independently of my perception, but the extreme empiricist position which he now adopts is bound to lead him eventually to question that assumption. For if all our concepts originate in experience, and if this is true even of our concept of space, the validity of geometry itself becomes dubious; so that Kant is driven to ask what the real nature of space may be independently of its presentation to consciousness.

The position of Leibniz had been that the activity of monads consisted in their power of 'representing', and consequently that space, as involved in my representations, must be analysable into a clear concept, namely that of an order of coexistence. But Kant has now demonstrated that geometry is a synthetic science which differs from philosophy in taking its objects from intuition and connecting them with one another. Space thus becomes an unanalysable but fundamental notion which does not admit of such a reduction to conceptual terms at all.

§ 5

DREAMS OF A SPIRIT SEER

So far nothing in Kant's published work goes beyond expounding the difficulties with which rationalism is embarrassed. The first real hint of the lines along which the critical solution is to develop occurs in the curious *Dreams of a Spirit Seer* published in 1766. This work is a critical examination of the doctrines of Swedenborg, a spiritualist who claimed to have actual intercourse with disembodied spirits; but Kant goes far beyond his ostensible subject and discusses the whole question of the relation between soul and body with a view to deciding whether the existence of the former apart from the latter can be rationally maintained and, if it can, whether our belief in the existence of such souls can ever extend beyond mere conjecture and hypothesis.

He begins by pointing out that the concept of spirits as immaterial entities which none the less are spatially located in bodies is itself extremely difficult. When carefully considered, however, it may be seen not to differ in principle from the similar problem dealt with in the *Monadologia Physica* of the spatial location of forces which also must be regarded as pervading space without being themselves extended.[5] Such an account of the character of spirit has the advantage of rendering unnecessary all discussions as to the seat of the soul in the body and also of making possible a distinction in kind between souls and material substances.

Kant admits[6] that his personal inclination is in favour of a view

[5] Ak. ii. 322.

[6] Ak. ii. 327.

of this kind, though he recognizes the great difficulties which the interaction of the soul with the body must present as soon as such a difference in kind is allowed to exist between them. If, however, these difficulties can be surmounted, and he does not regard them as necessarily insuperable, it will be permissible to inquire further into the possible relations of such spirits with one another. We might reasonably maintain that they are related not as the bodies with which they are connected are related in space, but immediately in what he describes as a *mundus intelligibilis*.[7] To such a world physical relations would be accidental and irrelevant. Now although the existence of such a spirit world is neither obvious nor demonstrable, there does seem to be sufficient evidence for it to make it something more than an empty hypothesis. The phenomenon which most favours our belief in it is the existence of a general will or rather of a moral or social sense shared by a number of individuals. For this readily admits of being regarded as the empirical manifestation of a real connexion between spirits just as the laws of gravitation[8] are a manifestation of the real though inaccessible *vis viva* which is the essence of material things.

But if this account is at all sound, it seems at first sight very odd that this spiritual reality behind empirically apprehended individuals is so little revealed to us.[9] This difficulty, however, is only apparent, for we must remember that the intuition by which a man recognizes himself as a member of the super-sensible world must necessarily be different in kind from his awareness of himself as a human being through a representation which has its origin in his physical body. He must be regarded as the same subject, though not the same person in the two worlds, and between these divergent ideas of himself there is simply no connexion whatever. For the representation of myself as spirit is an inference from the observed phenomenon of the general will; it can never be given in intuition or experienced, but we should be wrong for this reason to assume that all apprehension of a *mundus intelligibilis* is out of the question, for we might be able to represent to ourselves at least something analogous[10] to the reality which in

[7] Ak. ii. 329.

[8] Ak. ii. 335. It was presumably this idea which led Kant to treat the ethical views of Rousseau as comparable in importance to the physical theories of Newton.

[9] Ak. ii. 337.

[10] Ak. ii. 339.

itself is imperceptible to us. After all, the subject is the same in both its capacities, and therefore its ideas though admittedly quite disparate need not be entirely disjoined, but it could hardly be denied that even this limited degree of insight is at best the perquisite only of a limited number of individuals and must in its very nature be of subjective validity only.

Thus we can only conclude that there is nothing to prevent us from believing in the existence of a world of spirits if we wish to do so, but if we do, we must remember that there is and can be no proof of its existence, since the nature of spirit and therefore of life itself in so far as it is held to be essentially immaterial and non-mechanical is quite inaccessible to our intelligence.

Kant concludes from this that metaphysics regarded as a system of knowledge concerning a super-sensible world must be abandoned as a dream. All that we can claim to know are the mechanical laws which can be empirically verified as governing the movements of bodies, and even here we must admit that the reason why bodies obey such laws is necessarily out of our power to discover.[11] His position is even more agnostic than that of Newton had been, for although the latter admitted in the *Principia* that he had not yet discovered the cause of gravity, he suggested that this ignorance was due to a lack of suitable experiments which the future would doubtless supply, and not to any difficulty inherent in things. But what is more important than this approach to empiricism is Kant's notion of the universe as consisting of a *mundus intelligibilis* or world of reality contrasted with a world of sensibility or representation, and also his location of the true or moral self together with really efficacious material causes to the former, whereas those manifestations of force which are the subject-matter of mathematical assessment are held to belong to the latter. The *Dissertation* of 1770 and the three *Critiques* are essentially an elaboration and development of this general doctrine sketched in *Dreams of a Spirit Seer*; they differ from it not in any extension of our knowledge to grasp the super-sensible world, but in their claim to demonstrate that, as far as the sensible world is concerned, our knowledge is *a priori* and not merely empirical in character.

[11] Ak. ii. 371.

§ 6

THE ESSAY OF 1768

Von dem ersten Grunde des Unterschiedes der Gegenden im Raume

In this short essay[12] Kant at last recognizes quite explicitly the insuperable difficulties involved for his physical theory by both the Newtonian and Leibnizian doctrines of space and thus enters on the line of thought which results in the attempted solution of the *Dissertation.* The specific problem is, What account are we to give of 'incongruent counterparts', figures or bodies which are exactly similar but do not coincide when superimposed on one another, as, for instance, a right- and left-hand glove or screw[13]? For if we are to draw any distinction at all between them, we are bound to take for granted the existence of an absolute space in which both exist. To do this, however, involves giving up the notion of space as a predicate or quality of things, for it would appear that things must be regarded as presupposing space and not vice versa. Hence Kant abandons the rationalist doctrine completely and adopts the view of Newton and Clarke, namely that space is neither the product of abstraction from sensuous experience of things nor itself an object of outer perception but an actually existent real entity of whose nature we are immediately aware by 'inner sense'. Further, 'mensuration provides a convincing proof that absolute space independent of the existence of all matter and itself the ultimate ground for the possibility of the composition of matter, possesses a reality of its own'.

Since, then, everything which exists is in space and as such spatial, there exists no non-spatial, intelligible world as postulated by previous metaphysicians, and metaphysics itself, considered as the science of the super-sensible, must be regarded as mere illusion. The science of nature becomes the only genuine science which we have. This doctrine of space gives further support to the conception of geometry as essentially synthetic; for since intuited

[12] Ak. ii. 375–85.

[13] Let belated justice be done to poor Mr. Richardson whose translation of *Proleg.*, § 13, has been greeted with derision by his successors from Mahaffy (p. 39) to Lucas (p. 43). Kant meant 'snails', not 'spirals'. See '*Fast alle Schnecken . . .*', Ak. ii. 380. '*Contrary to all sense*' is not so good.

space is the ontological presupposition of mathematical objects, it is only to be expected that purely conceptual and therefore analytical thought will fail to penetrate to this sphere and that nothing but intuition can reveal to us the spatial combinations of objects.

The idea of absolute space in fact seems to provide the answer to Kant's difficulties in so far as these are concerned purely with geometry. It enables him to maintain against scepticism the validity and *a priori* character of mathematics while keeping an agnostic attitude towards the alleged super-sensible knowledge of rationalist metaphysicians; it also justifies the peculiar position which he ascribes to mathematics in virtue of its synthetic character, as contrasted with all other sciences including metaphysics, and it does this simply by bringing out the necessarily intuitable character of space which alone makes that synthetic procedure intelligible. None the less, as he realized, the view was by no means free from difficulties.

For Kant differed from Leibniz in that he always found the idea of an actual infinity of real entities intolerable. He had as a scientist accepted the notion of infinitesimals and therefore of infinity for purposes of calculation, but to assert as a metaphysical truth that a finite thing could contain within it an actually infinite number of real parts was a very different proposition, since to assert it would involve giving up not merely metaphysics but also his own physical doctrine of monads as centres of force; for if space is real and infinitely divisible it is impossible to conceive it as occupied by a determinate number of centres of force, yet their number, however great, must be determinate if the doctrine of the conservation of *vis viva* in the universe is to be upheld. Thus he was placed in an unfortunate position. He could not retain the Newtonian doctrine of space and thereby explain the synthetic and apodeictic character of mathematics except at the cost of sacrificing his physical theory; but he could not return to the orthodox position without giving up his conviction of the *a priori* validity of applied mathematics. He was thus in a dilemma from which he believed that the doctrine of the *Dissertation* offered the only hopeful avenue of escape.

§ 7

THE DISSERTATION (1770)

De mundi sensibilis atque intelligibilis forma et principiis

It is difficult to decide on the proper method of treating the *Dissertation.* It was Kant's Latin inaugural lecture as a professor at Königsberg, and all that is of material value in it was republished practically verbatim in German in the *Critique* eleven years later.[14] As Kant published nothing of even secondary philosophical importance during the interim, it is a document of great historical interest as a link between his pre-Critical and Critical doctrines. Its merit lies in the light which, taken in conjunction with his correspondence and fragmentary notes between 1770 and 1781, it throws on his distinction, never clearly elucidated in the *Critique* itself, between phenomena and the things in themselves of which phenomena are representations. This is an extremely difficult problem which is better considered as a whole at a later stage. At this point I shall merely indicate the doctrine of the *Dissertation* and the difficulties of the succeeding period and pass immediately to the mature view of the *Critique.*

Sensibility, Kant now holds, does not reflect things in themselves (noumena) in a confused manner as the rationalists maintain. It is not to be compared with a mirror, since it imposes on things specific forms which exist only in so far as things are represented under them by a perceiving subject. None the less, sensuous knowledge, so far as it goes, is perfectly valid and in no way the arbitrary product of imagination. But it is erroneous to suppose that such knowledge can ever be extended to things in themselves, since it is necessarily valid only of things apprehended under the forms of space and time, that is of representations. Turning now to the understanding, we find that it possesses two distinct functions,[15] namely a logical and a real employment. The former, which consists in the formation of concepts and judgements, needs no explanation. The latter is a capacity of representing that which by reason of its non-sensuous character cannot be perceived by sense at all, e.g. causation.

[14] He considered that it alone of his pre-Critical work was worth preserving.
[15] Ak. ii. 393.

Concepts of this kind are not derived by abstraction from the data of sense, and consequently should not strictly speaking be termed concepts but rather pure ideas,[16] which are native to the understanding just as forms of sense are to sensibility. They are not to be regarded as innate, but are derived by us from attention to the operations of the understanding in relation to experience, and since they are of this nature they must embrace not sensuous representations but things as they are in themselves. Mathematics provides the *a priori* science of the world of phenomena in virtue of its pure intuitions, while metaphysics provides the science of the intelligible world in virtue of the pure concepts of the understanding.

This view is a compromise between those of Leibniz and Newton, and we may suppose that the retreat from empiricism which it involves was the result of Kant's study of the *Nouveaux Essais*. It leaves him with a hopeless problem of how things in themselves can possibly be connected to form a world, since space and time do not apply to them, and here he is simply driven back on occasionalism. There can be no specifiable relation at all. Every monad must be conceived as complete in itself and therefore contingent except in so far as it can be regarded as divinely sustained. Clearly as an account of the real nature of the physical universe this is extremely unsatisfactory; indeed Kant himself admits that it reduces universal causality, the principle of the conservation of matter, and indeed all scientific principles outside the range of pure mathematics, to the level of heuristic fictions possessing no objective validity.

The development from the *Dissertation* to the *Critique*, then, consists in Kant's gradual acceptance of the pure concepts of the understanding as being of the same nature as space, that is as being objectively valid of phenomena but inapplicable to things in themselves, and the relegation of the super-sensible world to the state of unknowability to which it had previously been condemned in *Dreams of a Spirit Seer*.

[16] Ak. ii. 394.

§ 8

FROM 1770 TO 1781

The *Dissertation* teaches that things *qua* sensuous are apprehended by us through sensibility, whereas things *qua* intelligible are apprehended by means of the understanding. In contrast to the doctrines of Leibniz it maintains that each of these faculties within its own sphere provides *cognitiones verissimas*, but that any attempt to regard the spheres as continuous is doomed to failure at the start. The position is summed up in the sentence 'quas mens ab intellectu fert ideas abstractas, illas in concreto exsequi et in intuitus commutare saepenumero non posse'.[17] Sensuous knowledge, however far it is carried, will always remain sensuous and will never become transformed into conceptual knowledge as Leibniz had supposed would be the case, and the failure of the rationalists to observe this truth is responsible for the contradictions which arise as soon as any attempt is made to give an account of the nature of space and time in conceptual terms. Up to this point the view is identical with the critical position as expounded in the *Critique*. It is in respect of the character and intelligibility of the objects of the understanding that Kant's mature view differs from the earlier one.

Here again the *Dissertation* view is perfectly simple, too simple, unfortunately, to be retained for long. It is simply that whereas our sensuous knowledge is of the appearances of things, our intellectual knowledge is of things as they really are in abstraction from all conditions of sensibility. In other words Kant's view in 1770 was that the mind can reach genuine knowledge of independently existing objects by means of pure reason, provided that it is careful in doing so to abstract altogether from the sensuous conditions under which those things are given to us in perception; and the practical conclusion is that geometry deals with appearances while physics and metaphysics (not at all clearly distinguished from one another) give us knowledge of the real as it is in itself.

It seems to me likely that the decisive influence of Hume on Kant's thought occurred at this point, namely after the *Dissertation*, and it is easy to imagine exactly how the difficulty was

[17] Ak. ii. 389.

brought home to him. 'Does it contain experimental reasoning on matters of fact and existence? No. Commit it then to the flames, for it can contain nothing but sophistry and illusion.' So ran Hume's conclusion in the *Enquiry*, and this constituted a challenge which Kant could hardly ignore. The *Dissertation* manifestly did assert the possession by us of just that capacity which Hume so strenuously denied of obtaining knowledge of real existence by means of pure reason alone. Kant's development for ten years or so is nothing more than his gradual extrication of himself from this position.

For the metaphysical view of the *Dissertation* is that there exist both selves and things. These are all substances in the Leibnizian sense, but by the doctrine of *influxus physicus* no longer windowless monads. They can somehow 'affect' one another, though the manner of this 'affecting' is never satisfactorily formulated. But, granting its possibility, we can maintain that the operation of the real thing on the real self produces in that self a representation of the thing, a sensuous, spatio-temporal image. This image would not be an exact 'resemblance' of the real thing, but rather an analogon or symbol of it such that to every part of the representation there corresponded a part, not necessarily like it, in the real thing. Now the crux of this view is that it remains plausible if and only if I can rightly claim an acquaintance with the real thing independently of sense-experience. Locke had evaded this difficulty by his unsupported assertion that our ideas of primary qualities were like their originals, since on this understanding we can regard the ideas of secondary qualities of things as produced in us by the operation on our senses of minute particles endowed with primary qualities. Kant, when he composed the *Dissertation*, saw no serious difficulty in such a view, but he came to see one as a result of a more careful study of the central point in Hume's *Enquiry*. For what Hume is there maintaining is first and foremost that this fundamental assumption cannot be established.

Furthermore, the central problem for Kant in this connexion is bound to be the nature of our knowledge of the causal axiom, for the nerve of his position in the *Dissertation* is that real things affect our sensibility and are in fact the cause of appearances in us. Now if this is sound, only two methods are possible for reaching knowledge of real existences; either we must reach this knowledge by pure reason alone or we must obtain it inductively by arguing from effect to cause. But Kant cannot permanently accept either of these views. The first would involve the admission that physics as an experimental science is valueless, since the truth is accessible to pure reason without assistance from experience; the second would lead certainly to the conclusion that physics as an inductive science can give us probability only, not knowledge.

In view of this Kant's main interest ceases to be space and becomes causality; he regards the question 'How is physics possible as a science?' as the question which above all others requires an answer from philosophy. The outline of the answer seems to have occurred to him quite early. It was the elaboration of it which occupied so much time. In principle he regards the problem as solved at once by the introduction of 'forms of thought' or categories. For if it can be maintained that causality, substantiality, and the other fundamental concepts of physics are, like space and time, not properties of things in themselves at all but simply forms of my apprehension, it will be possible to understand how, by experimental physics, I can achieve *a priori* knowledge of real though phenomenal existences. Physics like geometry may then be deemed to provide *cognitiones verissimas* provided that its operation is restricted to the sphere of things as they appear to me and that it is forbidden to make any assertion as to the nature of 'things as they really are'. We may here anticipate Kant's working out of this scheme to the extent of observing its obvious implication as regards the status of the 'real thing' (not phenomenal, but noumenal). For, on the face of it, by transferring physics as well as geometry to the sphere of appearances Kant has to a great extent emptied the noumenal world of objects of investigation. He has also, by transferring cause to the phenomenal sphere, made the simple metaphysics by which 'real things' can be regarded as just the 'cause' of appearances, untenable. It is not clear, however, that he ever abandoned this view in principle. It is unfortunate that the *Transcendental Aesthetic*, which is derived wholly from the *Dissertation*, accepts it in a far more naïve form than is compatible with the more complex though substantially identical doctrine contained in the section on *Phenomena and Noumena* in the *Analytic*.

PART II

THE ARGUMENT OF THE CRITIQUE

I

INTRODUCTION TO PART II

ALTHOUGH the repetition of well-known doctrine and the study of unexciting philosophers and immature Criticism which any historical approach to the *Critique* involves is certainly laborious, I believe that it is not merely justified but is the only sensible method of going to work. It is unlikely, however, that many readers will agree with me, for the conviction that any serious book about philosophy must be judged by its capacity to answer those philosophical questions which are recognized as urgent now is very strong; so, too, is the belief that a philosopher whose terminology is ambiguous can be refuted once and for all by the exposure of that ambiguity even though it arose from an attitude towards reality which the author could hardly avoid adopting and for which he was certainly not responsible.

'Kant', it will be said by critics of this type, 'formulated a question and claimed to answer it. The question was, "How are synthetic propositions *a priori* possible?" What we need to do in order to estimate the philosophical value of the *Critique* is to discover precisely what questioning thought corresponds to these words. When we have done this we can proceed to inquire whether the *Critique* gives any satisfactory answer to Kant's question. Pre-Kantian philosophy and pre-Critical Kant may throw some light on the history of philosophical thought but have no bearing on philosophy.'

I disagree with this view.

The method of dissection has been tried on Kant's question many times and led nowhere. It cannot be successful because Kant, as we have seen, was concerned not with one question but with several. They were not isolated, but the connexion between them is exactly what the *Critique* as a whole reveals. There was for Kant a problem of space, a problem of cause, and a problem of free will. He believed that he had discovered a method which led to the solution of all of them, and this method was employed in his transcendental philosophy. But no amount of preliminary analysis of his question will indicate what these problems were, and no dissection of the *Critique* conceived as a timeless contribution to philosophy will do much to reveal the nature of Kant's solutions. This does not mean that Kant was himself always confused or uncertain as to what the questions were which he wanted to answer, but rather that he understood, as some of his critics have failed to do, the peculiar nature of philosophical inquiry. No mathematician whose questions are ambiguously formulated is likely to meet with much success. But Kant had realized years before he started work on the *Critique* that the distinction between mathematics and philosophy was fundamental and that definitions which are the starting-point of the former are the aim of the latter; and since for better or worse this was his view, we cannot hope to elucidate his work by an analysis, however painstaking, of his opening remarks. The Introduction to the *Critique* is not the few pages of text which are called by that name. It is the historical process which culminated in the production of the book, and it is of this that I have given a summary account. If these considerations are borne in mind, it is not misleading to describe Kant's purpose as being the justification of empirical scientific method without prejudice to the validity of Euclid, Newton, or the moral law. His method was transcendental philosophy, and he proposed to survey the field of human knowledge as Locke had done, but from an entirely different point of view. Kant was interested not in knowledge as such but in *a priori* knowledge. He proposed to discover and examine the validity of just those concepts of which he believed that empiricism had no satisfactory account to offer, and the aim of this Critical inquiry was to prove

(*a*) that Euclidean geometry is valid of objects;
(*b*) that Newtonian mechanics is valid of objects;
(*c*) that the metaphysics of Leibniz as developed by the Wolffians is not valid of objects.

The general proof of these contentions depends on the already familiar distinction between things as phenomena and in themselves which is the basis of all the three *Critiques*. Special interest belongs, however, to the *Transcendental Analytic* in the *Critique of Pure Reason* by reason both of its extreme difficulty and of the problem with which it is concerned: 'How is pure physics possible?' Kant's argument here depends almost entirely for its force on his belief that the empirical psychology of Locke's successors, including their views on the formation of concepts and similar problems, is essentially correct. What he claims to demonstrate is that it is not truly self-sufficient, but needs to assume that certain specifiable *a priori* propositions are known to be true.

In this Part, I shall sometimes simply summarize Kant's own exposition in the *Critique* and sometimes give a restatement of my own which does not claim to do more than express the outline of his thought on a particular problem; I shall also add explanatory comments on the more controversial aspects of his general view.

As I do not believe that the first and second editions differ from one another in principle but only in the importance they attach to the special problem of time and inner sense, I have thought it sufficient to give references throughout only to the second edition. In the *Transcendental Deduction*, however, I have attempted to conflate the first and second edition's versions, as I am even less confident than Kant was that the psychological background which the second edition almost entirely omits can be left out without serious damage to the whole thread of the argument. It is necessary for the exposition if not for the proof of his deduction.

II

THE PREFACES AND INTRODUCTION TO THE CRITIQUE

SUMMARY OF PREFACE B (B vii–xxxvii)

To decide whether a particular branch of study is entitled to be called a science or whether it is still in the stage of mere conjecture and guess-work we must satisfy ourselves first as to the extent to which it leads to results of unquestioned validity and importance and second as to the measure of agreement among those who profess it as to its fundamental propositions and the methods of pursuing it. Judging by this standard, we may say that in three departments of its activity human knowledge is essentially scientific in character, namely in logic, mathematics, and physics. Among these logic is peculiar in that its aim is not, like that of the other two, the obtaining of knowledge about objects but is simply the study of the formal conditions of valid thinking without any reference to the objects with which such thought may be concerned. Hence its task is comparatively simple, and indeed it was completed by Aristotle and has never since required substantial alteration or amendment. Mathematics and physics are in a different position in that each of them can be seen to have required a revolution in our common method of thinking before it could claim to be genuinely scientific.

This revolution is required to bring about the transition from mere collecting of specimens to the elaboration of explanatory theories which hold good generally, and do not need confirmation by specific instances. In the case of geometry this transition was achieved so long ago that all record of it is lost. It consisted in the recognition that the properties which belong necessarily to a figure can be discovered neither by simple inspection of particulars nor by analysis of the concepts of which those particulars are instances, but by concentration on the act by which the figure has been constructed and by realization that no property can be known to belong to it necessarily except those which have been incorporated in it by that act of construction. In physics a precisely similar revolution was brought about, though at a much later date by the introduction of experimental methods. Here, too, it was recognized that neither mere observation nor analysis of concepts could lead to the discovery of laws of nature. The experiment fulfils precisely the same function as the constructing of the geometrical figure. When we attend to our own activity in performing it, we are similarly aware that the outcome is not merely a particular occurrence but exemplifies a law which is universally valid.

If we now turn to the other great department of human knowledge, namely metaphysics, we are bound to admit that no similar development has occurred, for no advance has taken place since ancient times, and no single proposition can be formulated which will command general assent among metaphysicians themselves. The nature and existence of God and the self, the validity of the causal axiom, and even that of mathematics are all called into question. In this predicament we may well ask whether a revolution similar to those already made in the other sciences may not be practicable and lead to similar beneficial results. The aim of metaphysics is to study the real as such, that is the universe in general, not this or that special department of it. Hence this revolution requires the hypothesis that the universe in general, in so far as it is capable of being known, contains certain elements which are contributed to it by the mind. This, however, will involve the further supposition that by 'the universe in so far as it is capable of being known' we mean 'the universe in so far as it is capable of being experienced', for then we might hold that, inasmuch as experiencing is an activity, it does contribute something to its own object by imposing on it a determinate form; and if this is so, we may hope to discover that form and in so doing to find out what are in fact the laws to which nature *qua* object of experience is subject.

Such an hypothesis would be not unlike that introduced by Copernicus into the sphere of astronomy. For just as he succeeded in explaining what had previously been regarded as the real motion of the fixed stars as an apparent motion due to the real change in the position of the observer relative to them, so we should be explaining the most general laws of nature, which we normally take to be entirely independent of our apprehension and inherent in things, as being actually contributed by ourselves and relating not things as they are in themselves but things as they appear to us under conditions of sensibility. Naturally such a view can be put forward in the first instance only as an hypothesis. It requires confirmation, just as Copernicus's hypothesis had to wait for the discoveries of Newton before it could be taken as scientifically established, and this confirmation is precisely what the *Critique* will provide.

This demonstration, however, has an implication which is at first sight disquieting. For suppose we succeed in proving that our knowledge of general laws can extend to things in so far as they are objects of sensuous experience, but no farther, we shall admittedly have refuted sceptical doubts, such as those of Hume, as to the possibility of achieving knowledge by the experimental method, but we shall have done so at a price. For we shall be driven to admit that other objects such as God and the self, since they are not capable of being perceived by the senses, do not admit of being known by us. This consequence, however, is found on reflection to be less alarming than it appears. Indeed it provides prima facie confirmation rather than refutation of the hypothesis which we are to consider. For the assumption that we do possess knowledge of God and the self in the same sense in which we possess it of the laws of nature is inconsistent with the existence of free will as required by moral philosophy, whereas by distinguishing between things as they appear to us and things as they are in themselves we render a belief in the existence both of God and freedom perfectly consistent with the validity of a scientific knowledge of phenomena.[1]

For in the first place it is evident that, so long as we consider causality as a relation which holds between things in themselves, among which the self must be included, freedom must in the end be illusory and God a piece of inconsistent mythology. We should

[1] The term 'phenomenon' has not in itself any idealist or subjectivist implications, but is simply the standard word used in seventeenth- and eighteenth-century philosophy to denote the objects with which natural science deals. Cf. Newton's Preface to his *Principia*, 'Since the ancients made great account of the science of mechanics in the investigation of natural things; and the moderns, laying aside substantial forms and occult qualities, have endeavoured to subject the phenomena of nature to the laws of mathematics, I have in this Treatise cultivated mathematics so far as it regards philosophy.'

The precise meaning of the term for Kant (and of *Erscheinung*, which is its German equivalent), especially as contrasted with its correlate 'noumenon', is controversial, but except in passages where this contrast is explicitly under discussion it has no specifically Kantian meaning.

be committed to a thoroughgoing materialistic mechanism in which religion and morality could be preserved only at the impossible cost of abandoning all claim by the human mind to obtain knowledge by scientific methods. If on the other hand we distinguish, as we propose to do, between things as they are in themselves and things as they appear to us in sense perception, this difficulty immediately disappears, since freedom and determinism can then both be postulated of the same entity when considered from different points of view.

And in the second place we may realize that the limitation implied by the new hypothesis is more apparent than real. Admittedly knowledge, strictly so called, of God and the self is now shown to be impossible, but it may be doubted whether the claim to such knowledge which has been put forward by the Schools has ever carried much weight. The plain man's hope of immortality does not depend on his confidence in a Scholastic argument based on the doctrine that the soul is a simple substance, his belief in God does not derive any help from the ontological or cosmological proofs, and his consciousness of freedom rests wholly on his clear apprehension of duties as opposed to inclinations. Now these notions of God, freedom, and immortality are perfectly consistent and intelligible thoughts, and even though we are led to admit that we can never scientifically demonstrate that they have objects corresponding to them, they are not thereby shown to be empty or meaningless. Provided that they do not contradict either themselves or the necessary postulates of the scientific investigation of phenomena (as on the Critical hypothesis alone they can be shown not to do), we are entitled and indeed constrained on moral grounds to entertain them as matters of faith.

Thus the distinction between things in themselves and phenomena, with the contention that the latter and the latter only are possible objects of scientific knowledge to us, is what the *Critique* claims to demonstrate, and if it is successful in doing so it will lay a foundation for a rational view of the relation between science, morals, and religion at no more serious cost than the sacrifice of a large number of Scholastic and theological sophistries.

THE AIM OF THE CRITIQUE

Comment on Kant's Prefaces

Kant's own formulation of the aim of the *Critique* is to be found in the *Prefaces* to the first and second editions (1781 and 1787) and in the *Prolegomena* (1783). The differences between these are matters of emphasis rather than of substance, and the *Preface to B*, summarized above, is much the most important of them. I shall therefore comment on this at some length. Brief references to *A* and *Proleg.* may also help to explain what Kant thought that he needed particularly to stress about the Critical Philosophy before and after uncertainties and difficulties as to the meaning and purpose of the *Critique* had developed among his colleagues.

COMMENT ON PREFACE A

The theme here is the problem presented by the antinomies, that is, by the paradoxes which reason cannot escape from concerning the infinite extent and divisibility of space and time and also the existence of God and the freedom of the will. Kant was worried by these puzzles because, as he claimed, he could produce impeccable arguments based on 'principles which are unavoidable in experience' but leading to contradictory conclusions in reasoning about them, and 'the battlefield of these endless conflicts is known as Metaphysics'.

This position he found intolerable, indeed the antinomies seem to have moved him in much the same way as the mathematical paradoxes were later to provoke Bertrand Russell, and it is interesting to notice that late in his life he writes that the discomfort they produced was what woke him from his dogmatic slumber.[2]

Whether the claim to 'impeccable arguments' is justified or not is unimportant here. Most people now would say that it is not. Kant, however, thought that it was and therefore begins his *Preface* with the words 'Human reason is in a predicament in that it is faced with questions which it cannot avoid because they spring from the nature of reason, but which it cannot answer

[2] Letter to Garve, 21 Sept. 1798; Ak. xii. 258.

because they transcend the competence of human reason'. This is an intimidating start, especially when it is formulated as it is later in the *Critique* in the awe-inspiring language of the Unconditioned, but Kant's point is familiar enough. Many of us do get puzzled, as soon as we begin to think seriously, by the antinomies; it still seems logically queer to say 'The Universe never started', and equally queer to say that it did. It sounds even more queer to say that neither of these statements is true.

There is, however, no doubt that both statements (the thesis and the antithesis of the antinomy as Kant calls them) are *a priori*. We can attach no meaning to the idea of an empirical verification of them, and yet they purport to refer in some way to matter of fact. Hence it certainly looks as if something has gone wrong with the functioning of our reason—we should now prefer to say, with our language—and that 'the only method of escape from this dilemma is to undertake the criticism of pure (*a priori*) thinking, to consider the competence of our thinking in any attempt to gain knowledge independently of all experience' (i.e. without a genuinely empirical premiss).[3]

There are several points of importance here. In the first place the central difficulty in Kant's complex of problems struck him in 1781 as being a logical point, and his solution is that of a logician. For what his distinction between things in themselves and phenomena amounts to is simply a rough theory of types. His answer to his paradoxes, especially those concerning God and freedom, is one which was eagerly taken over by some theologians in the nineteenth century, namely, 'It makes no sense (or is linguistically improper) to suppose that questions which can properly be asked about particular events or things in the Universe can equally well be asked about the Universe'; for 'if all clothes are concatenations of stitches, absurdity results from saying that all stitches are themselves very tiny clothes'.[4] Kant, in fact, was being a logician rather than an epistemologist both in his formulation of the question and in the answer which he gave to it by stressing to the exclusion of everything else the antinomies to which traditional metaphysics has given rise and the need for philosophers to do something about them.

It is also noteworthy that at this point he thought of his predecessors as 'Dogmatists' and 'Sceptics' (represented by Locke)

[3] A vi.

[4] Ryle, *Concept of Mind*, p. 214.

and not as 'Rationalists' and 'Empiricists'. He was not stressing the problems of scientific explanation—indeed they hardly get a mention.

Finally, he was in this *Preface* consistently rude to the Dogmatists[5] and rather friendly to the Sceptics.

Now this is not altogether helpful as a guide to the *Critique* though, as Professor Martin has pointed out,[6] it does focus attention on an ingredient in it which is extremely important and frequently neglected. 'The *Critique of Pure Reason* is a sea which is fed by two great rivers. One is the new philosophy of nature, the other is the old ontology.' The metaphor is not quite a happy one since, as Martin clearly shows, Kant did not suppose that he was reconciling the views of Locke and Leibniz. He claimed that both were wrong and that he was superseding them. It is, however, the rationalist in him who is the dominating figure in *Preface A*.

COMMENT ON PREFACE TO PROLEGOMENA

Comments and reviews on the *Critique* soon convinced Kant that he had been misunderstood. His criticism of rationalism had been taken as the whole of what he had to say, and he appeared as a somewhat shamefaced supporter of Hume. Hence the *Proleg. Preface* is almost entirely devoted to a statement of what, in Kant's view, was right and what was wrong with Hume's empiricism, especially with his assault on the causal axiom. The point is this: 'The question was not, as Hume's critics had supposed, whether the concept of cause is correct, useful, and in respect of all knowledge of nature indispensable, for this Hume had never held in doubt; but whether it is thought *a priori* by reason, and in this way has an inner truth independent of all experience, and hence also has a more extended usefulness, not limited merely to objects of experience.'[7]

The emphasis is now changing, and the central point of the *Critique* is coming to be the rehabilitation of natural science against Hume rather than the solution of the antinomies.

[5] *Veralteter wurmstichiger Dogmatismus*, A iii. Also A xiii.

[6] Gottfried Martin, *Immanuel Kant*, Köln, 1951, Preface. My references are to the English translation by P. G. Lucas, *Kant's Metaphysics and Theory of Science*.

[7] Ak. iv. 258.

COMMENT ON PREFACE B

§ 1

The *Preface to B* is a serious, but not a very successful attempt to clarify the complex aim of the *Critique*. It does some justice both to Kant's claim to have given a more comprehensive account of scientific procedure than Hume had done and to have established by means of the critical hypothesis the boundaries between science and metaphysics. Unfortunately it is so condensed as to require a good deal of elucidation. The first distinction Kant makes, and it is maintained throughout the *Critique*, is between 'mere groping about' and 'the secure path of a science'. This is important. It is very much the same distinction as Professor Toulmin[8] has in mind when he talks of the natural history stage of science as distinct from scientific theory. In the beginning there is simply collecting and classifying, and it is only at a later stage that theories or explanations are produced.

It is hard to define the extent to which Kant fully understood and accepted this distinction. There are passages in the *Analytic* (especially in the *Deduction* and the *Analogies*) when he seems to recognize it perfectly clearly and to be on the verge of formulating a theory of scientific reasoning well in advance of his time; more frequently, however, he uses 'induction'[9] in a much less satisfactory way. In *Preface B* he certainly holds that we can test the claim of any branch of study to have achieved the secure path by asking (*a*) does it make steady progress? (*b*) are the professional researchers in it agreed as to the basic truths which it has already established and as to the correct method of prosecuting further investigations? Judged by this standard he thinks that logic, mathematics, and physics have all obviously established themselves and that metaphysics obviously has not. Hence the first aim of the *Critique* must be to settle what is the difference between metaphysics and the other studies which is responsible for the unsatisfactory state of the former and the success of the latter. Logic presents no difficulty. The distinction between the safe path and blind groping, between natural history and scientific theory, arises only in studies which deal with matter of fact. Logic is not

[8] E. S. Toulmin, *The Philosophy of Science, passim.*
[9] Ak. ix. 132.

one of these. It is concerned solely with the validity of arguments and therefore could not have a natural history stage. Hence it needed no sudden development or revolution, as mathematics and physics did, to raise its status. It had no need of a genius to set it on the right road because it was not and never could have been off the right road.

This claim is less manifestly justified than Kant supposed. In the sense in which he claimed that mathematics had a natural history stage, he might well have argued that logic had one too. Why should people not have discovered what reasonings were valid by noting which gave reliable results? Indeed, how otherwise can they have discovered? God did not make men rational and leave it to Aristotle to teach them to think. This point needs no further discussion here, but Kant's assumption that logic sprang fully armed from the head of Aristotle is not in keeping with his views on mathematics and was responsible for some of his later troubles concerning general and transcendental logic. As far as *Preface B* is concerned, however, the weight of the argument is carried by the mercilessly overcondensed discussion of mathematics and physics which follows.[10]

Kant maintained that mathematics and physics alone are truly theoretical sciences, and his terminology here needs a little clarification. When he speaks of mathematics, what he has in mind is always Euclidean geometry; pure mathematics was not regarded as philosophically puzzling until the advent of Frege and Russell. Admittedly Kant sometimes gives mathematical, or rather, simple arithmetical illustrations ($7+5=12$), but his treatment of them shows that for him geometry is the real trouble. He was not very competent either as a mathematician or as an amateur scientist,[11] and it is useless to press him far in such matters. His word *Physik* is not really translatable (though one has to say 'Physics', this is misleading). What he is thinking about is almost entirely what is now generally known as 'mechanics', namely the study of levers, pulleys, the behaviour of moving bodies. Roughly, it is what Newton discussed in *Principia*. Rudimentary chemistry comes in too, i.e. phlogiston theory, since heat, light, and sound are included in *Physik*. For Kant *Chemie* does not strictly mean 'Chemistry', but rather the qualitative study of different sub-

[10] B x ff.

[11] Adickes, *Kant als Naturforscher*, examines this question in great detail.

stances, sulphur, iron, &c. It was not a theoretical science.[12] In fact, Kant's nearest equivalent to 'science' in our extended use was *Physiologie*[13] quite generally, 'the study of Nature'.

To return to his view of mathematics and physics in *Preface B*, what he says is:

> Mathematics was at first in the groping stage. It was set on the safe road by the Greeks. The light dawned on the first man who *demonstrated* that the angles at the base of an isosceles triangle are equal. He found that this demonstration did not depend on what he saw in the figure or even in his empirical thought about it, but on what he himself put into it by constructing it in accordance with a rule which he himself had predetermined.[14]

This is a large part of Kant's answer to 'What is the point of the *Critique*?'; it is restated in *Proleg.*, § 38.

The comparable revolution in physics was achieved by Bacon, who is quoted on the title-page of the *Critique*. Kant does not explain why Bacon is comparable with Thales, but presumably he was thinking of Bacon's emphasis on experiment as an essential ingredient in scientific discovery. It must be remembered here that Bacon's conception of experiment was the over-simplified notion of the *experimentum crucis*, which Descartes and others had embraced in modified forms. In general it was that *a priori* reasoning about matter of fact can, at least sometimes, reach the point at which we can say with certainty, 'if my guess (hypothesis) is correct, so and so will be observed to occur under suitably arranged conditions; if it does not occur, my hypothesis is disproved'. More clearly, '*A priori* reasoning can lead us to see that A and B are both possible. Experiment can then tell us which is actual.' Kant gives three examples to illustrate this point:

(i) Galileo calculated what would happen to balls on an inclined plane.

(ii) Torricelli calculated the height of mercury in a tube which a column of air would carry.

(iii) Stahl calculated something, and Kant knew what it was. It was one of the phlogiston experiments, and a detailed account is given in Wolf, *Science and Technology in the XVIII Century*, *s.v.* Stahl.

The crucial point in all this is Kant's explicit claim that these

[12] See *Preface to M.A.N.*, Ak. iv. 468.

[13] See Eisler, *Kant Lexicon*, art. *Physiologie*.

[14] B xii.

experiments were literally and precisely parallel to his geometrical example of the isosceles triangle; in other words, he thought that setting up an experiment in accordance with previously made calculations was just like drawing a figure in accordance with a predetermined rule or formula.

The point is that Euclid's conclusions follow from the definitions and transformation rules of his postulational system, and not from observation of (or groping among) the properties of particular figures. They may therefore be said to be put into the figures and not just found in them. Evidently it requires some straining of the word 'experiment' to say that the procedure of the experimentalist is precisely similar. It was, nevertheless, penetrating of Kant to observe that there is a lot more deductive reasoning in actual scientific procedure than earlier analyses of it had allowed.

The upshot is that experimental physicists 'understood that reason grasps only that which she produces herself in accordance with her plan', or that the result of an experiment is the answer to a precisely formulated question and is therefore radically different from any casual observation; and this is what Kant's distinction between 'blind groping' and 'the secure path of science' amounts to.

Certainly this formulation is too condensed to be intelligible if taken by itself. It merely gives a hint which the *Transcendental Analytic* has to elaborate as to what Kant meant by phrases like 'the understanding prescribes laws to Nature', 'theoretical science depends on *a priori* reasoning', 'objects depend on the mind, not the mind on objects', and so on. What it comes to is that all demonstrations about circles depend on the fact that the rule for constructing any circle (i.e. for drawing it on a piece of paper) is given by 'a plane figure bounded by a single curved line which is everywhere equally distant from a point within called the centre'. We can calculate with certainty the characteristics which any figure constructed in accordance with this definition will have. In just the same way we can calculate with certainty how balls will behave on an inclined plane or mercury will behave in a tube by reasoning from the concepts 'mass', 'force', 'velocity', &c. But this will work only if our theorizing includes the construction of a model by the imagination; the experiment then is the realizing of this model in real life.

This line of thought is far beyond the Baconian 'experimentum crucis'. It is much more like the Marxist story of the unity of theory and practice.[15] There are plenty of defects in it as an elucidation of geometrical and physical reasonings, but it is not difficult or mysterious as far as it goes.

§ 2

The idea that we understand only what we have in this sense constructed in accordance with a predetermined rule or plan provides when fully worked out the answer to Kant's first question, 'what entitles us to say that mathematics and physics are on the secure path of science?' It supersedes 'steady progress' and 'agreement on principles' which are criteria only, not explanations. It remains to deal with metaphysics. One would naturally expect this to be disposed of very quickly. For if by metaphysics we mean (as in *Preface A*) *a priori* demonstrations about God and the Universe, it is manifest that what we have here is a mere groping about and not a theoretical science. More than this, we have a mere groping about among concepts. This, from Kant's point of view, is the worst kind of intellectual time-wasting. He believed, and had developed this line in *Dreams of a Spirit Seer*, 'that one might have some empirical evidence for the existence of disembodied spirits by collecting instances of their alleged manifestations. This would indeed be very weak and mere groping, but it would be something, whereas arguments for survival derived from the *a priori* premiss "The soul is a simple substance" were utterly worthless.'[16]

Hence if the question is to be 'Can traditional metaphysics be placed on the secure path of science by a revolution in thought comparable to that brought about by Thales in geometry and Bacon in science?' the quick and final answer is 'Of course it cannot be'. It is plain nonsense to suppose that God, Freedom, and Immortality are possible objects of experimental study, even in the odd sense in which Kant thinks of geometry as involving experiments. What could it conceivably mean to talk about constructing a working model of God?

[15] See H. B. Acton, *The Illusion of the Epoch*, pp. 54 ff.
[16] B xxxii.

In fact that is just what Kant does say for almost the whole of the *Transcendental Dialectic*. Unfortunately he confuses both his readers and himself by arguing that in a different and important sense metaphysics is possible and can be set on the secure path of a science, and further, that the *Critique* has done this job. What he has in mind here is supposed to be explained by his comparison of himself with Copernicus,[17] from which the stock phrase 'Kant's Copernican Revolution' is derived. This phrase is liable to be misleading, but it needs to be considered fairly carefully because some of the most important commentators have placed considerable weight on it.

The introduction of Copernicus conceals a genuine and not surprising obscurity in Kant's own view of what he had achieved in the *Critique*. It is not surprising because it is a common experience at the end of much shorter and less ambitious works to find that the question which has been answered is not strictly the question that was posed at the outset. At first sight it often looks as if this can be adjusted by a few minor alterations, but this is never true. What has shifted is the point of view and emphasis, and a new book would have to be written to allow for this; and then the same trouble might easily recur.

What happened in the *Critique* was that Kant's reflections on the procedure of geometers and physicists expanded into a long and complicated consideration of synthesis and apperception. He finally committed himself to the view that all coherent thinking has the same essential character as scientific thinking. Now whether this view was sound or not, it was difficult for him to say how this bit of reasoning was itself to be described. To put the puzzle shortly, he began with meta-talk or second-order talk about the way in which mathematics and science are done. This can perfectly well be described as metaphysical, since it is clearly talk about physics which cannot occur unless physics is there to talk about. Nowadays we prefer on the whole to call it just 'philosophical' as Ryle does in *Dilemmas*.

Kant, however, had more or less committed himself (as members of the Wiener Kreis were to do later on) to the view that the only way of talking which could advance knowledge was the scientific way. Hence he is pushed into claiming that he has set second-order talk about science on the secure path of science, and

[17] B xvi.

this leads to the obscurity of *Preface B* in general and of the Copernicus passage in particular.

Before going into this in greater detail, I must emphasize that I am not attempting here or later to revive a patchwork theory of the *Critique*. Professor Paton is absolutely right in holding that this is nonsense.[18] Of course, Kant did not write down casual jottings on the backs of envelopes and then string them together more or less at random for publication. But Paton wrote his paper in *P.A.S.*[19] while the work of Professor Norman Kemp Smith, based on the analyses of Vaihinger and Adickes, was still the leading authority on Kant in this country. Therefore he sometimes tended to argue the extreme opposition view that there are hardly any serious philosophical muddles in the *Critique* at all. This was a most salutary antidote to Kemp Smith, but I think one can see now that it was rather overdone. My own view is that Kant never did get the distinction between scientific talk and philosophical talk really clear; and that is why one is often in doubt in crucial passages (especially in *Deduction A*) as to whether he is functioning as a philosopher or an *a-priori* psychologist.

§ 3

To return from this digression to the 'Copernican Revolution', what Kant says is this:

> Hitherto it has been assumed that all our knowledge must conform to objects. But all our attempts to extend our knowledge of objects by establishing something in regard to them *a priori* by means of concepts, have on this assumption ended in failure. We must therefore make trial to see whether we may not have more success in the tasks of metaphysics, if we suppose that objects must conform to our knowledge. . . . We should then be proceeding precisely on the lines of Copernicus' primary hypothesis. . . . A similar experiment can be tried in metaphysics as regards the *intuition* of objects.[20]

The introduction of Copernicus here as if his achievement in getting rid of the geocentric theory from astronomy was exactly comparable to those of Galileo and Torricelli is rather curious. Actually Kant himself does not say that Copernicus brought off

[18] Paton, *Kant's Metaphysic of Experience*, vol. i, Introduction, §§ 2 and 3.
[19] *P.A.S.*, vol. xxx, 1930.
[20] B xvi.

a revolution (as Thales and Bacon are held to have done) but that he invented an hypothesis or made an experiment, and these were both hospitably vague phrases. In B xxii, however, he does refer to a revolution, and seems at any rate (especially in the footnote) to assume that all the scientists he has mentioned were doing pretty much the same thing.

But if he did think this, one can only say that he was confused. What Galileo and Torricelli were doing was to frame hypotheses and test them; what Copernicus did was to suggest a new way of looking at accepted facts. One could not possibly frame an experiment to decide between Copernicus and Ptolemy, since either could account for all the observations. Copernicus achieved, or at least showed the way to, a tremendous simplification; he discarded a number of epicycles which are not required in order to explain the movements of the stars but which will explain them. In fact he produced a new and better theory. But pre-Copernican astronomy was well beyond the groping or natural history stage. Its defect lay in the fact that it was not a very powerful theory. It did not link astronomy up with anything else. As Kant rightly points out,[21]

> the laws of motion determining the orbits of the heavenly bodies which Copernicus adopted as a hypothesis gained established certainty and demonstrated at the same time the invisible force that holds the universe together (Newtonian *gravitatio*) which would have remained undiscovered if Copernicus had lacked the courage to look for the explanation of planetary motion paradoxically but correctly not in the fixed stars but in the observer.

In fact Kant had two extremely important insights into scientific methodology but failed to distinguish them from one another. They were:

1. The move from natural history to scientific theorizing (Galileo, Torricelli, and Stahl).
2. The move from disconnected theories to a unified theory. Copernicus is not the best instance of this. Newton himself would have been much better. The Newtonian theory included the astronomical theories of Kepler and Galileo, and a good deal more besides, as special cases. Einstein later on did the same for Newton.[22]

[21] B xxii n.

[22] For a much fuller exposition of this see Professor Karl Popper, *Logik der Forschung*, &c.

I think Kant half realized that two different lines of thought were involved here, but he implicitly conflated them in his talk of setting metaphysics on the secure path of science, and the result is some real confusion both in *Preface B* and in the central parts of the *Critique*. He was not clear whether what he wanted to do was to replace groping by theorizing or to supersede a theory by a wider and stronger theory, or to do something quite different from either, namely, to philosophize about science.

§ 4

What, then, was the revolution which he claimed to introduce into metaphysics? At first sight, part of his achievement was analogous to what Copernicus had done for astronomy, and may be stated in terms of his embarrassment with the metaphysical puzzles which was prominent in *Preface A*. It had been generally taken for granted that the entities with which metaphysicians especially concerned themselves, namely God, the universe, and the self, were the same kind of things as those with which scientific thinking in physics and psychology were concerned; or, to put it differently, that the words 'God', 'self', and 'universe' behaved logically in the same way as 'John Smith' and 'Westminster Abbey'. But what Kant claimed that we had to do in order to steer clear of confusion and paradox was to regard them as different in type, that is to say, that statements which could significantly be made and questions which could properly be asked in one department were nonsensical in the other. To help in making his point, he coined some new terms, or rather, used some existing terms in a new and semi-technical way. 'Things in themselves' or 'noumena' or 'transcendent objects' cover entities in Group I (God, &c.); 'phenomena' covers entities in Group II (planets, animals, &c.).

The decision to draw this distinction is his Copernican experiment, and the justification for drawing it is on B xviii (footnote). 'If we find that, when we treat things from this two-fold point of view, we have agreement with the principle of pure reason [i.e. we escape from paradoxes and contradictions], whereas if we treat them from a single point of view, reason inevitably contradicts itself, then the experiment decides in favour of this distinction.'

This, however, is only half the story. Certainly it fits Copernicus, but it leaves Galileo, Torricelli, and the secure path of science out of the picture. They belong to the second part of the enterprise. For as Kant comes (in the *Transcendental Analytic*) to develop his distinction between noumena and phenomena, what emerges is that the latter, unlike the former, can have *a priori* and therefore metaphysical truths asserted about them (e.g. the causal axiom). It may be argued that this is just analytical. Kant has really ensured by definition that phenomena are the kind of things which can be understood, can have valid and testable scientific theories propounded about them; and that noumena do not admit of such treatment. There is something in this.

The unavoidable consequence of Kant's critical distinction is that it becomes logically impossible to make use of scientific arguments in theology and ethics or metaphysical arguments in scientific discussion. Hence a field is cleared logically for the theologian and the moralist. This is the burden of *Preface A*. The question remaining is 'What field?', and this can be answered only by making precise the area which is now open to science; what is it, in fact, which scientific theorizing as distinct from mere groping is qualified to study? This is what is added in *Preface B*.

If this is correct, it is clear that Kant's comparison of his work with that of Copernicus, though superficially attractive, is misleading if pressed at all hard. He did not himself attach much importance to it. It was an afterthought. Equally, the talk of setting metaphysics on the secure path of a science is misleading and not at all clear. The *Critique* is concerned with philosophical questions. It is no part of Kant's job to frame and test novel hypotheses about matter of fact or to invent wider hypotheses which will include more partial theories as special cases, and in fact he does not try to do either except possibly in the *Subjective Deduction of the Categories*. He was, however, doubtful about this from the start[23] and tried to get rid of it in B.

§ 5

In the course of this lengthy disquisition on Kant's *Prefaces* I have already referred to a distinction which needs to be remembered all the way through his Critical writings, namely the

[23] A xvi–xvii.

distinction between the substance of what he has to say, which is always serious, and the form in which he presents it, which is often trivial. This needs to be emphasized, because some phrases, the 'Copernican Revolution' is only one example, which really belong to the form, have often received much more attention than they deserve and have been pressed so much as to obscure what is genuinely important.

What is here in question is often discussed under the impressive heading, 'Kant's respect for Architectonic', and something more may usefully be said about it at this stage. To confine the discussion to the *Prefaces*, we have already seen that all of them, taken as statements of what is going on in the *Critique*, are at least superficially misleading. *Preface A* tells us roughly what in 1781 or earlier Kant had planned; *Proleg*. is concerned with one important but limited problem, namely his view of Hume and of the causal axiom; *Preface B* reveals more or less what in 1787 he decided to stress as his great achievement. Each of the three is rather obviously tailor-made, and each in its way encourages us to look at the suit of clothes rather than at the man who is wearing them. Kant had weighty things to say both about scientific procedure and about the logical defects of traditional metaphysics, but his view is concealed rather than elucidated by the formal dress in which he presents it. It will not do to excuse him by saying that Prefaces tend to be propaganda and to present a much too tidy and buttoned-up view of what is to come. They do; but with Kant the trouble was deeper than that. Partly, no doubt as a result of the almost total absence of philosophical discussion in which he thought and wrote at Königsberg, he was rather too confident that he knew just where he was going and just where he had been. 'In this enquiry I have made completeness my aim, and I venture to assert that there is not a single metaphysical problem which has not been solved, or for the solution of which the key has not been supplied [in the *Critique*].'[24] This is typical of his general attitude.

Königsberg, however, was not solely responsible. Kant's conviction also sprang from his original and never abandoned faith in the logic of Aristotle, which encouraged him to believe that all genuine knowledge could be neatly formalized and assigned its place in a single coherent system. To say of a philosopher, even

[24] A xiii.

of Aristotle, that at least in one respect he was methodical but not systematic was, for Kant, to make a damaging criticism.

But Kant was a pedantically tidy man, fortunately for only part of the time. It is true that all the stories which survive of his daily life prove conclusively that he was. But although he was a tidy actor, he was not at all a tidy thinker.[25] He made a terrible mess, but was scrupulous about concealing it.

It seems to me, therefore, that both Vaihinger, Adickes, and Kemp Smith on one side and Paton on the other have drawn attention to essential ingredients in Kant's method of philosophizing, and have materially over-emphasized them. It is not true that Kant worked with a mental box full of pigeon-holes which he was determined to fill with something at any cost; but it is not true either that he was just orderly in his exposition and never allowed his anxiety to present a tidy picture to obscure the substance of what he had to say. Hence it is always necessary (as in reading the *Prefaces* it obviously is) to avoid pressing very hard on the framework within which he expounded his view, because often it is just a framework and does not matter, and sometimes it cannot be really fitted on to the substance of what he has to say. Often the connexion is more or less arbitrary and we reach only pseudo-problems if we look for a better fit than is to be discovered.

To say this is not to charge Kant with any major philosophical lapse. He had some insights of genius to communicate and was over-optimistic as to the possibility and desirability of a tidy explanation of them. That is all that needs to be said.

§ 6

To conclude this introduction to Kant's contribution to the philosophy of science, I will briefly restate what I take to have been his considered view and compare it with what may roughly be called modern philosophical thought on the same subject. Kant has been severely treated, especially by Russell, and it is therefore worth asking whether he might have any answer to later empiricist criticisms. What I have to say here is not fully intelligible in the light of the *Prefaces* alone, but nevertheless a

[25] The facsimile of a page of this *Nachlaß* in Ak. xvi is good enough evidence for this. It is a horror [Ak. xvi ad fin.].

preview of the line taken in the *Aesthetic* and *Analytic* may be helpful at this stage. It would be generally agreed now that Kant's distinction between theorizing and mere groping about, though he may be said not to have formulated it very well, was perfectly sound; in particular, he was right and the first philosopher to be right (though Hume[26] had an idea on the same lines) in pointing out that there had been a groping or natural-history stage in geometry. Since the time of Plato at any rate it had been popular to talk of geometry as involving 'innate ideas', 'self-evident truths', and so on, and to ignore the fact that a revolution in Kant's sense must at some time have taken place. Yet it is undoubted that the Egyptians and Babylonians at any rate knew plenty of truths about the properties of triangles and circles, even though presumably they lacked *a priori* demonstrations of them. They could predict eclipses and build pyramids. The transition which Kant stressed from this kind of empirical knowledge to geometrical proof was real and notable.

On the other hand, his conception of it as 'seeing what was put into the figure by the act of constructing it according to a rule' was dubious and controversial. It needs to be contrasted with the answer generally given by Hume's more sophisticated successors, such as the members of the Wiener Kreis, especially Moritz Schlick[27] in the 1930's. This account of what happened to geometry runs approximately as follows: it eventually dawned on the Greeks that calculations made in accordance with a set of selected but conventional axioms, definitions, and transformation rules would give more rapid and reliable predictions in the relevant area of matter of fact (land measurement, engineering, architecture, and astronomy) than can be achieved by the process of simply observing regularities and basing predictions on them. The limit of the area within which such calculi can be relied on, however, is itself always something which must be settled empirically. It cannot possibly be discovered *a priori* or, in Kant's language, by pure reason divorced from all experience. Kant was just wrong when he supposed that the applicability of Euclidean geometry to phenomena was unrestricted, though his mistake was pardonable enough since the limitations of it had not yet been realized. Equally, it did not occur to him to be critical of pure mathematics

[26] *Treatise*, I. II. iv.

[27] Moritz Schlick, *Philosophy of Nature*, New York, 1949.

or formal logic, though both of them were equally vulnerable.

If, *per impossibile*, he had realized this, he might also have realized the potentialities of post-Aristotelian logic and non-Euclidean geometries as well as the logical foundations of mathematics; and then he might have cancelled 'put into the figure' and substituted 'put into the postulational system', which would have been correct but would not have given the answers he wanted to his question 'How is a pure science of nature possible?'

If we pursue this line, which clearly has much to recommend it, we reach something like the following conclusions on Kant's general position. Admittedly his account of logic, mathematics, and physics had the beginnings of a sound analysis in it, since it did make the essential distinction between *a priori* deductive systems and empirically observed regularities. On another essential point, however, he was quite wrong, since he thought that 'seeing' or 'intuition' or 'imagination' were needed as an integral element in scientific reasoning. Perhaps figures and models may sometimes help us to get at the right deductive system, but they have nothing more than psychological importance. As a result of this mistake Kant was led to mis-state his metaphysical problem (in both his uses of 'metaphysics').

(i) In immanent metaphysics (or the philosophy of mathematics and science) he had no need to ask 'How are synthetic *a priori* propositions possible?' They are not, and anyway we do not need them. He thought we did because he wrongly supposed that the connexion between theory and fact was *a priori* and not empirical.

(ii) In transcendent metaphysics (God, Freedom, Immortality) he would have realized, as he sometimes seemed to do, that there was really no future at all. Such words are just symbols which may indeed be manipulated in accordance with conventionally determined rules, but the conclusions reached by such manipulation are worthless since there is no empirical interpretation of them. They cannot be cashed, that is, used to explain or predict phenomena. Hence as contrasted with the symbolic systems engendered by Euclid and Newton they are empty, meaningless, or, in logical positivist language, literally nonsensical.

Thus the root of Kant's error which ultimately wrecks the whole of his Critical Philosophy, is his unquestioning assumption that Aristotle, Euclid, and Newton had each of them pronounced some last words about the structure of the universe, whereas in each case a wider and tougher theory has been developed within which their work is included as a special case.

It might perhaps be urged that it is still premature to jump straight away to the opposite extreme and hold that all theoretical systems are entirely conventional and it is therefore a pure accident that any of them serve any useful purpose at all. Surely, it may be argued, the astronomical conclusions of Copernicus were true whereas those of his predecessors were false. This line is not a profitable one. It is not difficult to give grounds for holding that the choice between rival postulational systems is determined solely by pragmatical considerations. Physicists turn to the mathematics of quantum theory and wave mechanics because the simpler systems of Euclid and Newton will no longer provide efficiently the explanations and predictions in which they are interested. Some symbolic system is a necessary condition of our being able to calculate or even to communicate with one another at all, but that is all we can say.

In short, while Kant in *Preface B* was correct in claiming that all theoretical systems are *a priori* and that therefore every rational study has an *a priori* ingredient,[28] he was fatally wrong in supposing that our preference for one theoretical system over another is dictated by anything but practical considerations. It makes no sense to ask which of them is true, and the purpose of the *Critique* can therefore be seen at the very outset to be doomed to frustration.

This brief preliminary outline of a standard modern criticism of Kant demands a similar sketch of a line of defence which he might have taken to meet it.

He could, it seems to me, have accepted a good deal of it and still have claimed that his defence of metaphysics, based on the critical distinction between things in themselves and phenomena, was at least a considerable advance on any view which had preceded it. He could certainly have argued with a great deal of force that the wholesale conventionalism which would put him out of court straight away is too sweeping to be acceptable as an account of scientific theorizing or ordinary reasoning processes.

The point at issue is the slippery but indispensable phrase 'matter of fact', which I have hitherto employed without com-

[28] *M.A.N.*, Preface, Ak. iv. 469.

ment. We tend, following Hume, to suppose that it refers significantly to what is there, what is given, what forces itself upon us, and that there is no uncertainty or doubt as to what this is. We find out about it in the first instance by looking, listening, smelling, tasting, and touching, and by simply recording or recollecting the results of these performances. Then we formulate theories, some of which happen to work, to explain and predict.

This simple story seems on examination to leave out something which Kant noticed, and which in his criticism of Hume he tried to recover. It is not really good enough to urge, as Hume did (and later sense-datum theorists have followed him, though they have employed a more refined and sophisticated vocabulary than that of 'impressions' and 'ideas'), that sensa or impressions are just there as the 'furniture of the world'. We can and do say a lot more than that. We see, hear, and so on in virtue of a special arrangement of organs, retina, optic nerve, cortex, &c. These are pretty much alike in most human beings and therefore we can give a fairly precise meaning to statements like 'A and B are looking at the same house'. Hence it can fairly be argued that for beings constituted as we are ('for us men' is Kant's phrase) there is in fact nothing near to a free choice of postulational systems. With very minor qualifications which have been pointed out by Gestalt psychologists and the rather more extensive variations which can be produced by drugs we cannot choose to see or smell things in a way different from that in which we normally see and smell them.

To go as far as this is no doubt to overstate the degree to which the idea of a standardized matter of fact or given manifold should be accepted. Kant was by no means out of the grip of the view he was criticizing. What he wanted to emphasize was that it is at least reasonable to talk about the way things look to standard human observers, but it is blatant nonsense to talk of the way things look to fishes, dogs, or angels. Such talk has a veneer of plausibility only because we can at least attach meaning to guesses at the way things would look to us if we had the optical apparatus of dogs or fishes but remained otherwise as we are. Equally, we think as we do because of the way in which our higher nervous centres are organized.

None of this commits us at all to a strange belief that the things we look at, houses, trees, &c., are created by the people who see them. It states no more than the familiar and unmysterious truth that the way we see and the way we think depend on our being the type of creatures we are and not another type. It is only in fairy stories that animals and trees can talk like human beings.

If this is accepted, and I do not see any good reason for rejecting it, two of Kant's contentions are still significant and important:

(*a*) The distinction between noumena and phenomena must be accepted in principle. It surely does make sense to say that there is something at which two men under different conditions or even a man and a fish are both looking; and it is at least misleading to argue that 'matter of fact' will cover this in all cases.

(*b*) It can be held that things look as they do to us because we are as we are.

Certainly we may criticize the way in which Kant puts his view, but even his statement that forms of sense and understanding determine objects of experience need not be very misleading, though it needs a lot of clarification. His point is ultimately that *a priori* does not have to mean 'unrelated to the way in which we experience *in general*'; it can mean 'independent of any *particular* experience'. We cannot say significantly that our way of seeing, hearing, &c., is shared by other living things. Hence, except in a rather arbitrary sense, it is pointless to ask 'What does the house *really* look like?'

I am not convinced that this will do as a view and I am even less sure that Kant would have accepted it without a lot of reservation. But it is useful to have it in mind as the sort of thing he might have said in answer to a logical positivist and conventionalist line of criticism; and although he would have objected to it as not giving enough scope for moral philosophizing, it certainly is part of what he said and meant. He was perfectly clear that our equipment with two forms of sense and twelve forms of thought was an empirical matter which might be otherwise. We cannot deduce it from any non-empirical premisses. This is one of the cardinal points on which Hegel disagreed.

What Kant did in *Preface B*, then, largely because of his imperfect insight into the way hypotheses and experiment figure in scientific method, was seriously to overstate the place of logic and deduction in the empirical sciences. But just because of this he got on the right track as regards philosophy. He saw, though he failed to state the point clearly, the importance of asking questions about language, both technical and natural. Metaphysics in his new sense is largely a philosophical inquiry, but the technique he uses in pursuit of it is not and could not be scientific; so the Copernican Revolution is at least partially a fraudulent prospectus.

SUMMARY OF THE INTRODUCTION (B 1–30)

It is evident that in point of time all our knowledge begins with experience, but not that it is derived from experience, since the latter may be the indispensable stimulus which moves the mind to an activity of its own. Hence it is important to decide whether we do possess knowledge which is independent of experience (*a priori*) as distinct from that which is merely empirical (*a posteriori*). Such knowledge must be expressed in propositions which are necessary or universal, for these characteristics can never belong to empirical propositions which merely assert facts and do not enunciate laws. It is obvious that mathematics and physics depend on propositions of this *a priori* kind. Furthermore it should be observed that the immense success of these sciences in producing results which are both confirmed by experience and of the utmost practical value has hitherto been considered to absolve us from asking for any theoretical justification for their procedure and to justify us in assuming that we are capable of formulating propositions expressing laws which necessarily hold good of the real world. In other words it has been assumed that the mind is competent to obtain *a priori* knowledge by pure reason alone and without any assistance from experience, and we have been encouraged to hope that such knowledge may be extended beyond all experience so as to include the specific objects of metaphysics, namely God and the self. This hope is illusory, but it has been rendered plausible by the assumption common among philosophers that every advance in knowledge consists in a more thoroughgoing analysis of our conceptions of things than has hitherto been made. Now it is true that some of our knowledge is really obtained by this analytical method and that it is of great importance to understand exactly what is contained in the concepts which we use. But propositions which express such knowledge, though they are indeed necessarily true since they are guaranteed by the principle of contradiction, merely make explicit what we already know and do not add to it. They are explicative, not ampliative, in character. To possess the latter property a proposition must assert of its object something which is not contained even implicitly in the concept of that object, that is, it must be synthetic and not analytic. The importance of this distinction has not been observed before, mainly because it has been taken for granted that the axioms of arithmetic, geometry, and physics are all analytic in character; but this is a complete mistake. For if we consider the assertion that $7+5=12$, we find that in the end its certainty depends not on the analysis of the concepts of seven, five, addition, and equality but on the actual process of counting which requires sensuous intuition rather than conceptual analysis; and it is even more clear that geometrical knowledge ultimately depends not on the analysis of the concepts of triangularity, straightness, &c., but on the construction (whether on paper or in imagination) of geometrical figures. Hence, although the demonstrations of arithmetic and geometry are analytical and may be made by means of the principle of contradiction, their axioms are all synthetic as well as *a priori* in character.[29] They are propositions which claim universal validity in spite of the fact that their predicates are not contained even implicitly in the conceptions of their subjects.

The same assertion will be found on examination to hold good both of physics and of metaphysics. The concept cause cannot be discovered by analysis of the concept of an event, and propositions which assert the freedom of the will or the immortality of the soul are certainly synthetic, since they can be denied without self-contradiction, which would be impossible if their predicates could be shown by analysis to be contained in the concepts of their subjects.

Hence our first attempt must be to discover what it is that justifies us in formulating propositions of this kind (synthetic *a priori*) in mathematics and physics,[30] for in view of the success of these sciences it cannot reasonably be doubted that we are justified, and we have therefore only to discover the reason. We must then consider metaphysics, but in this case our problem is twofold. On the one hand it must be admitted that here, too, we do formulate

[29] B 14.

[30] B 20.

synthetic *a priori* propositions, but on the other it cannot be denied that such propositions do not and in the nature of the case cannot receive the same kind of confirmation from experience as do those of mathematics and physics. Hence we must examine first the origin and second the possible validity of such propositions, and our four questions are:

(i) How is pure mathematics possible?
(ii) How is pure natural science possible?
(iii) How is metaphysics possible as a natural disposition?
(iv) How is metaphysics possible as a science?

The answers to these questions form the essential basis for all rational investigation both in science and philosophy, and the *Critique* which discusses them is therefore to be regarded as the propaedeutic to a system of Pure Reason. The inquiries contained in it are called transcendental inasmuch as they are concerned not primarily with our knowledge of things but rather with the possibility of knowing things *a priori*. They are therefore reflexive or self-conscious. I may accept the propositions 'All bodies are extended' and 'Everything that happens has a cause' without proceeding to investigate the question 'How is such *a priori* knowledge possible?' Hence the *Critique* is a critical investigation of the possibility of *a priori* knowledge in the three departments in which such knowledge is commonly but uncritically held to exist, namely metaphysics, physics, and mathematics. Logic is exempt from such criticism in virtue of its purely formal character. It does not claim to give us *a priori* knowledge of things.

Kant has now formulated his difficulty as a logical problem. His attempt to deal with it begins in the *Aesthetic*. But before turning to this, it is as well to consider at some length the epistemological thicket into which somewhat absent-mindedly he had wandered.

III

THE AESTHETIC

KANT'S EPISTEMOLOGICAL EMBARRASSMENT

Stage I

From the Dissertation to the Transcendental Aesthetic

§ I

KANT was not primarily an epistemologist. It was, however, inevitable that his discussion of the boundary between metaphysics and science should involve him in epistemological difficulties. To begin with, these are concentrated on the question 'What does it mean to say that any entity is "a thing" or "an object"?' In Kantian language What is meant by 'Thing in itself' and 'noumenon' on the one hand and by 'phenomenon' and *Erscheinung* on the other?

As a preliminary to investigating this it is helpful to ask why all attempts to elucidate it are so terribly confused. The chief reason is this. One can distinguish roughly between three areas in which human inquiries are prosecuted.

1. We can explore the behaviour and constitution of things and animals, and such exploration makes up the physical and biological sciences. It does no harm at the moment to group these together as Kant himself tended to do, though in the *Critique of Judgement* he came to realize clearly that there was a frontier to be drawn between them.

2. We can study the constitution and behaviour of human beings. Equally vaguely this is the job of sociology (psychology, economics, politics, ethics, and jurisprudence). There is here another boundary dispute arising from the controversy between naturalist and non-naturalist theories of ethics. This also may be ignored for the moment though it was responsible for much of Kant's difficulty in the *Critique of Practical Reason* and the *Grundlegung*.

3. We may note and comment on the fact that the linguistic

conventions accepted in investigations (1) and in (2) are different and that these differences are at least capable of generating confusions and paradoxes. Thus the logical grammar of physics and that of psychology needs investigation, since questions which are eminently askable in the latter are nonsensical in the former. We can ask 'What is Mr. Jones trying to do?' but not 'What is the table trying to do?' Possibly Mr. Jones is not in fact trying to do anything in particular, but he might be; so we say that in this case it makes sense to ask the question. It makes no sense to ask about the table, for it is neither trying nor idling.

Now these fields of inquiry are not clearly marked off from one another, though for didactic and expositional purposes it is handy to pretend that they are. At first sight the distinctions may look clear enough. We should be able to distinguish between 'X has a novel hypothesis about the way in which rats learn to run mazes' and 'X has done something to clarify the meaning of "learn"'. But the more one tries to apply the distinction in actual cases as distinct from made-up, tidy models, the less confident does one feel about it. What purports to be linguistic analysis and conceptual cartography frequently wanders into the department of psychological and physical hypotheses.

I do not suggest that such wanderings are reprehensible, though this is not the place at which they should be defended; but they should be noticed. Modern philosophers at least are sensitive to the need for clarification, Kant on the whole was not; or rather, he did not think of what was needed in those terms. He came nearest to doing so in his *Preface to M.A.N.* Indeed he was just beginning to get clear the distinctions which I have drawn and which are now philosophical platitudes. But they were clear to him only for part of the time and then only operationally. He frequently played the game as if he had read books on the theory of it; but he had not, since there were none. It is because he played as a natural philosophical genius that other people have been able to work the theory out.

Turning now to Kant's view of objects or things, it is only too clear that all three forms of inquiry are mixed up in it.

1. There is a pyscho-physical theory, assumed rather than explicitly formulated, a doctrine involving rays of light, retina, optic nerve, and cortex.
2. There is a psychological theory concerning intellectual

operations which Kant is trying to make up and expound, a theory involving inner and outer sense, synthesis, apperception, and choice. This is especially important in the *Aesthetic*, the *Deduction in A*, and the *Third Antinomy*.

3. There is throughout a genuine philosophical problem about the confusions which the languages employed, especially in ethics and science, seem inexorably to generate.

Since these territories are not precisely determinable, and since Kant never explicitly recognized that (1) and (2) were distinct from (3), his wanderings between them were a good deal more uncharted and irresponsible than those embarked upon by some of his modern successors. It is not worth while, even if it were possible, to disentangle his exasperated transitions from physics through psychology to philosophy and back again all through the *Critique*. I shall draw attention to some of them in Part III. At this stage I shall simply offer an historical account of the way in which the *Ding an sich* puzzle developed for him, and this account will repeat without comment the transitions I have mentioned.

§ 2

We have already seen in a very general way what Kant's epistemological problem was. It may be described either as the problem of perception or the problem of objects, and the fact that it still presents itself to serious writers, especially scientists, as a genuine one suggests that what is involved is not simply a verbal confusion. It is a problem which is bound to arise as soon as we attempt to say in an unconfusing way what goes on when we see things or think about them. I shall first attempt to formulate this problem as it emerged for Kant in his gradual development from 1770 to 1781 and to explain the line along which he moved in his attempt to dispose of it; later on I will restate it and suggest what seems to me a more promising method of approach.

The point of this procedure is that Kant's own doctrine in the *Critique* seems to me frequently to approximate to the second line, but he certainly did not hold consistently to it, and the fact that he did not may with considerable plausibility be attributed to his unconscious retention of a part of the view he was engaged in discarding.

What I have in mind here may be illustrated by a comparison with the epistemological development of Russell. One is puzzled by the occurrence in his *Human Knowledge; its Scope and Limits*, published in 1948, of many of the formulations of his problem which date back to the *Problems of Philosophy* (1912), though it is obvious that the position taken up in *Logical Atomism* and revised in the *Analysis of Mind* and in the *Enquiry into Meaning and Truth* requires something much more sophisticated than these. The explanation appears to be that Russell, like Kant, starting from the prima-facie view of the scientist, has never quite escaped from the problem which Eddington, Adrian, J. Z. Young, and many others have found so embarrassing. When Kant is off his guard, he goes on talking as if 'seeing', 'hearing', &c., referred to the end results of a causal transaction between a thing and a person. When the commitments of such a view are clearly stated, nobody can seriously believe it, but it is as difficult to avoid as it is impossible to accept. As Ryle has shown, it is part of the legacy of the Cartesians to Western Europe, and the fact that our philosophical and physiological vocabularies have it built into them at the outset makes it almost impossible to eradicate when we are not actually attending to it.

It is in this context that Kant's attempt to deal with perception and objects needs to be criticized, and it must be remembered throughout that his description of space and time as 'forms of sensibility', on which his analysis of them depends, was carried over with hardly any change from the *Dissertation* to the *Aesthetic*. It is important, too, to emphasize, as Martin[1] does, that in Kant's own view the two pillars which supported the Critical position as a whole were the transcendental ideality of time and space and the idea of freedom. Kant's position in 1770, then, to repeat what has already been briefly mentioned in connexion with the *Dissertation*, was as follows. He had introduced a novel technical term, 'form of sensibility', to refer to something, not clearly specified, which he thought was involved in our perception of things, and this device enabled him to dissolve the antinomies within physics. It further satisfied him that Euclidean geometry was valid of 'objects of perception' or 'phenomena'. A new and intractable difficulty, however, arose with regard to Newtonian mechanics. For 'forms of sensibility' suggests that the

[1] Op. cit., p. 134.

percipient, in virtue of his psychological or physiological constitution, shapes or moulds data which are given to him, but that what is given to him depends not on him but on an external object. This is an incurably muddled way of describing what goes on when we see and hear, but at first sight it is not obviously nonsensical. The underlying idea is that I possess a piece of apparatus called 'a mind' which is a very special kind of camera or wireless set, located at the receiving end of a complex causal transaction. Physics and physiology between them give a reasonably comprehensive account of the process involved.

The question then is, 'How do I know that the end product of this bit of machinery, the idea, representation, appearance, or whatever we choose to call it, is "like" the original at the transmitting end?' This sounds a sensible question because we know what it means to say that the result produced by a modern recording is very like the real thing and that colour photography has made great progress in the past twenty years. I will leave this model for the moment and return to it shortly.

Now Kant's version of this story even in 1770 seems rather more advanced than those of his predecessors, though it is not at all easy to say exactly what it was or how it relates to the formulations of Locke and Leibniz; but although it is more sophisticated, it turns out on examination to have made a bad muddle rather worse. For if we take the causal story seriously, as Russell, for instance, did in *Problems of Philosophy*, we can at least make some sort of case for saying that we can infer empirical truths about the objects which cause our perceptions by reflecting on the perceptions which they cause. This is the 'prisoner in the dungeon' myth, and it is not difficult to see that it breaks down. When it does, we are tempted to reject the causal story and the 'external world' altogether and attempt to work out an alternative statement either in theological language, with Berkeley, or in the mystical terminology of nineteenth-century idealism.

None of these lines is satisfactory, yet it seems fruitless to say, as Kant did in the *Dissertation*, that Euclidean geometry is valid of appearances because it is imposed on them by the nature of our minds, while mechanical and physical laws are somehow recognized by our minds as being valid of things in themselves. Hence his first move away from the *Dissertation* view was to claim that, just as space and time are forms of sensibility, so cause and substance and the other categories required by Newtonian mechanics are forms of thought. Clearly this is exceedingly difficult to work out, and in any case it is at first sight hardly distinguishable from idealism, which Kant considered no less a scandal to philosophy than the antinomies which his doctrine of time and space disposed of. Nevertheless, the aim of the *Critique* as a contribution to epistemology was to do just that. It was to conceive the categories of mechanics as forms of thought while standing firmly by empirical realism. Kant wanted a theory of knowledge which would both meet the claims of science to discover truths about reality (including the claim of physiology to explain the mechanism of perception) and also make sense, that is, not conflict with our ordinary beliefs expressed in the language of seeing mountains, reflecting about the nervous system, and choosing our course of action.

Hence there is much to be said for the view that his true aim, though he did not formulate it in that way, was to think out and clarify our ordinary use of perception words, since this is what 'having a theory of knowledge' means. A theory of knowledge is not a theory in the scientific sense of 'theory', since it cannot be empirically disproved.

This, however, is for consideration later. What is wanted at the moment is some elucidation of the mystifying phrase 'form of sensibility' and of the statement that space is the form of outer sense. Time has important problems of its own which I shall not consider here.

As a preliminary it may be noted that there is at least a verbal advantage in Kant's 'form of sensibility' locution. It preserves us from saying

(i) 'Space' is a proper name standing for a very special and peculiar thing. This is in effect the line taken by Newton and Clarke.

(ii) 'Space' stands for an odd kind of quality.

(iii) 'Space' stands for a complicated system of relations holding between things. This is the line Leibniz had attempted to develop against (i).

Kant held that we involve ourselves in verbal paradoxes by using 'space' uncritically in these distinct and irreconcilable senses, and also that none of them by itself is adequate to our needs. What has now to be asked is whether it is significant to say 'Neither thing, nor quality, nor relation, but form of perception'.

Difficulty arises here because 'form' is ambiguous anyway, and for Kant it is extremely vague as well. We therefore cannot say with confidence whether, when he talks about forms of sensibility, he has in mind a linguistic convention for discussing our visual experience (what it means to say 'I see a house') or whether he is actually propounding a psychological hypothesis to explain the origin of the spatial character of some of our perceptual data. The standard view, which seems to be accepted by Paton and many other commentators, inclines towards the latter interpretation. 'Form of sensibility' then stands for a piece of psychological apparatus which ensures that most if not all of our awareness of what goes on in the world is spatial.

I doubt whether this does justice to Kant's final position, but it is certainly convenient and mostly right as a starting-point; and I agree that, as a matter of history, he never quite succeeded in freeing himself from it. In its crudest form it is something like this. We can distinguish between the form and the matter of what we perceive. It is hard to say just what this distinction amounts to, as Kant's terminology is neither precise nor stable, but generally speaking he uses 'sensation' (*Empfindung*) to refer to neat or non-spatial data as contrasted with 'intuition' (*Anschauung*) which refers to normal (visual) perception. He then takes for granted a psycho-physical hypothesis as to what happens when I see something.[2] Objects, or rather light rays reflected from objects, operate on (affect) the optic nerve and generate impressions which in themselves are neither spatially nor temporally ordered (*Empfindungen*). In addition to being receptive of these impressions, our minds have a form-imposing structure of their own. This is presumably an ordinary empirical scientific hypothesis, and it suggests the question 'Might the form of outer sense be atrophied or destroyed and impressions still be received?' Kant seems generally to have favoured an affirmative answer,[3] and modern experiments confirm this.[4] He knew, too, of Locke's discussion with 'the think-

[2] Immanuel Kant's *Menschenkunde oder philosophische Anthropologie*, Leipzig, 1831, pp. 64 ff. Compare Kant's Letter to Sömmering, Ak. xii. 31.

[3] See his discussions of unsynthesized manifolds, A 115 ff., and references in Eisler, *Kant Lexicon*, '*Mannigfaltig*'.

[4] J. Z. Young, *Doubt and Certainty in Science*, pp. 61 ff.

ing Mr. Molyneux' and later controversy on the same point.[5] But he certainly did not think he was propounding a scientific hypothesis.

The whole of this story is probably best thought of by the analogy of coloured spectacles, as Paton does, though perhaps the camera or even the sausage machine are even more suitable. Kant seems rather surprisingly to have found no difficulty in holding (*a*) that there were both spectacles and data observable *in theory* without spectacles, (*b*) that he could examine the spectacles (in the *Aesthetic*) and find out how they worked and what they did, (*c*) that he could not *in practice* examine the pre-spectacular data, the raw materials, and give a description of them. He could inspect the sausages and the sausage machine, but not the sausage meat before the machine had formed it. All this he seems to regard as just obvious (though it ceased to be so when he began asking questions about synthesis). It is dismissed in a paragraph[6] of the *Critique*. Probably it seemed to him the concern of physiology and he would have referred a questioner to Haller's textbook[7] for further information.

No doubt the absence of experimental psychology made it very difficult for him to be clear on this point or to ask whether he was in fact propounding a testable hypothesis about vision, though surprisingly he does use a sort of empirical argument to confirm his view that the space-spectacles are open to our inspection whereas the pre-spectacular data are not. He can easily think of space with no objects in it, but not of non-spatial objects.[8] We may concede that if the existence of this piece of psychological machinery is accepted, though the reasons Kant offers for accepting it are mainly linguistic, the non-empirical validity of Euclidean geometry might be held to follow, provided that 'non-empirical' meant 'inescapable by human beings'; and indeed that is precisely what Kant does mean by *a priori* nearly all the time. What he is claiming is that he knows about spatial relations without deriving this knowledge inductively from the study of particular spatial situations, just because space is part of the furniture of the mind; but he did not ask whether the furniture of the mind

[5] Locke, *Essay*, II. ix. 8 and footnote (Fraser); Kant, *Menschenkunde*, p. 63.

[6] B 34.

[7] Haller, *Elementa physiologiae corporis humani*, 1762. See Ak. xii. 34.

[8] B 39.

was certainly open to thoroughgoing inspection by the owner of the mind. Hence he could claim to know *a priori* that everything which is perceived by outer sense is *ipso facto* subject to Euclid's rules.

As we have already seen, this psychological doctrine of perception, though it harmonizes quite well with the language of phenomena and things in themselves at first glance, is bound to collapse as soon as it is pressed at all hard. For the essence of it when fully understood is that spatio-temporal relations do not hold either between neat sense impressions or between the physical objects by which such impressions are generated. Kant need not perhaps have worried too much about the former, but he simply could not ignore the latter since the behaviour of physical bodies (atoms, light-waves, &c.) is the subject-matter of physics. In fact he saw from the start that there was a fatal gap in his critical view at this point. His weak conclusion in the *Dissertation* was an admission of this, and amounted to a confession that he had not yet found a consistent meaning for 'physical object'.

His next moves, contained in his letter to Herz[9] of February 1772, deserve careful study for the light they throw on the build-up of the *Transcendental Analytic*. The virtual collapse of the early 'forms of sensibility' view is expounded as follows:

> I asked myself on what ground rests the relation between that in us which we name 'representation' to the object? If the representation contains only the mode in which the subject is affected by the object, it is easily understood how it should accord with that object as an effect with its cause, and how this determination of the mind should be able to represent something, i.e. have an object. The passive or sensuous representations have thus a comprehensible relation to objects and the principles which are borrowed from the nature of our mind have a comprehensible validity for all things in so far as they are objects of the senses.

In other words, if there were a mechanical explanation of the origin of our ideas, we should be satisfied. There is such an explanation of the end product of cameras and radios. We can say how the trick is worked. But perception is not a trick. Kant goes on, 'If that in us which is called a representation were active in

[9] The relevant passages are translated by Kemp Smith, *Commentary*, pp. 206–20.

relation to the object, that is to say, if the object itself were produced by the representation, the conformity of objects with representations might be understood.'

Unfortunately, however, if the form-of-sensibilty view is taken seriously, both these routes are closed. I do not create the material things which I see, nor do my representations of houses and trees provide me with any information about their causes. Only the matter of sensation is given. Hence, as before, we are driven back on some pre-established harmony view or an arbitrary resemblance postulate, and these explain nothing. Forms of sensibility alone will not deliver the epistemological goods, since 'object' remains an intractable puzzle.

What lies behind the condensed statement in the letter to Herz is indeed the general difficulty that the new way of ideas developed in different ways by Locke and Leibniz is inherently incapable of making any sense of Newton. Newton's laws govern the behaviour of bodies, and bodies are not the kind of things which depend on the wishes, beliefs, or perceptions of human beings. The motions of the planets are not dependent on our knowledge of them. So Kant realized that he was faced with a dilemma. If, as Locke had claimed, there was a 'resemblance' of our ideas of primary qualities and the things themselves, i.e. if our ideas of figure, solidity, extension, motion, and number were genuine copies of non-mental originals, there would be a plausible ground for holding that Newton's laws governed the planets. But then this would be merely an empirical proposition based on the unproved and unprovable assumption of a pre-established harmony, and it would certainly not fit in with the psychological postulate which Kant was using to solve the antinomies and to demonstrate the factual validity of Euclid. For figure, &c., involve space; but Kant had dissolved the antinomies at the price of saying that real things, the things that generate impressions, are not spatial at all. Nor, though he did not observe it at this stage, does the simple *Ding an sich-Erscheinung* disjunction enable him to include a physiological theory of perception in his complete view. For if perception happens as the result of a direct affection of minds by *Dinge an sich* via the forms of sensibility, what need have we of the apparatus of retina, optic nerve, and so on to produce it?

But if we accept this conclusion and admit that we do not come by the ideas of cause and substance empirically, there seem to be only two alternatives. Either I must claim to know about physical laws by some kind of intellectual intuition, which is wholly non-informative, or I must go right back to Descartes and admit that it is sensible to ask 'How do I know that the physical universe (atoms, &c.) exists at all?'

This letter to Herz is a most important milestone in Kant's intellectual progress. It marks the transfer of his main preoccupation from the problems of space and time in the interest of metaphysics to the problem of things in the interests of science, and this transfer led incidentally to a much more concentrated study of epistemological problems than he had made previously.

Hardly anything is known of the details of his development at this time. The only evidence is that contained in the *Duisburgsche Nachlaß*[10] and the scattered fragments which Adickes with vast labour collected in the Akademie Ausgabe;[11] all that can be extracted from these sources has been definitively set out by de Vleeschauwer.[12] As this is a matter of purely historical interest, I shall not go into it here.

It is, however, to be remarked that, in the same letter to Herz, Kant shows that the general line of his final solution had already occurred to him.

> How comes it that the axioms of pure reason about these objects agree with the latter when this agreement has not been in any way assisted by experience? In mathematics such procedure is legitimate because its objects only are quantities for us and can be represented as quantities only in so far as we can generate their representation by repeating a unit a number of times. Hence the concepts of quantity can be self-producing and their products can therefore be determined *a priori.*[13]

This quotation already contains the germ of what Kant was later to call *a priori* synthesis, and this is the idea on which he finally based his solution to 'What does it mean to say that something is a thing or an object?' (*empirischer Gegenstand*). His position at the start (in the *Aesthetic*) is that he must use *Gegen-*

[10] *Der Duisburgsche Nachlaß und Kant's Criticismus um 1775*, edited by T. Haering, 1910.

[11] Ak. xiv–xix.

[12] *La Déduction transcendentale dans l'œuvre de Kant*, vol. i.

[13] Quoted by Kemp Smith, *Commentary*, p. 220.

stand in such a way as to enable Newton's laws to be described as (*a*) objective—not just hypotheses, but statements of the laws in accordance with which real things behave, (*b*) non-empirical.

I do not think that this can be done, but Kant's attempt to do it is an immensely powerful one, and his failure, if he did fail, unquestionably dominated other attempts to formulate the philosophy of science in a more tractable way.

NOTE ON 'PRE-CRITICAL'

There has been much discussion by commentators of the so-called 'pre-Critical' character of Kant's account of space in the *Aesthetic*, and certainly there is some force in the arguments which have been brought against him. Technically it is awkward that the early doctrine of space and perception which I have outlined here is simply taken over from the *Dissertation* and embodied in the *Critique*, although during the twelve-year period of development which intervened Kant had certainly moved a long way. To a great extent he had thought himself out of the simple 'camera obscura' doctrine of perception and the too simple *Ding an sich-Erscheinung* disjunction, which inconsistently was made to go with it, into a much more tenable and sophisticated view. So why, the critics ask, should he retain the old formulation almost unchanged in the *Critique*? This point is actually one of the main props of the old patchwork theory,[14] but it is not really very strong. I should say that the *Aesthetic* is non-committal. It has to be interpreted in the light of what follows. We can interpret it if we choose so as to make nonsense of Kant's final view, but we need not. All the same, I think he had better have rewritten it to avoid needless mystification of his readers. The use of 'pre-Critical' as a straightforward chronological word with no pejorative implications is convenient and harmless.

TRANSCENDENTAL AESTHETIC (B 33–73)

[How is pure mathematics possible?]

The *Preface* and *Introduction* have already shown that the axioms of arithmetic and more obviously those of geometry require for their apprehension something beyond the accurate analysis of concepts, namely the immediate apprehension of

[14] Kemp Smith, *Commentary*, pp. 88–98.

what is put into a figure by our act of constructing it. Hence if we are to understand the nature of our *a priori* certainty with regard to them we must investigate our faculty of immediate apprehension [*Anschauung*], since, whatever may be the position of beings differently constituted from ourselves, it must be admitted that sensibility is the only form of immediate apprehension which we possess. Now the object of sense is an appearance [*Erscheinung*] of something which affects us, and these appearances may be analysed into matter, which is their sense-content, and form, which brings it about that such content is arranged in a specific manner and which therefore cannot be itself regarded as belonging to sense-content but rather as something already present in the mind and therefore capable of being apprehended in abstraction from all content. Such apprehension is pure (as distinct from empirical) intuition, e.g. the apprehension of the extension and shape of a body in abstraction from all its other properties.

The purpose of the *Aesthetic* is to consider these pure forms of sensuous intuition, and introspection shows that there are two of them only, namely space and time, which condition respectively the outer and the inner sense.

When we consider space, we find that it is both *a priori* and sensuous in character. It is *a priori*, as opposed to empirical, since it is necessarily presupposed by and inseparable from all immediate awareness of particular appearances of things outside us. For I cannot perceive things as outside myself or one another except in so far as I perceive them as related in a single all-embracing space, and it is impossible for me to abstract them from space and consider them as non-spatial in the same way as I can abstract space from them and consider it by itself.

Hence space is a necessary, that is, an *a priori* condition of the existence of all appearances to outer sense. Furthermore, this condition is sensuous and not intellectual in character. For if it were the latter, it would be a discursive or universal conception and the parts of space would be related to the whole of space as instances are to a universal, i.e. as particular patches of red colour are to redness. This, however, is obviously not the case, since the parts of space are themselves spaces, and stand to space itself in the relation of part to whole, not that of particular to universal. Space is a particular, and my notion or concept of it must be intuitive and not discursive in character.

Hence pure mathematics is possible as a science; for inasmuch as we have an intuitive awareness of pure space as being at once sensuous and *a priori*, there is no difficulty in seeing how we can apprehend necessary connexions within it independently of any conceptual analysis.

But further consideration of the implications of the view is called for, and from this it may be recognized[15]

1. That space cannot be a condition of things as they are in themselves, for to say that something is 'in itself', i.e. has true independent existence, when it presupposes the antecedent existence of something else (space), is a contradiction.

Therefore

2. Space must be the form, not of things in themselves, but of all appearances of these things to the mind in perception; it must be the subjective condition of sensibility under which alone immediate awareness of appearances of things as outside us is possible for us. And since this is the case, it follows that applied geometry also is valid of all appearances which objects can occasion in us through outer sense.

The same arguments which hold of space are also valid of time, which is the form of inner sense, or of consciousness strictly so-called. All that needs to be added is that time is in fact more all-embracing than space. For whereas the latter is a condition only of appearances of what is independent of us, time is the form of consciousness in general and therefore may be termed the immediate condition of appearances of our own self and the mediate condition also of appearances of what is independent of us.

Further Explanation

This account of the nature of time and space is essentially different from both the leading views which have previously been held. Newtonian physics has maintained that space in particular is something real in which things exist but which is by itself nothing, though it must be conceived as infinite, self-subsistent, and eternal, a view which, when pressed, leads inevitably to self-contradiction. The school of Wolff and Leibniz, on the other hand, have rejected this view and have attempted to explain space

[15] B 42.

and time as relations of appearances abstracted from experience and confusedly apprehended. This must lead to the conclusion that mathematics is invalid of real things in space. Both these difficulties are avoided by the Critical view which regards space and time as forms valid only of sensible objects, that is, as being empirically real but as having no applicability to things when considered in abstraction from our actual or possible sensuous awareness of them. For the Newtonian difficulties spring from the notion of space as something independently real and the Leibnizian from the notion of it as a relation confusedly apprehended; both views must therefore be regarded as erroneous.

It may, however, be objected that in treating space and time as the forms of appearances only and not of things in themselves, the Critical view reduces bodies to mere illusion and even makes it impossible to draw any genuine distinction between illusion and reality. This is a complete mistake arising from a failure to take account of what is being asserted. To make matters more clear it should be pointed out that the term 'appearance' is somewhat ambiguous and is often used, especially in common speech, for that which is illusory or dependent for its existence on the perceptual peculiarities of particular individuals. The whole of what are sometimes called the secondary qualities of things are subjective and therefore to be regarded as appearances in this sense. Spatio-temporal properties, on the other hand, are usually and rightly distinguished from these and regarded as the realities of which the secondary qualities are only 'appearances'. This too is in accordance with the Critical view which holds that space and time as forms of sensibility are empirically real, and possess complete objective validity for all percipients whatever. The innovation of the Critical view is to conceive yet another level of reality, namely that of things as they are in abstraction from all experience, and to point out that in relation to these even space and time and the objects in them with which applied geometry and physics are concerned must be regarded as appearances,[16] that is, as transcendently ideal.

It might further be objected that the view, though plausible in respect of space, is inadmissible in respect of time, since by common consent we apprehend ourselves in time, and thus time at least is shown to be the form not of an appearance but of a thing

[16] B 63.

in itself. This, however, is an error since the object of my internal consciousness is always a series of acts and never the true subject whose acts they are. The latter is as much hidden from my inspection as are the things in themselves which appear to my senses as objects in space outside me.

This summary of the argument of the *Aesthetic* shows Kant's constantly increasing embarrassment with the epistemological implications of his view, and we must now return to these.

KANT'S EPISTEMOLOGICAL EMBARRASSMENT

Stage II

The Mind–Body Problem

§ 1

Kant's considered view of the *a priori* nature of space on which his conception of the non-empirical status of the physics categories depends was in the end that we do not need to learn from experience that the world is three-dimensional. There never was a time when we had to learn that physical objects have backs and insides. That this is itself a factual statement which is probably false did not often occur to him and was from his point of view almost irrelevant. He was concerned with normal, adult human beings, and believed that they at any rate have the kind of eyes, ears, and central nervous system which ensure that their perceptual data are spatio-temporally ordered. Naturally these do not protect us from error about spatial location and other relations in particular cases; we may mistake a looking-glass reflection for a person or a room. In general, however, we cannot even imagine what it would be like to apprehend data which had no spatio-temporal order, though we can, by concentrating on the spatio-temporal ordering, create in imagination a kind of formalized schema which might be called an abstract idea of space and time.

What mattered to him is our inability to attach any meaning to 'non-spatial seeing and imagining'. He held that apes or angels might (logically) differ from us in having non-spatio-temporal experience, but if they do, what happens to them is indescribable by us. One might say that for us any significant speech must have four pairs of co-ordinate words, 'above-below', 'in front of-behind', 'to the right-to the left', and 'before-after'. And the 'must' here is in an unexplained way both factual and logical. This point is not seriously attacked until the *Analytic of Principles.*

If his view is stated in this way, it does not matter whether he is said to have maintained that space is a form of perception or a formal perception. Both are harmless when what he means is clearly put. Such a statement, however, as he found out, simply cannot be made without a thorough clean-up of 'perception' and 'object'.

So far, following Kant in his early stage, I have deliberately used such words as 'perception', 'impression', and 'object' in a most imprecise way. This is inevitable if any plausibility is to be given to the view contained in the *Dissertation.* To make any progress in deciding what was his considered position, it is essential to come to some conclusion on a point of substantial importance. What we have to ask is, did Kant or did he not attempt to expound a two-world view of mind and body? Did he regard them as different kinds of things, both real, but somehow mysteriously joined to one another? It has generally, and with some reason, been assumed that he did accept this view and that one important job which the *Critique* attempts to perform is to explain the linkage. I now think that this is at least partly a mistake. I do not mean that he explicitly rejected a two-world view, but that it never seriously presented itself to him as a philosophical worry.

This point is of more than purely historical interest, since much of what Kant writes in the *Analytic* can be and has been interpreted as an unsuccessful attempt to escape from an 'egocentric predicament'. But if he did not consciously accept or reject the two-world view which generates the predicament, he could feel no need to escape from it, and his reasoning will bear a different and perhaps a more satisfactory explanation.

To elucidate this it is necessary to go back to the spectacles and sausage machine model of perception which has already been mentioned and consider in greater detail the history and philosophical importance of the two-world view.

In varying forms it is a very old view. Men did not have to wait for the advent of Descartes and Locke to come by the notion of a human being as a kind of double entity, a soul and a body, either of which could perfectly well exist without the other, and which were in fact separated at death. But this notion in its primitive form was essentially different from that of the *Ghost in the Machine,* since, although there were important differences between them, the soul and the body were basically the same kind of things. Odysseus could not embrace his mother's soul, but souls drank blood and could be kept away from it by a drawn sword. The inmates of the *Inferno* were not different in kind from living people.

This story, however, achieved an entirely different status and significance with the discovery of the rules of perspective and the development of a scientific theory of optics. The piece of apparatus which deserves to be particularly remembered in this connexion is a very simple one known as the camera obscura.[17]

If we take a candle and place a lens at the right distance between it and a screen, we get on the screen an image of the candle laterally and longitudinally inverted, i.e. the wrong way round and upside down. If we have a looking-glass instead of a screen and reflect the image on to a horizontal table, we get a correct image. This used still to be a popular diversion at sea-side resorts fifty years ago. One entered a dark room and saw on a table a picture of what was going on outside. The same device was used for making astronomical observations in the sixteenth and seventeenth centuries.

The epistemological consequences of reflection on this and similar devices were momentous. One notices at once that a person in a camera obscura chamber might be deceived and might suppose that he was 'really' seeing through a window or aperture the events depicted on the screen; and a similar line of thought is suggested by the fact that artists, when they come to know about perspective and foreshortening, can produce illusory appearances of three-dimensional scenes on a two-dimensional canvas.

Now the camera obscura illusion could easily be dispelled by exhibiting the mechanism and showing how the trick is worked. The observer would then say, 'Now I understand. What I am looking at is not the real thing though it looks just like it. It is an appearance, species, or idea generated by the reflection of light through a lens.'

The second scientific discovery which led to epistemological

[17] Kant mentions it in *Menschenkunde*, p. 63.

confusion is that the retina of the eye has many of the properties which are to be found in an artificially constructed lens. One may say that it is a kind of lens.

The stage is now set for the emergence of the belief (which is the causal theory of perception) that we are all the time, in our seeing at any rate, the victims of a sort of camera obscura illusion. Objects are all the time being reflected through a lens (the retina) into a dark room (the interior of the skull) where we must suppose that the appearances (ideas) of them are literally thrown on to a blank sheet (or tabula rasa). And there is Locke's theory of perception and the essential part of his semi-technical vocabulary. We need, it is true, a further piece of physiological machinery to rectify the inverted image, but this is a minor point. We also need an observer, and for this part we have ready-made the notion of the mind or soul. This now becomes an odd little imp located somewhere in the skull and gazing at the pictures on the tabula rasa.

I doubt whether anybody ever took this story quite seriously. It has so many obvious weaknesses. Yet in a vague way it has survived and still survives as the background of serious physiological talk about perception. For, after all, whether epistemologists like it or not, the retina is a sort of lens, and why should it be a lens except to work the camera obscura trick? To say, as is sometimes done, that what we have here is just a model which is heuristically helpful but without ontological commitment is simply to give up the game and admit that we have here an unanalysed linguistic muddle.

Philosophically it is simple enough to show that the two-world view is wildly wrong. Descartes, Leibniz, and Berkeley all knew that it would not hold water, but none of them and none of their successors in the nineteenth and twentieth centuries have stated clearly any acceptable alternative. For no alternative can be accepted which makes nonsense of optics, physiology, and physics. The crucial point indeed was understood clearly enough by Berkeley though he put it in a most misleading way. Quite simply it is that the mind–body story, either in its traditional or in its seventeenth-century dress, is epistemologically beyond redemption. It is hopeless. There just are not two different kinds of stuff influencing or causing modifications in one another, and therefore we waste our time when we search for the essential differences between the substances, mind and body, and the hidden link by which they are hitched together.

Leibniz, too, said something important when he talked of perception as the representation both of something that happens in me and of something that happens outside me.[18] It does make sense to say 'I am looking at a mountain'; it can make sense to say 'I am looking at my brain.' And this makes it nonsense to say 'The operation of my brain causes me to see.'

It is this haphazard introduction of 'cause' which does more than anything else to get us into hopeless tangles by leading us, as it did the camera obscura theorists, into a fatal misconstruing of 'see' and 'hear'. For if 'A causes B' is interpreted as 'The occurrence of B (my seeing a mountain) is always correlated with A (an observable modification of my cortex)', then there is nothing queer in talking about the causes of perception. But then it will not do to say that all events have causes, for there are some events, e.g. deliberate actions, for which it makes no sense to look for cortical correlates. If, on the other hand, 'cause' is used only to refer to the mechanical interaction of physical bodies, it is perfectly legitimate to say 'Everything which is describable in the categories of physics has a physical cause.' But then my seeing a mountain is not a physical occurrence within the meaning of the definition, and it is nonsense to talk of it as causally related to physical events.

To give a helpful analysis of 'X is looking at a mountain' we have to give up talking of seeing as a relation (presumed to be causal) between an observer and a physical object and say something like: '"X is looking at a mountain" is a short description of what happens when an organism constituted as follows is placed under specifiable conditions in a specifiable position relative to an object constituted as follows.' The blanks in this formula need to be filled in by the physiologist, the physicist, and the optician, but the only values which will qualify are observable data. Admittedly this does nothing about 'Yes, but the retina is a sort of lens', but there is no need to do anything about it. Lenses can do lots of jobs besides working the camera obscura trick. They make quite good burning glasses, for instance.

What matters is that none of Kant's authorities (he knew very little about Berkeley) had even suggested that the mind–body

[18] Kant also maintains this. *Menschenkunde*, p. 62.

difficulty is a linguistic and not a factual puzzle. Hence it is important to decide what his position on this issue was. Did he hold explicitly or take it for granted that perception statements, especially visual perception statements, should be elucidated by translation into camera obscura language or had he a different method of analysis? To give a satisfactory answer we need, in addition to studying his major works, to pay a good deal of attention to what he said in his *Anthropologie in pragmatischer Hinsicht*.[19] This contains the final version of the lectures on empirical psychology which he delivered for many years, published with his approval in 1798; an earlier and in some ways a more interesting version compiled from notes made by his hearers was published in 1831.[20] The details are not important here. What puts him in principle against the vicious form of the camera obscura view, in spite of many concessions in formulation he makes to it, is that throughout his psychological exposition he follows Leibniz in drawing his major line of demarcation, not between mind and body, but between organism and environment. What bounds our persons is our skins, and 'outside me' means 'outside my body' which is in accordance with ordinary use, not 'outside my mind' which is without significance. Thus he avoided a trap which Berkeley, whether or not he was caught in it himself, left waiting for his successors.

None of this is surprising. In the last resort Leibniz and not Locke was Kant's chosen authority, and Leibniz, though he too conceded much to the prevalent fashionable view, was in principle opposed to an ideological body-mind disjunction. One may guess that the influence of Locke's firm disciple, Tetens, at a critical moment led Kant to over-emphasize in *A* the Lockean psychological theory which he never completely shook off and of which he never realized fully the essential untenability. We know that he read Tetens's *Philosophische Versuche* about 1778 and was greatly impressed by it.[21]

§ 2

It is fair to say that a great deal of Kant's admitted failure to make clear what he meant by 'knowledge of objects', 'objects of

[19] Ak. vii. 117.

[20] Immanuel Kant's *Menschenkunde oder philosophische Anthopologie.*

[21] Letter to Marcus Herz, April 1778, Ak. x. 232. Cf. Ak. x. 270.

perception', and 'objects of scientific inquiry' resulted from his tendency to use perception and sensation words which occur in both Leibnizian and Lockean ways of talking, without noticing the very different employment of them which the two systems require. In addition, his vocabulary of epistemological words was quite inadequate to the distinctions he needed to draw, and therefore his use of them is generally both ambiguous and vague. No clear analysis of his uses is practicable except at enormous and unprofitable length, and no English equivalents to his terms can be consistently employed in translation which are not seriously misleading. Roughly, however, his most important German words with the Latin equivalents of the Leibnizians and the English renderings of Kemp Smith are these:[22]

Kant	*Leibniz*	*Kemp Smith*
Vorstellung	Repraesentatio	Representation
Erscheinung	Phaenomenon	Appearance
Anschauung	Intuitio	Intuition
Empfindung	Sensatio	Sensation

These need some further comment.

1. *Vorstellung* is an umbrella word corresponding to Locke's 'idea', 'whatsoever is present to the mind when it thinks'. Hence it refers indifferently to concepts, thoughts, images, and any kind of apprehension. Feelings[23] are generally excluded.

The least misleading English equivalent is probably 'idea'. But Kemp Smith not unnaturally felt he must avoid this because Kant uses *Idee* technically to stand for the 'Ideas of Pure Reason', God, Freedom, and Immortality. It might be better to use 'notion' for these, following Berkeley, though Kant himself would not have approved.

2. *Erscheinung* is simply not translatable by any one word or phrase. Kemp Smith decides in favour of 'appearance', but this is misleading almost always. Frequently 'phenomenon', which Kant sometimes, though not often, uses as Leibniz had done, is preferable. The point is that for Kant it makes sense to say that *Erscheinungen* have backs and insides; that they are solid and obey the laws of mechanics. But these are not permissible ways of using 'appearance' in English. On the other hand, it is impossible to stick to 'phenomenon' or just 'thing' since Kant also wants

22 Kant's own table is at B 376. It is not very helpful.

23 See below, p. 259.

to say that *Erscheinungen* are *Inbegriffe der Vorstellungen*, and this produces the same feeling of cross-category discomfort as Berkeley's 'We are fed and clothed with ideas.' We do not use 'idea' and 'thing' like that in English.

Among professional philosophers, it is true, resistance to this kind of talk has been reduced by Russell's recommendation to make 'thing' equivalent to 'class of appearances' and to the phenomenalist contention of the 1930's that statements about material objects might be replaced without change of meaning by statements about sense-data. But this, too, is against ordinary use and I do not think Kant would have accepted it. He did not think he was using a technical language here.

My objection to translating *Erscheinung* by any of the 'appearance', 'sensum', 'sense-content' group of words is not merely on grounds of scholarship. It is rather that such translations tend to commit Kant to a two-world view with its egocentric implications. They push him into a terminology like that of Descartes and Locke in which it is linguistically proper to talk as if the furniture of the world contained both plates and looks of plates.[24]

3. *Anschauung*. 'Intuition' is not a good English equivalent since it at least suggests a special kind of faculty or achievement. We need rather a standard ordinary-language word to cover 'seeing' and 'hearing'. 'Perception' is probably the best available. In fact Kant seems nearly always to have seeing in mind when he uses *Anschauung*. When he wants to use a wider term he prefers *Wahrnehmung*, which Kemp Smith translates as 'perception'.

4. *Empfindung*. Kant's use has already been considered. See above, p. 110.

I shall continue generally to use Kemp Smith's equivalents, since his translation of the *Critique* is now the accepted English version.

The upshot is, though it must be repeated that Kant's handling of his own terms would by no means satisfy a legal authority, that to have an empirical intuition is to have an idea which is at least fairly clear and distinct. Further,[25] 'The undetermined object of

[24] Kant realized the unclearness of *Erscheinung* and tried to do something about it in the *Opus Postumum* by distinguishing between *Erscheinungen* and *Erscheinungen von den Erscheinungen*. Ak. xxii. 339 and 363–5. Too late!

[25] B 34.

an empirical intuition is called appearance', that is, the object of an idea is called 'thing' or 'phenomenon'. This is certainly vague and uninformative, but, as a preliminary statement, it is not at all mysterious. 'Undetermined' merely emphasizes the deliberate lack of precision in *Erscheinung*. Kant does not want to tie himself down to 'body' or 'material thing' in a restricted sense. A rainbow is an *Erscheinung*, so is a thunderstorm, and so is a writing-desk.

In fact Kant's perceptual vocabulary does not in German encourage or discourage the adoption of a two-world view. It is too vague to commit him to anything. The Kemp Smith renderings, which are too firmly established in this country to be altered without generating more confusion among students who do not use the German text, are much more committal. They all tend to edge Kant into the phenomenalist camp of the 1930's. The real criticism of Kant's epistemological vocabulary is not that it is technical or complicated but that it is far too simple to do the job he requires of it. He just has not enough words with which to draw the distinctions within 'perceiving' which he must draw in order to expound his concept of the 'object of perception'. Hence he uses *Erscheinung* to stand indifferently for:

1. Things as they look (sound, &c.) to a normal observer under normal conditions.
2. Things as they look to a specially equipped observer under more or less controlled conditions (microscopes, telescopes, X-rays).
3. Ideas, perceptions occurring to normal observers under abnormal conditions (Gestalt tricks, mirages).
4. Ideas, perceptions to abnormal observers under normal conditions (pink rats).

(3) and (4) are supposed to be called *Schein* rather than *Erscheinung*, but Kant does not always remember this. The footnote on B 69–70 shows where this inadequate vocabulary can lead him.

IV

THE ANALYTIC

INTRODUCTION

Transcendental Analytic (B 89–349)

[How is pure physics possible?]

THE aim of the *Aesthetic* was to demonstrate that the axioms of arithmetic and geometry are valid of the phenomenal world of our experience. The *Analytic* is designed to perform the same service for physics. The method adopted is in principle that of the *Aesthetic*, but in view of the complexity of the subject the proof is more elaborate and includes steps which in the *Aesthetic* had been omitted as obvious. Essentially it consists of four stages:

1. Demonstration that, just as sensibility has its proper forms of space and time which it imposes on matter presented to it, so thought or understanding has forms peculiar to it, namely the pure concepts of the understanding. These are discovered and enumerated in the *Metaphysical Deduction*. B 91–116.
2. The demonstration that these forms of thought, like the forms of sense, are necessarily valid of phenomena. *Transcendental Deduction*. B 117–75.
3. The explanation of how these pure concepts can be employed by the imagination so as to give rise to the fundamental axioms of physics. *Transcendental Schematism*. B 176–88.
4. The enumeration of these axioms and the demonstration that they are necessarily valid of all phenomena. *Analytic of Principles*. B 188–295.

To this is added a section on the critical distinction between phenomena and things in themselves, B 295–315, and a criticism of the metaphysic of Leibniz and Wolff, B 316–49. It is important to remember this programme, since it is common to regard Kant's purpose as having been much less complex than it actually was, with the result that much of his argument seems to be only repetitive. Had he merely wished to refute Hume's view that we can never justly claim to apprehend necessary relations between real existences, much of what he says would certainly be redundant. But in fact his aim was not merely to answer Hume but also to provide a metaphysical basis for Newton, and it is to this fact that many of his difficulties must be attributed.

TRANSCENDENTAL LOGIC

Sense and Understanding

§ 1

Kant's transition from aesthetic to logic is abrupt. It is not at first sight clear, except in a trivial way, what he thought it was or why he thought it mattered. A good deal of light can be thrown on both questions by considering the part which 'sensibility', 'understanding', and 'synthesis' play in his working out of the way in which 'scientific knowledge' is to be understood, indeed, it is fair to say that the entire plot of the *Transcendental Aesthetic* and the *Transcendental Analytic* is involved here, and that, to start with, all the characters seem extremely artificial. It is a great deal easier to see that his talk is queer than to feel the force of any genuine problems which were worrying him. To put this in a different way, it is fairly easy to do a verbal elucidation of Kant's language; we can say, 'Sensibility is passive, Understanding is active. We therefore need a bridge or a link between them. This is provided by Imagination, and the technical device by means of which Imagination bridges the gap between sensibility and understanding is called "synthesis".' This tells us nothing important about what Kant's difficulty was. It fails because none of the key words are cashed, except in terms of one another, yet they are not easily cashable. We do not learn about the purchasing power of sterling when we are told the rates of exchange prevailing between London, Zürich, and New York. I shall therefore give a preliminary clarification first of 'sense' and 'understanding' and then of 'synthesis' before going on to the doctrine expounded in the *Metaphysical Deduction*. This involves a certain amount of repetition and anticipation, but there is no great harm in that.

§ 2

Are the *Aesthetic* and the *Analytic* contributions to the solution of one problem, or are there for Kant two distinct problems to be faced before the task of dealing with metaphysics is undertaken in the *Dialectic*? As a matter of historical fact we have already seen that Kant originally thought that there were two, and that the solution of the first inevitably gave rise to the second. We can answer 'How is pure mathematics possible?' by pointing out that space and time are transcendentally ideal, that is, by describing them as 'forms of sensibility'; but this procedure seems to make 'How is pure physics possible?' insoluble. To avoid this conclusion, Kant gradually gave up the idea of two separate but related difficulties, though without fully realizing that he had done so, and substituted a single question, 'How is synthesis possible?' For this, or rather 'What does "synthesis" mean?' is the question he is putting in *Preface B*, the *Deductions*, and the *Principles*.

The answer he gives is that synthesis is possible in virtue of a 'blind but indispensable function of the soul' to which he gives the name 'productive imagination'. This is unhelpful. It is just adding another rate of exchange; and Kant never does cash 'productive imagination', so that we are driven to work out what he meant by it for ourselves. On the whole the most profitable approach to the idea, which has to carry most of the weight in the central part of the *Critique*, is to start from Kant's own rather casual account of the distinction between the processes with which the *Aesthetic* and the *Analytic* are concerned. This is itself shrouded in misleading faculty language and needs to be disentangled before it is intelligible.

Certainly Kant's basic distinction is between 'activity' and 'passivity'. 'Through sensibility objects are given to us, by the understanding they are thought.'[1] This is unpromising. 'Given' is a camera obscura phrase, while 'sensibility' and 'understanding' are slippery words to which it is difficult to give any precise meaning. All the same the idea Kant was trying to put across was a sound one, and it is one which our own natural language will not comfortably express, any more than his technical, psychological talk would do.

The trouble is that 'perceive', 'see', 'hear', &c., look and are often construed as if they referred to doing something, but this is not usually their job at all. 'What have you been doing for the last hour?' may be answered by 'Playing tennis', 'Hunting for

[1] B 74.

birds' eggs', or 'Reading the *Critique*'; but not by 'Perceiving' or 'Seeing'. The old gentleman who said, 'Sometimes I sits and thinks; sometimes I just sits' made an important distinction. When we just sit, we are seeing, hearing, &c. We can often recall what we saw if we are challenged. We do not, however, require a non-philosophical word to describe this situation, for, outside the theory of knowledge, such a word would have no genuine antithesis. If we want to deny that the speaker was seeing, &c., we must say that he was unconscious (anaesthetized); but 'conscious' is seldom used except in phrases beginning 'conscious of . . .' (except in contrast with 'anaesthetized'), and to say 'conscious of . . .' implies more than 'just sitting'. 'I was conscious of . . .' is equivalent to 'I noticed . . .' or 'I noticed that . . .'. Now suppose we decide to use 'conscious' as the antithesis, not to 'unconscious' but to the higher-order word 'self-conscious'; if we do this, we may also develop a kind of faculty language as Kant did, but we need not do so. It seems more correct and more in accordance with ordinary usage to describe the difference between 'just sitting' and 'sitting and thinking', not in terms of the presence or absence of an activity called 'thinking' or 'self-consciousness' but by means of an adverb such as 'observantly'. When we do this, we find that even 'just sitting' is seldom or never quite unobservant, since I can recall at least something of what had been going on around me unless I have been asleep.

In reality the distinction between attending closely to what is happening and idly seeing and hearing without noticing is nothing like as clear cut as faculty language encourages us to believe that it is. The two shade into one another, and we mislead ourselves if we demand that 'observant seeing' or just 'observing' be always analysable into two components, 'sensing' and 'understanding'.

If we work along this line, we tend to say that when I become interested and concentrate my attention on something, say, an odd noise or smell, I do not suddenly begin to do something, namely thinking, which I was not doing at all before. It is not like scratching when I feel a tickle. Rather, I am doing carefully something that I was doing before but was doing idly or casually. Our language is awkward here because, as I said to start with, 'seeing' is not a word for doing something yet 'looking at . . .' normally suggests a greater degree of concentration and interest than was actually present. We do not need words to describe all the possible degrees of attention between 'just sitting' and 'observing with extreme care', but aeroplane spotters and fire watchers know the difference and know that there are continuous gradations between the two.

This account of 'sense' and 'understanding' also indicates Kant's development of the notion of synthesis. To start with he regarded it as something very intellectual and high-powered which we perform only when we are engaged in solving geometrical and mechanical problems or, more generally, when we are definitely and consciously theorizing. As he developed this idea, he came to think that the same process is going on (*a*) in any coherent thinking, and finally (*b*) even when we are not in ordinary language 'thinking' at all but just 'perceiving' or 'being conscious'. But in this kind of context words like 'constructing' and 'connecting' which are appropriate enough when I am drawing a diagram or making a plan are clearly much too strong, even 'doing something' seems excessive. Thus there really is a marked distinction between the activity of the understanding and the passivity of sensibility, though the boundary between them is not clearly definable as faculty language misleadingly suggests that it is. I am trying to do something as soon as I begin to wonder what the scratchy noise or the queer smell is. I was not trying to do anything before. We may rightly object to describing this difference by saying that a new faculty has come into operation, that imagination is building a bridge between sense and understanding, but it is correct to maintain that my attitude towards the situation is now different from what it was before. The verbal change is important, but Kant's distinction, though not well stated, is a perfectly genuine one.

Supposing that this is correct, does it help to elucidate further the argument of the *Aesthetic*? We can see what Kant's original difficulty over geometry was, but if it was absorbed in the wider question of synthesis and if that question is dealt with, as he claims that it is, in the *Analytic*, why was it necessary to retain the *Aesthetic* at all? Is it there simply because his architectonic, derived from the faculty psychology, contained a pigeon-hole labelled 'sensibility' and something had to be found to put into it?

The answer may run as follows. Our passive perceiving is psychologically basic and it is always spatio-temporal. This is not just an empirical fact. The pillar-box might be green and not red, but it makes no sense to say 'It might not be spatio-temporal'. This was certainly Kant's considered view and I do not think that modern attempts to show that spatio-temporal characteristics are empirical in the ordinary sense have succeeded. The only qualification needed is Kant's admission that, as far as logical possibility is concerned, there may be and indeed probably are, sentient beings quite differently constituted from ourselves. For these (*a*) passive perception may not be psychologically basic ('they may have intellectual intuitions' is his way of putting it), (*b*) their passive perception may not be spatio-temporal. We cannot significantly ask why ours is spatio-temporal.

Although this sort of view may certainly be challenged (one might for instance question the significance of both (*a*) and (*b*)), it is at least arguable. What I take to be Kant's succeeding thought is much more dubious. His contention is that since the world which we passively perceive or observantly study is spatio-temporal, it follows that Euclidean geometry reveals to us truths about it—that is, we have some factual knowledge about it which is not derived from any empirical premiss but is purely *a priori*. He seems incidentally to make the same claim for arithmetic (in the section on Time) but this is not stressed. Put shortly, his claim is that, since we have pure intuitions of space and time, we can discover non-empirical truths about whatever is spatio-temporal, and the world as we perceive it is spatio-temporal. This is incorrect. It may salve the validity of Euclidean geometry if we take the 'pure intuition' of space and time for granted, ask no questions about the precise meaning of it, and accept it as being a sort of empirical premiss. But this requires an excessive dose of primitive credulity or natural piety. Certainly Kant is right in holding that we 'see' in some undefined sense the implications of the figures we construct. We do not regard them as ordinary particulars about whose properties it is appropriate to frame empirical generalizations. We have, too, sufficient insight into the way in which things normally behave to be confident that we can rely on our geometrical reasoning when we want to build bridges or predict eclipses. I think he is right, too, though this is less clear, in maintaining that our basic experience is necessarily spatio-temporal in the sense that we cannot say or imagine what non-spatio-temporal experience would or might conceivably be like.

Hence it will not do to say that geometrical axioms are completely arbitrary. 'Geometrical' here, however, is not equivalent to 'Euclidean'.

All the same Kant's hard and fast initial distinction between sense and understanding together with the demand that imagination, or any other psychological bridge-builder, should somehow connect them is a weak piece of exposition. It sounds unplausible. We must, however, accept the fact that he never doubted the propriety of the disjunction and could hardly have done so without a major recantation, for it was precisely this which he continued to put forward as his major advance on Leibniz. Without it the critical distinction between things in themselves and phenomena, which he rested on the transcendental ideality of space and time, could hardly have survived in the form in which he conceived it.

Admittedly Kant was seriously worried, and quite rightly worried, by the fact that we do recognize geometrical reasonings from figures as cogent though they are not analytical in his sense, and he would not have been comforted by any claim that rigorous analytical demonstrations can be substituted. His point was that Euclid's demonstrations were convincing. They still are.

Nevertheless Kant was really in trouble because his early faculty formulation and his mature synthesis formulation are not compatible with one another. They cannot be rendered consistent, nor is it in his power to renounce either of them. I believe he could have sacrificed the faculty story without loss to his philosophy of science, but I doubt whether his ethics or his theology would have survived the amputation.

The sharp distinction between *Aesthetic* and *Analytic*, between sensibility and understanding, originated in Kant's attempt to supersede Leibniz's doctrine that sense is confused thinking. But Kant could not stand by his disjunction and still give an answer to 'How is pure physics possible?' So he went in for psychological bridge-building, and this in any simple interpretation is doomed to failure. All that happens is that he restores in his undefined term 'imagination' the combination of sense and thought which his official terminology excludes. It is by developing the notion of synthesis that he succeeds in getting going again.

§ 3

The first formulation of the view to which Kant is committed by his attempt to treat the basic concepts of physics in the same sort of way as he had dealt with those of geometry is this: when we claim to know without any experimental evidence that some general statement about the physical world, Newton's Laws of Motion, for instance, is true, what we are doing is to recognize a form or pattern which is really present in things as we perceive them. But it is there solely because we are organisms of a specifiable psycho-physical variety.

This is a provisional statement only. It has too much of the camera obscura and sausage machine analogies embodied in it to stand up for long. If this limitation is recognized, however, it is not very misleading and is of some help in showing how the notion of synthesis was developed. What is wrong with it in principle is the suggestion of a precise boundary line between crude perceptual data (*Empfindungen*) and normal perceptual experience (*Anschauungen*), with the further notion that crude data occur first and are somehow transmuted into perceptual experience by the imposition of form. This is indeed much too simple for Kant's final view even though it does not seriously misrepresent his point of departure.

The next move is the one we have already met in *Preface B*. It is expounded again in B 713 ff. and in the *Axioms of Intuition*. What emerges here is that what makes our geometrical knowledge possible is our construction of figures. The idea of form as a sort of mould is being replaced by that of form as a kind of synthesis, and it is this which is to carry us over from Euclid to Newton. But although the germ of this is already present in the letter to Herz of February 1772, the development is not easy to follow. As far as Euclid is concerned, Kant clearly holds that both the cogency and the factual validity of his conclusions rest on three conditions.

1. I must construct a figure.
2. I must recognize the unity of my act in constructing it.
3. I must further recognize that my construction of it in that way has determinate consequences.[2]

The line of his thought here is intuitively clear enough, though

[2] Cf. *Proleg.*, §§ 7–13.

most mathematicians today would say that he was mistaken in searching for the foundations of geometry here. It should also be noted that he was by no means the first person to take this line. What is difficult is to see how the argument about geometry has any relevance to his further difficulty about pure physics.

For the sake of simplicity at this stage, let us assume that the basic notions involved here are those of substance and cause. Others are required, even for mechanics, but these are clearly indispensable. Space and time are needed too, but Kant has provisionally committed himself to the view that these are primarily, if not wholly, in the department of sensibility and not in that of understanding. Motion, for technical reasons, is reserved for treatment in *M.A.N.* But whatever is finally decided about these, 'cause' and 'substance' are certainly key words. They may, and do, later turn into 'mass' and 'energy', but this does not affect the main issue.

Now space has been dealt with at the level of geometry by introducing the notion of outer sense, time has been rather casually slipped into the same compartment as the form of inner sense. Mechanics is to be the concern of understanding, and cause and substance are to be forms of thought. This is verbally tidy, but what does the last sentence mean? I think we can begin, but only begin, to see light here if we put together Kant's three requirements for Euclidean geometry and his typically eighteenth-century worship, bequeathed by Galileo, of mathematical method in science. Mathematics was the language of God, and the study of nature was rational just in so far as it was mathematical.

Hence the paradigm of synthetic activity is mathematics, and, for Kant, the ultimate foundation of mathematics is counting; for it was by counting, as he held, that the natural number series was generated.[3] Now counting is a clear instance of synthesis or construction in Kant's sense, as we see from his account of $7+5=12$ in the *Introduction*. This is what he means by saying that arithmetic is synthetic, not analytic. Furthermore, counting is construction in accordance with a rule. We recognize the unity of the act, that is, that we move from 3 to 4 by repeating the procedure by which we moved from 1 to 2,[4] and so on. Some details

[3] Cf. B 104, A 103, and many other places in the *Critique* and elsewhere.

[4] Cf. Wittgenstein, *Foundations of Mathematics*, i. 1–4.

of Kant's development are given in B 104. Finally, there are the implications of this procedure which are the rules of arithmetic.

It would be a mistake to suppose that Kant was here making a preliminary move in the kind of analysis developed later by Peano, Frege, and Russell. He was perhaps sometimes near that territory, but only by accident. Indeed his view of arithmetic as well as of geometry is still by modern standards hopelessly intuitive; and of course his answer to this criticism would be that modern views make nonsense *a priori* of what he was trying to do. It is of some interest at this point to contrast Kant's general approach with that of Russell. The fundamental disagreement occurs because Kant thinks of the activity carried out in counting as basic and as the prototype of all logical thinking. He could really give no general statement of how 'synthesis' is used except to say 'Think about counting.' He tries to give such a statement by saying 'What I mean by synthesis in general is a blind but indispensable faculty of the soul of which we are hardly ever conscious but without which we should have no knowledge.'[5] Russell, on the contrary, regards mathematics as part of logic. For Kant arithmetic was the fundamental activity of which propositional thinking was a special case, Russell reversed this.

§ 4

How does this help to clarify the description of the physical concepts 'cause' and 'substance' as forms of thought? Kant's preliminary answer is that if we concentrate on the process we go through when we count and then analyse the performance we call thinking or theorizing about nature, we can recognize that the nerve of the latter is explicit in the former. In other words, all communication by thinking involves synthesis, that is, construction in accordance with a rule, and the rule is what gives unity to the act of constructing. It is part of this development of his thought that he tends to substitute 'function' for 'form'.

What is offered here is an abstract and superficially mystifying statement of what goes on in geometrical and arithmetical reasoning. The novelty of Kant's position consists in his attempt to generalize this account by linking it with Aristotelian formal

[5] B 103.

logic. It is essential for him to maintain, as he does emphatically in the *Introduction* and *Proleg.*, that the cogency of geometrical and arithmetical reasoning is not explicable by means of the principle of contradiction or as straightforward empirical generalization, though 'How are synthetic *a priori* propositions possible?' was not a very helpful way of stating his difficulty.

To put the matter differently, Kant is reflecting on his own procedure in a kind of thinking which he regards as obviously legitimate and fruitful, namely mathematics. He differs from both Descartes and Leibniz in that he denies the clearness and distinctness of our ideas in this field to be what guarantee the force of this kind of reasoning, and rests his confidence instead on his insight into the synthetic character of mathematical method. He goes on to ask whether all legitimate theorizing has this synthetic character and concludes both that it has and that he can analyse it so as to show this.

The line is:

1. All thinking involves synthesis, i.e. involves construction according to a rule and recognition of the unity of the process of constructing. As will appear, this is the contribution of the *Metaphysical* and *Transcendental Deductions*.
2. That the forms or functions of thought, that is, the unifying principles involved in all our thinking, are responsible for the specific notions, 'cause', 'substance', &c., which are basic to our theorizing about physical reality. This is what is discussed in the *Analytic of Principles*.

Thus all thinking is synthetic, and the special branch of thinking Newtonian physicists do involves a specialized synthesis determined by the special subject-matter with which they are concerned. What this means and what is the relation between ordinary and scientific thinking is considered later on. In fact Kant develops (1) and (2) simultaneously in spite of his official distinction between the *Analytic of Concepts* and the *Analytic of Principles*, and it is impossible to separate them without losing touch with his argument. For the moment, however, I will try to concentrate on (1) as it is treated in the *Metaphysical Deduction*.

METAPHYSICAL DEDUCTION

SUMMARY

Metaphysical Deduction of the Categories (B 91–116)

The procedure of thought (as distinct from that of sensibility) in providing us with true propositions about objects is discursive. Its method is to frame concepts and to unite these in judgements, so that its relation to the real may be described as mediate in contrast to the immediate apprehension of sense or intuition. But the relation between concepts which judgements assert is not always of the same nature, as is shown by the table of judgements (universal, particular, negative, &c.) with which formal logic provides us.[6] When I assert that A is B, I am asserting a different kind of relation between A and B from what I should be asserting if my judgement were 'A is not B' or 'A may be B'. To enunciate a judgement is to perform a synthetic act, comparable with the construction of a triangle; both processes involve the introduction of synthetic unity into a multiplicity or manifold, and we are therefore led to ask what ground there may be for the particular kinds of synthesis which the table of judgements exemplifies. The answer, Kant maintains, though he makes no attempt to prove the point, is that each form of judgement, when carefully considered, is found to assert between the concepts which it synthesizes just the kind of connexion which is expressed by one of the concepts corresponding to his (considerably revised) table of Aristotelian categories.[7]

For instance, the hypothetical form 'If A is B, then it is C' asserts the kind of connexion which is expressed in the conception of the relation of ground and consequent, whereas the categorical 'A is B' asserts the connexion expressed by the concept of the relation of a substance to its attribute.

What Kant means by this becomes clear when we recognize that the bare formulation of an hypothetical proposition implies that I understand the relation of something conditioned to that which is its condition. If I did not, then that particular form of proposition would be entirely meaningless to me. It is in this sense that the category of pure concept is held to make possible the judgement form which corresponds to it.

[6] B 95.

[7] B 106.

This is the central contention of the *Metaphysical Deduction*, and in the light of it Kant's line of thought may be thus restated. The specific activity of the understanding is to formulate judgements, that is, to perform acts of synthesis between concepts in one of the twelve distinct ways which are laid down in the table of judgements. The kind of synthesis which each of these forms effects is given by the category which corresponds to it in the table of categories. Hence the categories are described as functions of unity in the judgement. They are indeed the necessary forms of thought without which judgement, and therefore the human understanding itself, would be an impossibility.

METAPHYSICAL DEDUCTION

COMMENT

§ 1

The *Metaphysical Deduction* is notoriously one of the points in the *Critique* at which Kant's architectonic footwear pinches him badly. One needs, however, to resist the temptation to give the whole thing up as hopeless, for it contains a lot of important thinking.

A good deal of the criticism which has been expended on Kant here springs from his unquestioned belief that all thinking is the articulation of judgements and that all judgements are ultimately predicative.

The first of these beliefs is simply a consequence of his faculty psychology. His major faculties, which exhaust the essence of Mind, are Cognition, Conation, and Feeling. The cognitive faculty consists of Sensibility and Understanding. Hence it is not open to him to ask whether there is anything which can properly be called an intelligent activity which is neither of these and which cannot be satisfactorily analysed into a combination of them. We have already seen that this leads him into trouble over 'imagination'.

But since he is committed to his verbal framework, he has to ask himself whether the formulation of any judgement involves synthesis,[8] that is, whether I can frame any proposition without

[8] Kant is not suggesting that all propositions are what he calls synthetic, i.e. propositions in which 'the idea of the predicate is not contained in that of the

doing the same sort of thing as he holds that I do in geometrical and arithmetical reasoning.

§ 2

It is clear from this formulation of Kant's problem in the *Metaphysical Deduction* that his terms 'forms of thought' and 'categories' are not very well chosen. The second in particular is unfortunate, because it suggests a parallel with the thought of Aristotle which does nothing to clarify the issue. But, since it certainly requires clarification, we may begin by quoting Kant's own statement in the overworked letter to Herz of February 1772.

> While I was searching [he wrote] for the sources of our intellectual knowledge, without which enquiry it is impossible to determine the nature and limits of metaphysics, I divided this study into essentially distinct compartments and tried to reduce transcendental philosophy, i.e. all the ideas of completely pure reason, to a specific number of categories. But my procedure differed from that of Aristotle who took them as they occurred and arranged them arbitrarily as the ten predicaments. I found that they arranged themselves in groups in accordance with a few fundamental principles of the understanding.

The same point occurs again in the *Metaphysical Deduction*. 'I will call these pure concepts "categories", following Aristotle. For initially my purpose was the same as his, though my method of executing it was essentially different.' And in the corresponding passage in *Proleg.*, § 39, Aristotle is mentioned in similar terms.[9] In fact, on each occasion Kant merely takes it for granted that Aristotle's aim was to make an inventory of the most important furniture of the mind, and criticizes what he thinks was Aristotle's method of doing the job on the ground that it was methodical but not systematic.[10]

The important reason why consideration of what Aristotle was trying to do is an unfruitful way of approaching Kant is that

subject but stands in relation to it' (B 10). 'Synthetic' is used by him in three different ways. See Paton's excellent criticism of Kemp Smith, *Commentary*, vol. i, p. x, § 6.

[9] None of Kant's references to Aristotle suggest any detailed study of his works. See B viii, 105, 107, 324, 882. The point of introducing him seems to be only to draw attention to the fact that he anticipated Locke in providing an empirical ancestry for the pure concepts. Cf. A ix.

[10] See *Preface to M.A.N.* and cf. B 92.

Aristotle and Kant had radically different expectations or presuppositions as to the general character of the world of nature. This difference is not explicit, but it needs to be brought to light because it leads to divergent uses of the term 'category'. Roughly speaking, Aristotle viewed the universe as a very noble animal, while Kant viewed it as a highly complicated and admirable machine. Admittedly this difference must not be pressed too hard. Kant was aware, at least when he came to consider the question carefully in the *Critique of Judgement*, that the concepts of biology were not genuinely reducible to those of mechanics. 'We may confidently assert that it is absurd for men even to hope that another Newton will arise to make intelligible to us even the genesis of a blade of grass from natural laws that no design has ordered.'[11] Nevertheless, Kant's settled conviction into which his use of 'category' must fit, is that we never thoroughly understand anything except machines, and we understand them just in so far as we are competent to put them together, to construct them in accordance with a rule of synthesis.

Now this idea, which is more prominent in *Proleg.* and *B* than it is in *A*, is not immediately or obviously connected with problems concerned with general words, subsumption, classification, and so on. Kant's own key phrase is that his categories are 'functions of unity in judgement', and there is no reason to suppose that he considered this at all dark or mysterious. Perhaps it is not if we think of it in the light of what has already been said about synthesis and forms of thought; certainly it becomes more puzzling than it need be if we try to elucidate 'function' either on Platonic lines (thinking of ἔργον in *Rep.*, bk. i) or on mathematical lines (to say that *a* is a function of *b* is to say that *a* and *b* vary together). Neither of these, indeed, is quite wrong, but both are liable to act as red herrings and to lead further inquiry off in the wrong direction. On the whole a better clue to ordinary seventeenth- and eighteenth-century usage is given by Descartes. 'Postquam consideravimus omnes functiones quae pertinent ad solum corpus.'[12] It is concerned with the way in which something works, and, for Kant, the way in which anything in nature works depends solely on the way in which it is put together. On the face of it, however, this will not do at all. What Kant says[13] is:

[11] *K.U.*, § 14.
[12] *Passiones Animae*, i. 17.
[13] *Proleg.*, § 39.

> To seek out from ordinary knowledge the concepts which are not grounded in any particular experience and none the less occur in all knowledge by experience, of which they constitute as it were the bare form of connexion, presupposes no more reflexion or insight than to seek out from a language rules for the real use of words in general and thus to collect the elements for a grammar (in fact both enquiries are very closely related to one another) without being able to state the ground why any language has this and no other formal nature, and still less that exactly so many, not more or less, of such formal determinations of language can ever be encountered.

And this is followed by his criticism of Aristotle.

Yet Kant remains confident that his categories are ways of doing something. It is correct to call them ways of unifying (*a*) ideas in judgements, and also (at a later stage) (*b*) ideas (*Vorstellungen*) in an intuition. 'The same function which gives unity to the various ideas in a judgement also gives unity to the bare connexion (*bloße Synthesis*) of various ideas in an intuition.'[14]

But how is 'ways of doing something' being used in this discussion? The relevant *O.E.D.* use[15] is 'Manner in which something is done or takes place; method of performing an action or operation.' Compare 32*d*. 'As an instance or a mode of; in the capacity or with the function of . . .'; 'by way of epitaph', 'by way of a joke' are given as instances. I think this is the kind of idea Kant wanted to express by his 'functions of unity', but, if so, it is less obvious than he thought it was.

I can say 'There are several ways of playing this hand, but there is only one which will make the contract against any possible defence.' Bridge, chess, and other puzzles are fabricated on this basis, and there is at least something on these lines in Kant's mind which is the ground of his objection to the methods of Locke and Aristotle in tabulating them. If we assume, as Kant did, that the world either is or is just like a fabrication, a vast machine constructed by the Great Architect, then it clearly makes sense to say, 'There are many ways in which it can be described, but there is only one way which is entirely self-consistent. All the others will break down if you test them hard enough.' This might bring him to his Table of Judgements, but would it extend to his categories? He could say, and I think he meant, 'The forms of judgement exhaust all the ways in which we can combine ideas

[14] B 104.

[15] *Way* 14.

to give significant propositions.' If this were true, as Kant thought it was, he could argue that no other way of connecting ideas is usable by us, therefore no other kinds of connexion between things are describable by us. But then has he not proved too much? What job would be left for the categories to do? They would surely be made redundant by the Table of Judgements.

This is awkward. It is clear, however, that Kant wants to represent his categories as somehow standing behind, presupposed by, or, in his language, making possible the forms of judgement which correspond to them. How may this be elucidated? Possibly this suggestion may help. There are various efficient ways of hitting a golf ball. We can classify them as wood shots, iron shots, and also as lofted shots, recovery shots, and so on. None the less it is fair enough to say to a beginner, 'Don't worry about these yet. Just remember that in order to make any of them you have to keep your head still and watch the ball. These, and one or two other precautions, are the preconditions or presuppositions of your playing any golf shot properly.' Similarly, one may say, 'The basic idea of this game is . . .', or, 'There are various trick ways of riding a bicycle, but what really matters is that you should know how to keep your balance', or, 'There are lots of ways of playing bridge (called "systems") but you will never be able to use any of them properly until you know without thinking what cards are out.' We talk, too, of ideas or concepts in this way when we say, 'He has read plenty of books and had competent coaches but he has never really got the idea of the game at all.' Similar language is used of more serious pursuits such as governing and philosophizing. As we have already noted, Kant's most general word for the constructing activity we call 'thinking' is 'synthesis', and the outcome of it is what he calls 'a synthetic whole' or just 'a synthesis', e.g. the synthesis of imagination, recognition in concepts, and so on. I do not think he would have rejected my suggestion that my idea of a special kind of operation, e.g. cycling, is the idea of a synthetic activity. Certainly it is consistent with his own description of 'synthesis in general' in B 103 and B 179–81 (*Schematism*).

It would no doubt be pompous and pedantic to describe knowing how to play bridge or ride a bicycle as 'apprehending by the faculty of productive imagination the unity of the act of balancing, or counting playing cards'. But nevertheless I think that the kind of performance Kant had in mind when he formulated his Table of Categories to underpin his Table of Judgements was of this type. The point is that, quite suddenly, I get the idea or get the hang of it. In the case of judgements, he thinks I just see that to formulate an hypothetical presupposes the idea of a special kind of connexion in the real world. It is worth noticing, too, (*a*) that to get the idea, in this sense, is not to become all at once a competent performer, (*b*) that there are natural good players who get the idea with practically no difficulty; and, of course, when you have got it, you are 'seldom or never conscious of it'. Bridge players do not deliberately follow suit or count their cards.

If this is correct, the line Kant is taking in the *Preface to M.A.N.* is fairly clear. It is simply that the idea of something in nature following inevitably on something else is realized when and only when you are faced with a bit of intuitable, that is, imaginable, clockwork. It is the job of the *Analytic of Principles*, especially of the *Schematism* and the *Second Analogy*, to convince us of this, and 'clockwork' is hospitably used. It covers, for instance, jigsaw and other puzzles. What matters is simply that the bits have to be fitted together in a special way, and you can see that this is so when you try to put the thing together on a table or a blackboard.

§ 3

Can one do as well as this with the other pairs in the Table of Categories and the Forms of Judgement? On the whole, I think so, though Paton is surely right in saying that the connexions are by no means obvious. I am not even sure they are discoverable by reflection on the *Metaphysical Deduction* alone. This is not surprising. You could hardly get anyone to grasp the idea of a game or indeed of any other operation unless he could be shown or got to imagine instances of people actually carrying it out. It is considerably easier to give a meaning to Kant's notion of categories when we attend to seeing, hearing, and generally, perceiving things, than it is to consider them as determining the way we think and theorize about things, and I am far from clear why Kant is determined to regard these as, so to speak, different sides of the same coin.

There is, however, another difficulty which has to come in at this stage. It is simply that neither the forms of judgement nor the categories (assuming that they can be related to one another as I am assuming that they can be) seem in any way obviously to exhaust the possibilities or to form a system, as distinct from just a methodical collection, in the way in which Kant openly and repeatedly claims that they do. All commentators from Hegel to Ryle have observed this gap. It seems almost incredible that Kant did not believe either that it was not a gap at all or that it was and that he had successfully closed it. In fact the Table of Judgement Forms always seems to me more of an enigma than the Table of Categories. I shall not do more than suggest a few points about it here which deserve attention:

1. The inclusion of singular and infinite judgements seems to me in itself to be unimportant. Kant says that these are of interest to transcendental, not to general logic, i.e. they arise only when we consider categories rather than judgement forms. Apart from this, his list is fairly standard as de Vleeschauwer has shown. But how did Kant know that it was complete and derived from a single principle?[16]

2. Its completeness cannot be validated in the same way as, for example, kinds of triangle or conic sections, because these depend, and he knew they did, on intuition.

3. This links up with Kant's certainty that logic, unlike mathematics and science, did not need to be put on the secure path of a science. It did not have a period of 'mere groping' or pre-scientific natural history. It was all right from the beginning. 'That logic has from the earliest times proceeded upon this sure path is evidenced by the fact that since Aristotle it has not needed to retrace a single step.' It is 'a closed and completed doctrine'.[17] And the point is that the understanding has here 'nothing to deal with except itself and its forms'. So Kant's view seems to be that here alone we have a conceptual, not an intuitable whole whose articulations are clear, distinct, and thoroughly intelligible.

4. I cannot really understand what Kant means here, but it surely must be something like this. Whatever it is that guarantees the completeness of the Table of Categories the clue must be in the footnote to B 133–4, and it is the synthetic unity of apperception which is the idea behind both the unity of nature and the

[16] See Klaus Reich, *Die Vollständigkeit der Kantischen Urteilstafel*, 1932, 2nd ed. 1948.

[17] B viii.

Table of Judgements. I am not clear about what this means either. The point presumably has to be that the Table of Judgements is certainly a complete list of the ways in which we can talk significantly. The schematized categories reveal the special way in which we can talk significantly about physical objects, or nature. This needs much more elucidation to make it intelligible.

At this point I will leave the Table of Judgements and conclude with a reflection on the Table of Categories. All that I want to do here is to remove what seems to me to be a purely verbal discrepancy. In contemporary use[18] to ask about categories is to ask a semantic question about permissible types of statement; you cannot say 'Saturday had a bath this morning'—and so on. Those are questions about logical grammar, or conceptual geography. Now in a way this is what Kant was doing, but he was not mainly concerned with it in the *Transcendental Analytic*. He was concerned with it in the *Dialectic*. In his language to regard Logic as an Organon and not purely as a Canon was to make what Ryle calls a category mistake. It is especially clear in *Preface A* that the trouble with traditional metaphysical questions is that these are, in modern language, unaskable questions, though there is nothing grammatically wrong either with them or with the competing answers offered to them.

In this sense Kant starts with two categories only, the language of physics and the language of morals. In *K.U.* he tentatively adds a third, the language of Teleology. Within each of them he tries to settle what are the askable questions, and he thinks he has proved that within (1), i.e. physics, an exhaustive list of the askable questions is provided by the schematized categories which supply or elucidate the ways in which it makes sense to talk about physical objects. In the course of his exposition he finds that he is committed to a far more searching analysis of the different uses of 'is' in what he calls judgements of experience than any previous thinker had carried out, and in this respect the *Analytic* is concerned with categories in Ryle's sense; but it is essential to notice that this is not the place where Kant is primarily concerned with them.

[18] Cf. Ryle on *Categories*, *P.A.S.* 1938.

TRANSCENDENTAL DEDUCTION

SUMMARY

Transcendental Deduction of the Categories (A 85–130; B 117–69)

§ 1

In this summary I take no account either of the controversy as to the unity and coherence of the *Deduction* in *A* or of the precise nature and importance of the innovations made by Kant in *B*, nor shall I adhere to the order of his exposition. There is, I believe, no substantial difference between the positions maintained in the two editions, though the weight attached to psychological as contrasted with logical considerations is not the same in both of them. It should be remembered that in Kant's own view the second edition was really a supplement to the first,[19] not a cancellation of it, and that his thought is therefore likely to be represented by a conflation of the two rather than by concentration on either to the exclusion of the other.

The importance of the *Deduction* for the Critical Philosophy as a whole requires no emphasis. Kant himself repeatedly lays stress on the difficulty as well as on the originality of it. There are two points of view from which it may be approached. We may consider it as a contribution to the theory of scientific investigation in the broadest sense, in which case its purpose is to prove that the forms of thought as well as those of sense must enter into the constitution of all possible objects for beings with cognitive faculties such as ours are. Viewed in this way it really is the heart of the *Critique*, the subsequent discussions in the *Schematism* and the *Principles* being only a postscript designed to clear up uncertainties in the central doctrine. Or we may, on the other hand, regard it, as Kant himself did, as only a step, though an exceedingly important one, in his answer to the question 'How is pure physics possible?'

It is important to observe this distinction because, if we concentrate as I propose to do here on the first of these two points of view, Kant's argument, though it is difficult, can be quite briefly stated since much of the detail of his proof is superfluous. I hope

[19] B xlii.

to show later that a large part of it is strictly relevant not to the question 'Must we accept the existence of an objective world subject to the categories in order to explain the possibility of thinking in general?' but to the further and different problem 'Exactly what characteristics must we concede *a priori* that the objective world possesses if we are to account for a variety of psychologically verifiable facts?' Admittedly the *Transcendental Deduction* is not directly concerned with the second of these problems, since consideration of it belongs officially to the *Analytic of Principles*. Nevertheless the *Deduction* argument in both editions, but especially in *A*, is greatly complicated in order to prepare the way for what comes later.

§ 2

Kant's line of argument is as follows:

It is an undeniable fact that we do think and that our thinking is expressed in judgements. We have seen in the *Metaphysical Deduction* that the act of judging demands the employment of pure concepts or categories defined as functions of synthetic unity. But thinking has an objective as well as a subjective side to it; every judgement will be found on examination to postulate the existence of an 'object of representations' to which our thought refers. It is ultimately with the meaning of this phrase that the *Transcendental Deduction* is throughout concerned. When I formulate a judgement I am not, Kant maintains, simply registering the relation of my ideas to one another. What I claim to be doing is to say something about the object which those ideas represent. This is equally true whether the judgement is categorical, hypothetical, or an instance of any of the other forms enumerated in the Table of Judgements. But difficulties soon arise when I begin to ask myself more carefully what kind of thing this 'object' can be. We cannot identify it with any quality or relation, or with any complex of qualities or relations, for by definition it is that to which our ideas of particular qualities and relations are all of them referred. Must we then admit that we understand by it just a substratum, a mere unknown *x*? It is at this point that Kant's theory becomes difficult and important. He denies that such an admission will meet the case and thereby abandons any attempt to justify the doctrine either of rationalism or empiricism so far as physical things are concerned. Far from being a 'something I know not what', the object has in his view a very important and intelligible function to perform. Essentially it is that which provides necessary as distinct from accidental connexion among our representations. Experience in the strict sense must be clearly differentiated from day-dreaming, and the point of the distinction lies in the fact that every judgement as such claims to be valid generally for all men, not merely for its framer. Although it is not obviously the case, Kant believes himself able to demonstrate that unless the existence of a system of necessarily connected objects to which our thoughts refer is conceded, we are utterly unable to explain the existence of any coherent or unitary self at all. Indeed in the absence of any such reference we should have no experience, but only a 'mere play of representations, less even than a dream'.[20]

The point which he is making is most easily understood if the question is approached from the side of the self. It will be granted that every idea which can conceivably occur to me must be capable of conscious apprehension. It must admit of being accepted into that whole which I call my consciousness. To be thus admitted is to be apperceived, and the sign of such apperception is the prefixing to the idea of the phrase 'I think'. No idea, then, can be entertained by me which is not capable of being apperceived or of becoming an element in a unity of apperception. But the whole of the ideas which I entertain constitute together a unity which is my conscious self, and this unity is not a mere aggregate, for if it were 'I should have a self as variegated and diverse as the ideas of which I am conscious'. Rather it must be a synthetic or connected unity, intellectual and not sensuous in character. We are thereby enabled to distinguish between apperception and association. The latter might give a chain of ideas, but only the former can combine those ideas so as to give a properly conscious self which is aware of its own identity in apprehending what is manifold in them. The synthetic unity of apperception is not strictly speaking something produced by the understanding, it is simply the understanding itself. For to understand is nothing more than to introduce unity into the manifold of presented ideas, and ideas as synthesized into an intelligible unity are the understanding. To make this clearer we need only consider the operation of the

[20] A 112.

activity of the understanding, namely thinking or judging. We have said that to think is to unify ideas by receiving them into the synthetic unity of apperception. This process proceeds by relating our ideas to objects, since understanding is the faculty of knowledge, and therefore the understanding or, what is the same thing, the synthetic unity of apperception is possible only in so far as the ideas presented to us are capable of being thought as connected with one another in objects. Thus the fact that there is thinking leads to the conclusion that an object of thought in some more complex sense than that of a bare substratum of qualities and relations must exist. It is needed for the purpose of imposing a necessary unity on our ideas and thereby making possible the unity of apperception, which is the understanding. What, then, must we hold the nature of the object to be? As I have said above, the answer to this question is what the whole *Deduction* is supposed to provide, and the clue to it is given by Kant's fundamental conviction that by necessary connexion we must always and only mean connexion which is the product of *a priori* synthesis. The object is, therefore, to be conceived as a ground of synthetic unity. By this he does not mean that an object, such as an orange, is something which we make by putting together ideas of yellow, round, sweet, and so on. It is with the 'affinity' or necessary relatedness of phenomena, not the associability of representations that he is concerned. His view is rather that, in regarding the orange as an object, we conceive the qualities which we judge to belong to it as springing from or dependent on some necessary connexion *in rerum natura*, not merely as accidentally juxtaposed. To maintain that this connexion is synthetic implies that we are capable of understanding its nature, which is possible for us only if it exhibits the characteristics of construction according to a rule.

If we now proceed to ask what this rule can be, the answer is not far to seek. The main justification of Kant's whole account of the nature of the phenomenal object is that it is required in order to make thought possible. The *Metaphysical Deduction* has proved that thought is based on the employment of the categories, and the *Transcendental Deduction* has demonstrated that the existence of objects, conceived as grounds of synthetic unity, is a further requirement. We may therefore combine the two conditions and conclude that the nature of that synthetic unity is provided by the categories. They must now be regarded not merely as functions of unity in judgements but also as the ground of unity in experience if thought and the self which depends on it are to be possible. The unity of nature is an intelligible unity, and the phenomena of nature are things subject to the forms of our thought, without which subjection they could never be recognized by us as constituting a world or nature at all.

TRANSCENDENTAL DEDUCTION

COMMENT

§ 1

Commentators are unanimous in thinking that the *Transcendental Deduction* is very important, and this is not surprising. It is long and so difficult to read that Paton not unreasonably says, 'the crossing of the Great Arabian Desert can scarcely be a more exhausting task than is the attempt to master the windings and twistings of the Transcendental Deduction'. Kant himself seems to have regarded it as his supreme achievement. 'I know no inquiries', he wrote,[21] 'which are more important for exploring the faculty which we entitle understanding, and for determining the rules and limits of its employment than those which I have instituted under the title *Deduction of the Pure Concepts of Understanding*.' The fact that he rewrote this section of the *Critique* completely for *B* is further evidence of the importance he attached to it. The mass of comment and criticism which has been devoted to it is enormous, and de Vleeschauwer's three substantial volumes[22] are witness to this. Yet when we reflect in a cool hour and ask what the *Deduction* is for, what philosophical job it is supposed to do, the answer is very far from clear. The *Metaphysical Deduction* is for the most part an avowedly linguistic inquiry. Kant was asking questions about the logical structure of language, and it is not difficult to recast his discovery of the categories as a discussion of logical constants or formal logic in the post-Aristotelian sense. What happens in the *Transcendental Deduction* is that for the time being he withdraws his attention from the particular categories and concentrates on what he

[21] A xvi.

[22] *La Déduction transcendentale dans l'œuvre de Kant.*

regards as the more fundamental question, namely, what right have we to use the categories at all?

Now this is surely a very odd question to ask. It looks a little less odd if we restate it and ask, 'Since there are basic types of connexions which propositions assert in virtue of their form alone, can it be demonstrated that these connexions hold, not merely between the terms of propositions, but also between the facts to which propositions refer?'

But is this really any better? The short answer is, 'Of course they do! What conceivable point would there be in making up a language whose syntax enabled us to assert connexions which are not encountered in real life?' There is no mystery about applied arithmetic and geometry, and there need be none about applied mechanics either. So what is all the fuss about?

This would not do for Kant because he was trying to prove a much tougher proposition. He is not interested in showing that his categories are high-level abstractions or symbols in a calculus whose practical utility has abundant empirical support. That is just where Hume's critics went wrong.[23] The categories might indeed be called rules of language, but they are supposed to be more than merely rules of language; for, unless Kant makes this claim, he is committed to the positivist or pragmatist account of natural science which it is an important part of the main purpose of the *Critique* to avoid. It is essential to remember when attempting to make sense of the *Deductions* in *A*, *Proleg.*, and *B* that he really wanted to show that the principles of Newtonian mechanics were discoverable by some non-empirical thinking and yet to hold that we know them to apply to matter of fact and real existence.

Nevertheless, to escape from his own criticism of traditional metaphysics, he also wanted his non-empirical demonstration to be somehow anchored to empirically established fact. He was not prepared either to be a whole-hearted rationalist or to introduce a *deus ex machina* called Pre-established Harmony to make good his case.

Now all that he has to start from is the conclusion of the *Metaphysical Deduction* that thinking can be described in a non-misleading way as the assertion of connexions of a highly abstract order between concepts, that is, a synthesizing process in the technical sense he has given to 'synthesis'. Where this description

[23] Ak. iv. 257.

of thinking is not obviously appropriate, as it is not when he wants to think about things in themselves and not about the world of nature, he can without much difficulty maintain that thought directed to an object not subject to the categories is 'empty'. Provided that it is not self-contradictory it is permissible and may be valuable in morals and theology, but it is by definition unscientific, since we can know only that which we can construct synthetically.

The problem, then, is 'Can we know *a priori* that observable reality, the object of science, is organized in accordance with the rules implicit in the categories?' If we can, we are at least on the way to demonstrating the factual validity of Newtonian mechanics; if not we must be content with positivism.

§ 2

The Subjective and Objective Deductions in A

In *A* Kant put forward two proofs of his deduction. They were supposed to be supplementary to one another and were called 'subjective' and 'objective' respectively. He held[24] that the objective deduction by itself (A 92–93) was a cogent demonstration of the soundness of his position, the subjective deduction being something of a luxury. Later on, in *B*, he seems to do without the subjective deduction altogether, though in fact, as I shall show, he still needs it. The two sides of his argument are not as separable as he thought they were.

The proofs are as follows. They are not clearly separable in the text of *A* and have no headings to mark them.

§ 3

The Subjective Deduction

This argument derives its force from a piece of psychological theorizing. Kant does not dispute this. He points out that it is, or at least looks like, a psychological hypothesis, not an *a priori* demonstration in his sense. It might be better described as a description of what goes on in our minds when we realize that something is the case or that a proposition '*p*' is true.

[24] A xvi–xvii.

The nerve of the argument is not hard to trace. It is that, as Hume had observed, our consciousness is always temporal, but to say 'X knows that *p*' is to say that he has done some conceptualizing or classifying. This, however, can happen only if particulars are somehow identified in the 'stream of consciousness'. Hence there can be knowledge only if the perceptions (*Anschauungen*) of which consciousness consists are capable of being referred to permanent objects or things. Perceptions must at least be organized in groups before it can be said that we know that . . .. Furthermore, the system on which these groups are organized must be one that we can understand, and this commits us to asserting that the connexions between perceptual data must be the kind of connexions which our language is capable of formulating. The same understanding, by the same operation, must combine perceptions into things and concepts into judgements. Hence there must be what Kant calls a 'transcendental object'[25] if thought is to refer to anything at all.

This argument as used by Berkeley[26] and developed by modern phenomenalism is certainly not without force, but as an ingredient in the position which Kant wanted to hold it is unsatisfactory in two ways. The line of thought is that if we are to think or talk as distinct from just seeing colours, smelling scents, hearing noises, &c., we must postulate the existence of permanent things to which our perceptual data in some sense 'belong'. This may be granted, but it may still be argued that these things are just hypotheses or constructs. Clearly we do not see or touch them. So Kant is unable by this argument to prove that anything but the convenience or decision of a particular thinker settles what connexions there shall be between perceptual data or how those data shall be grouped together.[27] In his own language this proof does not demonstrate the necessity for an 'object of representations' in the sense in which he set out to show it. *De facto* it may be the case, though Kant has not proved it, that we must postulate one particular set of connexions in order to talk at all; but something tougher than a psychological hypothesis is needed to show that we cannot help synthesizing our data in the

[25] For Kant's use of 'transcendental object' as distinct from 'thing in itself' see p. 293.

[26] Cf. Warnock, *Berkeley*, Chap. 6.

[27] See Ayer, *Philosophical Essays*, pp. 165–6.

categorial way. Strictly speaking, there is nothing in Kant's line of argument up to this point to which Berkeley, Hume, or any consistent phenomenalist need object, since the most Kant could get out of it is that we have to construct some sort of 'transcendental object' in order to make sense of our scientific theories. This, indeed, or something very like it, turns out later to be his epistemological last word on noumena; but if it is the last word on phenomena too, then Kant's position is at best simply a variant on the problematical idealism of Descartes which he took special pains to refute in both *A* and *B*. It seems fair to suppose that he noted this and tried to deal with it by redrafting in *B* and by adding his new refutation of idealism. He seems, however, to have missed the second point, which is this.

The psychological theory in terms of which his difficulty is both stated and solved is extremely dogmatic and non-empirical. It certainly looks as if he were propounding an ingenious but inconclusive answer to a puzzle of the camera obscura type. He always takes it for granted that the statement 'consciousness is successive' is a genuine factual statement and is equivalent to 'I am always and only aware of a number of intrinsically timeless data which occur in an order to which I give the name "temporal".' This suggests the cinema model, developed by Gestalt psychologists as an improved version of the earlier camera obscura myth. If it is accepted, we have a genuine question of Kant's type, namely, what brings it about that the data occur in the order or sequence in which they do occur?

If we are talking of cinema pictures, we answer 'The order or sequence on the film (which is verifiable).' When sense data are concerned we must, he thinks, say 'The object to which thought refers them.' But here there is and can be no empirical evidence. What sense would it make to say there might be? Kant is either telling us about the way in which 'seeing', 'hearing', and, in general, 'perceiving' should be analysed, or he is suggesting a view as to the physiological correlates of perceiving. In the first case, what he says is not evidence for what he wants to prove, and in the second, his doctrine rests on a testable scientific hypothesis and its correctness could be established only by an appeal to the scientific procedure whose legitimacy he is attempting to demonstrate.

Hence his argument is doomed to vicious circularity. It is possible that he might have restated his position in phenomenalist terms to avoid this criticism, but then the hypothetical or 'constructed' character of the transcendental or empirical object would have been painfully manifest. On the other hand he could not afford to accept the temporal character of perceptual awareness as just a brute fact and introduce 'things' to make it at least respectable as an object of thought. To do so would lead to some sort of Bergsonian anti-intellectualist conclusion which Kant certainly did not accept.

Hence the verdict on the *Subjective Deduction* is that, while it contains some interesting and important points about thinking, considered as a psychological occurrence, it cannot by itself support the position Kant is trying to maintain. It is usually this that commentators, Kemp Smith for instance, have in mind when they condemn a large part of *Deduction A* as exhibiting '*Kant's subjectivism*'. The point is a good one,[28] though somewhat misleadingly put. The alternative view, which Kemp Smith calls '*Kant's phenomenalism*', belongs to the *Objective Deduction.*

§ 4

The Objective Deduction

The demonstration here starts from the notion of self-consciousness or the 'original synthetic unity of apperception'. Self-consciousness, Kant argues, is an empirically established fact; but it could not occur unless we knew about things. Therefore we do know about things, and things, categorially determined, do exist.

The final form of this argument is in the *Refutation of Idealism* added in the second edition[29] and slightly amended again in *Preface B*.[30] It is more difficult to meet than that of the subjective deduction, but it still will not really satisfy Kant's demands. It rests on two claims, viz.:

(*a*) I do recognize myself as an entity persisting in time.

(*b*) This recognition is inferential.

The support for (*a*) is straightforward introspection or intuition.

[28] See Kemp Smith, *Commentary*, 'Phenomenalism and Subjectivism', pp. 270–84.

[29] B 274.

[30] B xl.

I do recognize my own identity through time, and that is all there is to be said about it. 'I am conscious of my own existence as determined in time.'[31] This, however, is qualified by Kant's adherence to (*b*), which leads away from the position of Descartes to that of Hume. I never catch myself without a perception, and my perceptions succeed one another with inconceivable rapidity. When from these data I try to infer to or construct a permanent self, I find nothing I can establish except my capacity to think. Hence what needs to be added to Hume's conclusion, and it is a pretty important addition, is synthesis; and so my capacity to think (an empirical fact) must be regarded as the condition of self-consciousness (another empirical fact). This result, however, is less informative than it looks. What it comes to is the formal statement asserting the occurrence of the bare 'I think that . . .' which holds our statements together.[32] The content is provided by what I think about, namely empirical things.

The trouble here is that the evidence for this last and crucial statement is provided by the psychological theory given in the Subjective Deduction, and the fact that this is so is confirmed by the simplified form of deduction offered in *Proleg.*, § 18, with its distinction between judgements of perception and judgements of experience. The subjective deduction has not been dropped. The central assumption on which it is based recurs in the revised formulations of *Proleg.* and *B* in a slightly modified form.

Accepting this limitation, Kant's conclusion in the objective deduction may be stated as: 'No unity of consciousness without unity of apperception, and no unity of apperception without knowledge about empirically real objects.' The most serious difficulty about maintaining this position is that Hume's argument for the non-immediacy of self-knowledge is not one which Kant can accept without a good many qualms. It involves the acceptance of an unproved psychological hypothesis, yet, as we have seen, this cannot be completely discarded without a relapse into the problematical idealism of Descartes. The self, as Hume conceived it, did not do anything. It was simply the theatre within which ideas mysteriously became associated with one another. But this is precisely the view which Kant with his new idea of synthesis as the essence of thinking, is bound to deny. He has to claim intuitive acquaintance with his own activity of synthesizing,

[31] B 275.

[32] A 362. *Third Paralogism.*

or else the whole elaborate story of scientific knowledge as a kind of making or producing and not a passive contemplation of self-evident truths must collapse; and this is why the doctrine of inner sense is so terribly embarrassing when Kant tries seriously to disentangle it in *B*.

Put shortly, the situation is that Hume can regard the self as a construct and sacrifice the claim of science to achieve certainty, but Kant cannot. Yet Kant will not openly claim intuitive insight into the thinking activity of the self, since this would undermine the critical distinction between sense and thought by introducing an intellectual intuition. Implicitly, however, I think he did make this claim,[33] and he was right.

This problem is fundamental to the whole of Kant's critical position. Whether or not it can be solved on lines which Kant would have considered acceptable, his general line in the *Transcendental Deduction* may be formulated thus. We cannot doubt that there is something, call it Nature, about which we do make assertions. We do not therefore have to ask,[34] 'Do material things exist?' but rather, 'What does it mean to talk about "material things"?' or, 'Are there any properties which material things have to have in order that they should be talked about?' Kant's answer is, 'They must have the characteristics formulated in the doctrine of the categories, for, unless they had, we could not talk about them, since we should have no empirical concepts.' To put it differently, 'No categorially determined objects' commits us to 'No empirical concepts'; 'No empirical concepts' commits us to 'No thinking'; 'No thinking' commits us to 'No self-consciousness', since we have no direct acquaintance with our selves. Yet I am aware of my own existence in time.

In this formulation, it should be noticed, Kant takes it for granted that we do know that there are empirical objects without evidence and do not have to conclude that material things exist from our acquaintance with perceptual data. More precisely, what are called 'sensa' or 'looks of things' are incidental and are not substitutes for things. This is sound, but it is not the doctrine of the *Subjective Deduction*.

[33] Cf. Martin, op. cit., § 28.

[34] Cf. Hume, *Treatise* I. IV. ii. ''Tis in vain to ask, *Whether there be body or not?* That is a point which we must take for granted in all our reasonings.'

§ 5

'Jurists, when speaking of rights and claims, distinguish in a legal action the question of right (quid juris) from the question of fact (quid facti); and they demand that both be proved. Proof of the former, which has to state the right or the legal claim, they entitle the *deduction*.'[35] Kant explains this by pointing out that some words in ordinary use, such as 'fortune and fate', are what he calls 'usurpatory concepts', in that 'no clear legal title, sufficient to justify their employment, is obtainable either from experience or from reason'. Now as regards the categories he says 'we are faced by the problem how these concepts can relate to objects which they yet do not obtain from any experience'.[36]

One gets the impression that Kant was rather pleased with this legal metaphor, but it was nevertheless misleading. As a result of it, he came to conflate two distinct but related questions and to reach, as we have seen, an inconclusive result. The questions are (1) What right have we to suppose that there are physical objects to which our language refers? (2) How do we know that physical objects are the kind of synthetic wholes which they have to be if we are to have *a priori* knowledge about them? (1) is a silly question, but Kant sometimes took it seriously, especially when he was influenced by Tetens and when he was accused of being either a Cartesian or a Berkeleian; (2) was the question about which he was really worried. The case for saying that the *Transcendental Deduction* is strictly superfluous is that in fact Kant answered (1), or tried to, in the *Refutation of Idealism* and answered (2) in the *Analytic of Principles*. As far as *Deduction A* is concerned, I am inclined to accept this view. *Deduction B* is a rather different matter since it moves from (1) and (2) to (3), namely, 'How can we elucidate "apperception" and "inner sense", and what is the connexion between them?' This is for Kant a crucial question, though discussion of it is more appropriate to Part III than it is at this point. As regards *Deduction A*, then, one may either say irreverently, 'Kant was in rather a muddle here', or, more respectfully with Paton, 'We shall find a powerful and penetrating intellect struggling and twisting relentlessly towards its goal.' But the *Deduction*, to quote Paton again, is emphatically not the work of 'a pedantic old professor, armed with an external architectonic,

[35] B 116.

[36] B 117.

incompetently tacking together old notes of what he used to think'.[37] A little hard on the industrious Vaihinger, perhaps; but he deserved it.

GENERAL DOCTRINE OF SCHEMATISM

SUMMARY

Transcendental Schematism (B 176–87)

§ 1

The doctrine of the *Schematism* and of the principles derived by means of it requires some preliminary explanation. Its difficulty is the result mainly of excessive condensation and of the virtual omission of the central theme which connects it with the *Aesthetic* and the *Deduction*, namely the notion of phenomena as an objective order of things distinguishable on the one hand from subjective apprehension and on the other from things as they are in themselves. The *Transcendental Deduction* is held to have proved:

(*a*) that if understanding is to be possible, there must be such phenomena, since otherwise no judgement would have objective reference (except on the assumption that judgements refer to things in themselves, in which case they would all inevitably be *a posteriori*, and scientific knowledge as Kant understood it would be out of the question)

(*b*) that these phenomena must be subject to the categories, which are the foundation of our judgements and in terms of which therefore we must think if we are to think at all.

These phenomena are the reality about which, in so far as we think scientifically, we formulate synthetic propositions *a priori*, and the general purpose of this section of the *Critique* is to explain how we are able to do this. It is essential to show exactly what is meant by saying that phenomena are 'subject to the categories', and also what synthetic propositions *a priori* are made possible by their being so; and to this end we need more precise information about the character and status in reality of phenomena than is given by the proposition that they are objects whose function it is to provide the synthetic unity demanded by

[37] *Commentary*, vol. i, p. 56.

empirical apperception. It is this further information which the *Schematism* is supposed to provide. Substantially Kant's doctrine is that phenomena are hypostatizations or embodiments of the categories. The latter are pure forms of thought, and as such are incapable of being intuitively and immediately apprehended (since our only faculty of immediate apprehension is sensuous, not intellectual). On this account the material for such embodiment must be sensuous in character, but cannot be the actual data of sense, since these are wholly empirical. Hence it must be provided by time, which, as we have seen in the *Aesthetic*, is (*a*) sensuous, (*b*) pure, (*c*) the form of all our awareness both internal and external. The actualization of the categories by providing them with a temporal interpretation provides us with a system of rules in accordance with which we must construe the manifold of sense if we are to be able to apperceive it in a unitary consciousness. In other words we are to be shown the nature of the objective but none the less *a priori* cognizable order of things which we must recognize in order to amplify and harmonize subjective appearances if we are to recognize those appearances, as we are bound to do, as forming elements in a unitary system. Phenomena are nothing more than the pure concepts schematized by the transcendental faculty of imagination, and the world of science is a world of schemata, generated in a sense by our own activity but none the less objective in contrast to the 'subjective play of representations' which makes up our unreflective consciousness. In the principles (*Axioms of Intuition*, &c.) which follow the *Schematism*, Kant proceeds to demonstrate (not without some rather arbitrary assumptions) that the categories as actualized by the imagination do supply principles which are required for the scientific interpretation of nature and are also essential to the existence of a unitary self-consciousness.

§ 2

We have to ask how it comes about that the pure concepts are embodied in and therefore valid of our actual sensuous experience. At first sight this would seem to present no difficulty since, as discursive concepts, they must presumably be expressed in particular instances and be recognizable in those instances just as empirical concepts are. This, however, is not the case, nor could it possibly be so, since they are bare forms of thought which cannot as they stand be said to have sensuous instances at all. This becomes evident when we consider that, even in the case of general notions derived by abstraction from experience, instances must be ideal rather than actual particulars. Their use is to serve as rules enabling us to construct in imagination such ideal particulars or schemata, and it is to these latter that we relate actual perceived particulars and so indirectly bring the latter under concepts. The mediating character of these schemata depends on their participation in both intellectual and sensuous characteristics so that, without being tied down to a single perceived instance, they are none the less sensuous or imaginable.

Now time is the pure form of all our representations, and is also sensuous, not intellectual in character. Hence if we combine each of the categories with this pure form, we shall obtain a set of schemata which will enable us to recognize the manner in which the pure forms of thought are actually exemplified in our experience. For instance, the category of substance is merely the idea of something which is always a subject and never a predicate. But when we temporalize this conception we obtain the sensuous schema of that which is permanent in time or which underlies successive modifications and alterations of accidents, i.e. substance in the ordinary sense. Similarly the category of cause and effect when considered in itself is no more than the bare notion of ground and consequent or implication, whereas its temporal scheme is that of necessary temporal sequence, and so on with the other categories.

GENERAL DOCTRINE OF SCHEMATISM

COMMENT

§ 1[1]

It is important to distinguish schematism in general from *Transcendental Schematism.* The former belongs to ordinary conceptual analysis, and, although it was given a new and important addition by the importation of Kant's doctrine of synthesis, it had a history going back at least to Locke's account of general or abstract ideas. It was not considered to be mysterious or even particularly difficult to grasp. *Transcendental Schematism,* on the other hand, is highly technical. Kant's aim and argument were recognized by his contemporaries as obscure and only doubtfully intelligible. I shall here concentrate on schematism in general and leave *Transcendental Schematism* almost entirely for later consideration in Part III.

There are three main reasons why the general doctrine of schematism often seems much more esoteric and forbidding than it is.

1. Kant formulates his problem as one concerned with the subsumption of particulars under universals, and this in England and especially in Oxford is waving a large red flag in front of an angry bull. Automatically it starts the reader thinking about Plato; and when Kant says that concepts must be homogeneous with the particulars which are to be subsumed under them, he is asking for trouble. The 'third man' argument of the *Republic* and *Parmenides* is good enough to finish that off.

This is a false clue, but it has led many people besides H. W. B. Joseph[38] to spend time and trouble on refuting a view which Kant was not advocating.

2. 'Schema' (as distinct from 'Transcendental Schema') tends to be regarded as a rather difficult and technical word; but in seventeenth- and eighteenth-century use it was hardly technical at all. Newton, for instance, writes: 'In the publication of this work, the most acute and universally learned Mr. Edmund Halley assisted me with his pains in correcting the press and taking care of the schemes.'[39] 'Scheme' and 'schema' are alternative words for 'diagram'. This use is confirmed in Phillips's *New World of Words*, 1706, where 'scheme' is explained as follows:

> Model, draught, the drawing of any figure on paper etc., the representing of any geometrical or astronomical figure or problem by lines, so as to make it sensible to the eye, and this is otherwise called a *Diagram*. Among astrologers it is a representation of the celestial bodies in their proper places for any moment, or an astrological figure of the Heavens, which is often called '*schema coeli*', and the making of it, erecting or drawing a scheme.

3. We are so confident that Berkeley, whatever else he may have done, completely demolished Locke's theory of abstract or general ideas that we hardly notice what Locke said about them. It was this:

[38] Joseph, *Ancient and Modern Philosophy*, chap. x.
[39] Preface to *Principia*.

When we nicely reflect upon them, we shall find that *general ideas* are fictions and contrivances of the mind, that carry difficulty with them, and do not so easily offer themselves as we are apt to imagine. For example, does it not require some pains and skill to form the general idea of a triangle (which is yet none of the most abstract, comprehensive and difficult), for it must be neither oblique nor rectangle, neither equilateral, equicrural nor scalenon; but all and none of these at once. In effect it is something imperfect that cannot exist: an idea wherein some parts of several different and inconsistent ideas are put together.[40]

Of course Locke put it terribly badly, and it is not surprising that Berkeley found here a nice, knock-down argument against material substance. 'If any man has the faculty of framing in his mind such an idea of a triangle as is here described, it is vain to pretend to dispute him out of it. All I desire is that the reader would fully and certainly inform himself whether he has such an idea or not.'[41]

One may doubt, however, whether Locke was quite such a simpleton as his successor made out. At least he might have said, 'You can draw a pig on the blackboard, and it may be a perfectly recognizable drawing. A spectator who puts the questions "How old is it? What colour is it? How much does it weigh?" simply shows that he does not know what a diagrammatic representation is. What about the schemes in Sir Isaac Newton's *Principia*?'

Berkeley could have replied, quoting Locke against himself, 'It is true the mind, in this imperfect state, has need of such ideas, and makes all the haste to them it can. But yet one has reason to believe such ideas are marks of our imperfection.'[42] He could then have developed his view[43] that general words are symbols which refer to reality directly, without the intervention of either schemes or pictures. The point here is that in this controversy Kant would have been firmly on the side of Locke, and that Locke's position, though it may be mistaken, is much too breezily disposed of by Berkeley and his successors.

Bearing these points in mind, one can see without much difficulty the kind of doctrine which is over-briefly stated in Kant's exposition of general schematism. Roughly, it is Locke's view,

[40] Locke, *Essay*, IV. vii. 9.

[41] Berkeley, *Principles*, Introd., § 13.

[42] Locke, loc. cit.

[43] Warnock, *Berkeley*, chap. 11.

strengthened by the notion of synthesis to meet the obvious Berkeleian criticism.

Kant says,

> The schema is in itself always a product of imagination. Since, however, the synthesis of imagination aims at no special intuition, but only at unity in the determination of sensibility, the schema has to be distinguished from the image (*Bild*). If five points be set alongside one another, thus, ... I have an image of the number five. But if, on the other hand, I think only a number in general, whether it be five or a hundred, this thought is rather the idea of a method whereby a multiplicity, for instance, a thousand, may be represented in an image in conformity with a certain concept than the image itself. For with such a number as a thousand the image can hardly be surveyed and compared with the concept. This idea of a universal procedure of imagination in providing an image for a concept, I entitle the schema of this concept.[44]

The first point to notice about this passage is that *Bild* had and still has a wider use than 'image' or 'picture' have. Thus, when Karl Marx, for instance, talks of our ideas as *Bilder* he is not necessarily committed to a crude copying theory of perception. *Bild* certainly includes 'diagram'; 'picture' and 'image' both exclude it. Thus Wittgenstein writes, 'Wir machen uns Bilder der Tatsachen', and, 'Das Bild ist ein Modell der Wirklichkeit.'[45]

Kant's position, however, is not very clear. He fails to distinguish between two contentions:

1. 'Schema' means my knowing that $x^2+y^2=r^2$ gives the rule of procedure for constructing circles on paper or blackboards.
2. 'Schema' means my more general knowing how to construct formulae in accordance with which particular figures can be constructed.

The distinction is not very important to him here, but failure to draw it obscures his point. What he means to emphasize is that it is the ability to draw diagrams, &c., rather than the products of this activity that we need to emphasize in our analysis of general terms, and this it true and important. Collingwood, I think, had the same idea.

> A plan [he writes] is a kind of thing which can exist only in a person's mind. As a rule, an engineer making a plan in his mind is at

[44] B 179.

[45] *Tractatus*, 2. 1 and 2. 12.

the same time making notes or sketches on paper; but the plan does not consist of what we call 'the plans', that is, the pieces of paper with these notes and sketches on them. Even if he has put complete specifications and working drawings on paper, the paper with these specifications and drawings on it is not the plan; it serves only to tell people (including himself, for memory is fallible) what the plan is.[46]

Or, as Kant put it, 'the schema of the triangle can exist nowhere but in thought. It is a rule of synthesis of the imagination in respect to pure figures in space.'[47] One cannot, however, appraise a boy's ability to do sums except by marking the sums he does, so 'schema' in practice tends to suggest the products of ability rather than the ability itself, though the latter is what we are really talking about.

§ 2

It is possible to get a somewhat clearer idea of what Kant had in mind in his discussion of schematism if one looks at the situation from a different point of view. To do this is not to expound Kant since the line taken here was quite unfamiliar to him. It is rather to formulate the point which he appears to have been dealing with in an entirely different way in the hope that by doing so we may clarify somewhat his admittedly obscure and unsatisfactory explanation and treatment of it.

Let us, then, consider the section on *Schematism* as being in the first instance Kant's attempt to analyse or say what is meant by 'thinking'. To do this without being most misleading involves the admission that 'thinking' is here taken in a restricted sense, though the restriction is a fairly common and reasonable one to make. On one side we must exclude day-dreaming, parrot-repetition, imagining, and so on, since Kant at any rate regarded these as the subject-matter of anthropology and not of epistemology. On the other side pure deduction or analytical thinking would also be excluded, i.e. the manipulation of symbols within a postulational system carried out by formal logicians. This second point is inevitably imprecise for the simple reason that Kant was not sure of his own ground. At first sight one would certainly say that he did in this sort of sense admit the occurrence

[46] *Principles of Art*, p. 132.

[47] B 180.

of non-schematic thinking, It may reasonably be argued that the development of postulational systems, of which formal logic was the typical example, seemed to him both legitimate and valuable; at any rate it was capable of being valuable since the systems might turn out to be cashable or schematizable later on. Trouble arises only if we mistakenly suppose either that all soundly constructed postulational systems are as such cashable or that there is among them one privileged one which we can prove to be cashable without consideration of the *de facto* conditions of experience.

It is hard to deny that in the *Critique* Kant was at any rate implicitly guilty of the second of these errors, though he withdrew considerably from this extreme position in *K.P.V.* and came near to abandoning it in *K.U.* This, however, is really incidental to the present point. It is mentioned only to draw attention to the fact that in the *Schematism* he is concerned with 'thinking' as a performance. It is not the development or interpretability of postulational systems which is being examined here, but rather the meaning of phrases such as 'thinking out', 'trying to solve', 'planning', and so on. The simplest instances which come to mind are provided by bridge or chess problems, train journeys, and battles.[48]

All these involve the exercise of intelligence, and the procedure adopted to deal with them is identical. I have an idea, though not a precise or detailed idea, of the result I want to achieve; but although it is not precise, it is not a mere truism like 'I want to capture his King', 'I want to get to Calcutta', 'I want him to surrender unconditionally'. It is more specific than this and in some cases is pictorial or quasi-pictorial 'I want to win from this position against this opponent, I want to get there before 6 p.m. on 5 April', and so on.

What we normally do here is to guess a suitable opening move and follow it up with a number of 'if . . . , then' statements which lead to the desired conclusion. Aristotle, indeed, suggests reversing this procedure, which is sometimes sound but which postulates a more definite and precise idea of the conclusion than we usually have except in simple puzzles. Hence to make this typical

[48] These are not all of the same logical type. For some purposes it is important to distinguish between difficulties, problems, and puzzles. But the distinction is not relevant here.

is to over-emphasize the extent to which technical skill is involved and correspondingly to understate the element of creation which is present in quite ordinary planning. Like so much Greek thinking it overstresses deductive theorizing as against scientific method, and it was with scientific method that Kant was trying to concern himself.

Now the inadequacy of the simple instances I have taken, if they are treated too seriously, is that in matters like train journeys the environmental set-up is highly conventionalized by the normal conditions of civilized life. In games the conditions are almost completely formalized. Battles are rather more interesting, but in order to plan them we need to do a great deal of formalizing by way of abstraction. We ignore the possibility that the opposing commander may be stung by a scorpion at a crucial moment. It is this kind of abstracting and formalizing which good planners do well and others do not. The word 'well' here needs a little definition. It means merely in such a way that inferences drawn from the data provided in the schematic diagram or model give reliable predictions as to what will be met with on the railway station or the battlefield. The test here, while it is pragmatic, is not pragmatic in the simple sense. A good prediction and a consequent win may be the result of luck rather than of good planning. It is not a valid objection to a Field-Marshal's planning to say that he demanded more resources than he actually needed to do the job. It would be a valid criticism to say that he demanded more than he would have needed even if the opposition had put up the best possible defence.

To return to Kant; if we adopt this type of test, it is correct to say that the Newtonian system of mechanics was a highly efficient formalization of the normal behaviour of physical bodies. By deeming it to be the over-all plan of the physical universe and elaborating subordinate plans which worked within it for special operations, one was able effectively to predict eclipses, build bridges, make guns, and so on.

This is a more modest claim than Newtonian enthusiasts usually made. 'God said, "Let Newton be", and all was light', was a typical expression of their over-confidence.

Kant was more sensible and more critical. He had an idea of what was going on and asked himself 'Just how is this piece of formalization done?' or 'What are the ingredients out of which the Newtonian system is constructed?' His answer is 'The ingredients are space, time, and things; things again analyse into substance, cause, and the other schematized categories, while space and time themselves have the determinate structure which this type of thinking demands only when they are conceived as conditions or forms of things.'

What Kant has to maintain is that this formalization underlies and makes possible all serious thinking, though of course we are not aware that it does so until we go through the transcendental analysis of the *Critique*. Put shortly, if we reflect on what process we go through when we think, we find that the general space–time–categories diagram or schema is the basic assumption on which any thinking which is to have predictive value has to be based. It is the governing plan in terms of which we have to interpret and make sense of all the subordinate plans, and it is so pervasive that we do not normally become aware of its presence as a condition at all.

Whether this kind of view can be worked out in detail seems to me highly dubious. Even now it is doubtful whether we know enough of our physical and psychological constitution to be confident about it, and even Kant was manifestly over-enthusiastic. In any case it does not seem genuinely to meet his own objections to any positivist theory. The crucial question which inevitably arises is 'Do I find these (or any other) patterns in nature, or do I just make them up, retain them if and for so long as they are useful, and discard or modify them when they fail to do the job for which I invented them?' Kant is manifestly saying the former, though with an important addition. His answer is 'You do find them; but you find them because your constitution (or central nervous system) brings it about that they really are there. If they were not, your special kind of perceiving could not take place.'

This has a most unsatisfactory ring about it. How 'could not', and what kind of 'because'? On the other hand one needs to ask whether the embarrassment which gives rise to this uneasiness is itself justified. Am I perhaps worrying because, on this type of view, I seem never to discover what is really there in nature, what things are really like? If so, my difficulty is not a genuine one though the conviction that it is genuine is deep rooted and hard to get rid of permanently. It amounts to asking 'What would things look like if they didn't look?', 'How would they appear if they didn't appear at all?'[49] This is simply a survival of the camera obscura view mixed up with theology, and I do not think that Kant was gravely handicapped by it. He knew he could get nowhere by trying to anchor his theory of knowledge to an inaccessible *Ding an sich*. Yet he wanted to anchor it to something specific, so he tried the device of regarding space, time, and the categories as fixed and immutable. This would not do, because the schemata derived in this way are not the only ones possible. The result of pretending that they are is to achieve the kind of scientific dogmatism which pays dividends for a time (as for most of the nineteenth century) but is certain to be self-defeating in the end unless the world is a lot simpler to understand than we have any ground for supposing that it is.

GENERAL DOCTRINE OF THE PRINCIPLES

SUMMARY

Principles of Pure Understanding (B 187–294)
Introduction (B 187–97)

The schemata are too abstract and general to help us to answer the fundamental question, how a science of nature is possible. For this we need certain specific *a priori* principles which relate to particular representations. We need to be assured that we can recognize instances of the transcendental schemata by means of the faculty of judgement just as we can recognize instances of empirical schemata. This we cannot do directly. We have first to ask ourselves what principles or laws of nature are implied by the various schemata; and to show that these laws of nature are really valid we must confirm them by demonstrating that, unless they are, no unitary experience of nature will be possible for us. For, as we have already seen, the laws of nature which are vital for science are all synthetic, not analytic in character, and whereas laws of the latter type can be demonstrated by means of the principle of contradiction, the former can be accepted only when we

[49] Cf. A. D. Lindsay, *Kant*, p. 54, and the parallel difficulty or pseudo-problem concerning objectivity in morals and aesthetics.

can show that, unless they are, the existence of a synthetic unity of apperception is an impossibility.

GENERAL DOCTRINE OF THE PRINCIPLES

COMMENT

§ 1

In the *Principles* Kant claims to expound the principles of synthetic unity which any study which can qualify as scientific must recognize as determining its subject-matter. In *M.A.N.* these are amplified by the introduction of the special conditions (bodies in motion) which are required by the special study of Newtonian mechanics. Kant, in fact, works out his main theme along the line of diminishing abstractness or increasing concreteness, beginning with the synthetic unity of apperception and passing through categories, schemata, and principles to actual laws of nature such as gravitation.

When the development is stated in this way, any modern reader will protest that this kind of thing will not do at all. It is manifestly illegitimate to derive any empirical conclusion without at least one genuine empirical premiss. Self-consciousness, as expounded in the *Transcendental Deduction*, is not a possible source for such a premiss, nor are the definitions put forward in *M.A.N.*

This objection is formally unanswerable if we attend strictly to Kant's exposition in the *Critique*. To some extent, however, the fault here lies with Kant's method of formulation. What he had to say was not so completely at odds with modern philosophies of science as it appears at first sight to be. I have already considered this point in discussing Kant's prospectus in *Preface B*, and some repetition here can hardly be avoided without constant references to what was said earlier. On the whole, I think the repetition is the lesser evil.

A good deal, though by no means all, the difficulty which unquestionably obscures what Kant has to say in the *Principles* about the foundations of science is the result of his determination to have nothing hypothetical or merely probable included in his proofs in the *Critique*.[50] To gain at least the appearance of having

[50] See *Preface A*.

satisfied this requirement he inverts the entire course of his argument in the *Transcendental Analytic*. The main result is to make his line of thought exceedingly baffling and much less plausible than it would be if a more natural line of development were taken.

So far I have followed fairly closely the order of statement in the *Critique*, but at this point I think it is helpful to consider whether a radically different order would not be an improvement. In Kant's language the question involved is whether a synthetic or an analytic order of exposition is to be preferred in a philosophical treatise. We do not use that sort of language nowadays, but in the days and places where formal treatises were well thought of, the point at issue was a commonplace. It must be noted that the use of 'synthetic' and 'analytic' in this context has no connexion either with Kant's use of 'synthesis' to stand for the constructive basis of thinking or with the distinction between synthetic and analytic propositions. The distinction between synthetic and analytic method is a standard one in textbooks on Euclidean geometry. Kant refers to it on several occasions.[51]

The analytic method takes what is to be proved for granted and draws inferences from this until some other proposition which is already known or postulated is reached (or contradicted). The synthetic method takes its start from axioms or accepted facts and argues from these to the required conclusion. On the face of it, therefore, a synthetic demonstration is logically preferable to an analytic one, and Kant's claim is that his proof throughout the *Analytic* and indeed throughout the *Critique* is entirely synthetic.

Formally this claim is valid. He does begin with logical axioms in the *Metaphysical Deduction* and with what he claims as indubitable facts of consciousness in the *Subjective Deduction*; and he does proceed from these through the *Schematism* and the *Principles* to *M.A.N.* But his proofs are never rigid (they could not be since he is not engaged in formal logic or geometry, i.e. in manipulating a postulational system) and sometimes they just break down.

A good instance is the main argument of the *Second Analogy*, which is circular. Kant's claim is that our recognition of the occurrence of a public time order proves that there is objective, necessary connexion between phenomena, i.e. causality in nature;

[51] See *Proleg. Preface, ad fin*; the *locus classicus* for it is in Pappus Alexandrinus (*Mathematicae Collectiones*, Lib. III *ad init.*).

but we have to recognize causality in nature as a condition of recognizing the possibility of a public time sequence.

Hence it is at least worth considering what his view would have looked like if he had started at the other end and proceeded, in his language, analytically. In more useful terminology, what would have happened if he had admitted (what he really did admit) that he was accepting the factual validity of Newtonian mechanics as his basic datum and was inquiring into the epistemological consequences of doing so. His question 'How is pure physics possible as a science?' could be reworded to read 'What are the presuppositions of Newtonian mechanics?' The defect of this procedure from the point of view of a logical demonstration is shown by the occurrence of the word 'presupposition'. 'Presupposition' is not equivalent to 'entailment'. Normally it means a credible or plausible genetic or historical account of the way in which something comes to happen. In Leibnizian terminology it is an argument from sufficient reason and not from logical necessity, and the principle of sufficient reason if it is to do its job is not, and Kant knew that it was not, derivable from the principle of contradiction. In more modern language to give a reason is not the same as to give a logically cogent demonstration. The root of the matter is that there may be and usually is more than one possible explanation of a given set of facts though there may well be only one which, as we say, makes sense in a particular context; and Kant, unlike Leibniz, had specifically cut himself off from making use of Pre-established Harmony to extract himself from this difficulty.

Suppose, however, that Kant had ignored this technical defect and had been content to talk the language of 'presuppositions', how might his answer to 'How is pure physics possible?' have been set out? Clearly it would begin with something like *M.A.N.* and work back to the categories; it would indeed be a kind of progressive analysis of (logically) higher-order presuppositions culminating in the categories or (perhaps) in the synthetic unity of apperception. The gist of the matter would then be (what it really is in the *Critique*) the exhibition of the technical terminology of Newtonian mechanics as a development out of the syntactical conventions of ordinary speech. I think that Kant's alarming battery of abstract words would be much more readily explainable if the argument were avowedly along these lines.

It might have run approximately as follows: In *M.A.N.* we assume that Newtonian mechanics is not merely a postulational system but that it is a system of true, general propositions about matter of fact—i.e. we assume that pure physics is possible as a science. We proceed to inquire what are the presuppositions or hypotheses which it makes no sense for the physicist, in this restricted use of 'physicist', to question. We know that his procedure is to frame definitions or hypotheses, to test these experimentally, and so discover general truths or empirical laws which hold of matter of fact. What we want to find out is what the higher-order principles or hypotheses are which he accepts as the basis of his experimental technique and which, as such, are not themselves empirically verifiable. Suppose that, in the case of Newtonian mechanics, these principles were found to be Newton's Laws of Motion, then these laws would be the starting-point of that particular science. Theoretically Kant should have asked a similar question about other sciences, but, as he points out in the *Preface to M.A.N.*, there were none. A study on his view is strictly scientific only in so far as it is mathematical, i.e. can 'construct its objects in pure intuition'. Even chemistry was very far from being able to do this.

In the *Principles* we should consider the presuppositions of scientific thought as such. These are more general and more abstract than the special presuppositions of a particular branch of study, such as 'motion' = 'translation in space', since we should now want to include psychology and sociology as at least theoretically possible sciences. But some sort of causal law and some sort of conservation principle (substance) are indispensable. Possibly, as Kant was claiming, these can ultimately be boiled down into 'objective temporal sequence'. It is part of the job of the *Principles* to discuss this.

In the *Schematism* the process would be carried farther since the meaning of 'thinking' in general and not merely of specifically 'scientific thinking' is in question; and this would lead on to the notion of the categories as basic forms of thought and perhaps to the synthetic unity of apperception. At least it can be said that if we understand it in this sense Kant's 'How . . . possible?' is recognizable as a significant question.

One might develop this point by saying that Kant was often in the same area of inquiry as modern philosophers of science who try to make clear the connexion between theories and inductive generalizations, or who try to elucidate the position of deduction in scientific research. One may be a thoroughgoing positivist without attempting to question the fact that both in scientific inquiry and in ordinary thinking we do make use of axioms and definitions, and that we could make no progress without them. Furthermore every scientist employs, usually unconsciously, hypotheses based on axioms which are not verifiable at any rate within the branch of study which makes use of them. Frequently these axioms are obvious and trivial, e.g. some sort of uniformity principle, but they are none the less indispensable.[52]

Yet these highly abstract assumptions are not incorrigible. Take the case of Euclidean geometry. It would have made no sense for physicists to set about trying to establish experimentally the truth of Euclid's axioms.[53] Euclid constructed a postulational system whose internal consistency can be tested by formal logicians. But physicists did set themselves to verify empirical laws within physics, and eventually they decided that for some purposes the Euclidean system was inconvenient. So they modified it and made it convenient. In other words the working out of a number of empirical laws led to a redrafting of the *a priori* axioms and definitions within the framework of which the empirical laws had themselves been worked out.

At a more abstract level the extremely tight causal axiom which physicists down to the end of the nineteenth century took to be the statement of an indubitable truth has been found inconvenient for some purposes in quantum physics and has been partly replaced by a statistical theory. Einstein always found this unacceptable.[54] But nobody has ever thought that it might make sense to try to verify or disverify the causal axiom experimentally.

Kant's main defect from our point of view is that in spite of what he says in *Preface B*, he never considered hypothesis and explanation seriously and therefore has nothing to contribute to

[52] Popper, *Logik der Forschung*, not translated, but summarized in *The Open Society*, chap. xxv. Also Popper, *British Journal for the Philosophy of Science*, Aug. 1952, 'The Nature of Philosophical Problems', and Popper, *Logic without Assumptions*, *P.A.S.* 1947. See also 'Philosophy of Science', *British Philosophy in the Mid-Century*, pp. 155–91.

[53] Cf. M. Schlick, *Grundzüge der Naturphilosophie*, especially §§ 6 and 10.

[54] See Born, *Natural Philosophy of Cause and Chance*, and *Physics in my Generation*, pp. 80–91.

the elucidation of them. This was due partly to the fact that the function of experimental technique was not understood in the eighteenth century; the old Baconian and Cartesian idea of it as a method of deciding between theories which were both logically possible was still accepted without serious question. It was due even more to the fact that neither the axioms of Euclid nor the tight causality of Laplace was actually inconvenient at that level of inquiry. It was the serious study of electrical phenomena that eventually gave rise to all the trouble.

Hence Kant was extremely anxious to have his *a priori* scientific hypotheses guaranteed by other and more abstract principles. It is only when he reaches the end of the road in the unity of self-consciousness or the synthetic unity of apperception that he feels the need to attach himself again to observable data of some sort, and we are presented as facts with highly questionable statements such as 'All my experience is successive.' Thus he never admits even as a possibility that his schemata and categories are at least in principle corrigible. But they are. Both the logical and the scientific frameworks which he took to be beyond question have been revised, not because they failed to accommodate some refractory observed fact but because they were inadequate for saying what people wanted to say. They were found inappropriate for expressing empirical generalizations which had been developed by means of them. We might manage with a logic in which relational statements were barred, but it would be extremely inconvenient and misleading to do so. Perhaps this is the core of sense in dialectical talk about abstract opposites, moulds bursting, and so on. But the language of Hegel is not well adapted for stating it or indeed for stating anything in a non-misleading way.

To return to Kant's distinction between synthetic and analytic method and his uncompromising preference for the former, his considered view was that his attempt to deal with Hume's scepticism would fail unless he could demonstrate that his categories were in no sense assumptions or hypotheses but were known to be ingredients in nature. Their reality and function therefore had to be proved without introducing as premisses their contribution to scientific thinking. That is why he attached so much weight to his 'Clue to the discovery of the pure concepts'. He wanted to derive them from pure formal logic and not to base them on scientific methodology. If this could be done, since formal logic was universally accepted as an indubitable datum, he would be able to claim that his doctrine was synthetically proved and not just analytically credible. He would have his unity of apperception as a unique kind of factual premiss, an *ἀνυπόθετος ἀρχή*.

This is not a feasible project. Nothing, or anything, can be said to follow from 'the fact of self-consciousness', as becomes evident as soon as Hegel claims to deduce particular categories from it; there is nothing but arbitrary verbal manipulation to be achieved on this line. I think Kant deluded himself because the categories of physics were never far from his mind and he never had to ask whether his was the only system of categories and schemata which would be logically tenable.

But in spite of all this and admitting that Kant tried to give philosophical analysis more to carry than it could hope to bear, I think the regressive argument from *M.A.N.* to schemata as set out above has considerable force, and the further move back to the categories has something to be said for it. The rules of syntax are not arbitrary in the sense in which the colours of postage stamps are arbitrary, though on the other hand they are not as fixed and definite as Kant wanted them to be.

Kant's point about self-consciousness still remains obscure. Possibly the root of his trouble was something like this. The rationalist half of him demanded a kind of Cartesian certainty and precision in knowledge at almost any price, and he was clear that he could never achieve this unless he was able to prove his conclusions *a priori* from data so clearly and distinctly perceived as to admit of no doubt by any sane man.

Self-consciousness (or the *Cogito*) struck him as it had struck Descartes as being a unique datum for this purpose. But it was not open to Kant to accept awareness of his own existence as an immediate (=not inferred or constructed) datum, since he recognized that this type of view would commit him to Descartes's problematical idealism. So his doctrine is transformed into the view that his own continued existence, which is a fact, could not be a fact unless certain specifiable conditions were satisfied, and he believes he can demonstrate that these conditions are the truth of the axioms of Newton as far as the observable world or nature is concerned. This really is the official *nervus probandi* of the *Critique*.

But the scientific half of him wanted to establish the validity of scientific reasoning against Hume's criticism at almost any price. He was not very clear as to what this entailed, but in his language scepticism as to the principle of induction was as reprehensible as idealism; Hume was as troublesome as Berkeley. Hence he has to establish and elaborate his doctrine of categories or pure concepts of the understanding.

Verbally his doctrines can be got to reinforce one another, but I do not think they ever genuinely get together. The final question is the one which comes to light in the *Refutation of Idealism* (added in *B*). Can it be proved that the validity of the pure concepts, especially 'space', 'time', 'substance', and 'causality' is a necessary condition of the existence of self-consciousness as a fact, not just a 'presupposition' of it? I do not see how this could be proved. All that can be done is to restrict and pervert the meaning of 'self-conscious' in such a way as to make the conclusion a truth of language.

As far as the actual list of categories is concerned the strength and the weakness of it are fairly obvious. The point to remember throughout is that Kant had both the synthetic and the analytic approach constantly before him while he was working it out. Hence it is inevitably something of a compromise. His anxiety for a proof (synthetic) led him to look for a tidy list closely and clearly linked with the forms of judgement blessed by formal logic; but his anxiety with regard to physics moved him to produce a practically useful list closely and clearly linked with the Newtonian axioms. It is therefore not fair to say he cooked the list to get the right answers. The position was rather that he knew the answers in advance and was searching for a synthetic proof by which he could demonstrate that they were correct.

On the other hand it has to be admitted that Kant's actual argument, especially in the section on *Schematism*, the *Second Analogy*, and *Transcendental Deduction in B* is terribly complicated by his special psycho-physiological account of Inner Sense with time as its form. This has really nothing to do with his general doctrine as regards scientific method. The position is that he was driven to regard schematism as basically temporal in order to make the empirical self a possible object of study at all. But this is done only at the cost of making psychology as a science impossible, since he cannot get his machine and therefore cannot get his necessity.[55] Furthermore, as he keeps on discovering, even as a physical concept time in abstraction from space is not an intelligible idea.

In spite of all this he never abandoned his belief that the distinction between time and space was fundamental and insuperable. This was the unhappy legacy of the camera obscura view which he never closely thought out and never explicitly rejected. It is the unrecognized influence of this disastrous doctrine that invalidates much of Kant's argument for the validity of his categories. But of course they might be valid in spite of Kant's failure to prove that they are.

The upshot is that Kant, like his contemporaries and many of his successors, suffered badly from his conviction that the method of gaining knowledge of the world initiated by the researchers of the sixteenth century (Galileo is the typical example) ought in the end to yield the same kind of certainty as was given by pure mathematics. This conviction has taken many forms. The effects of it can be clearly seen in the work of Descartes, Leibniz, and Spinoza. It is still there in a modified form in Russell's reiterated demand that philosophy should do something to demonstrate the validity of inductive reasoning. What it did for Kant was to inspire him with an exaggerated belief in physics as the only genuinely scientific study and with an associated belief that all other sciences were in the end physics rather badly done. Kant cannot justly be blamed for this opinion. He merely saw clearly and stated with considerable force the implications of the general seventeenth–nineteenth-century belief that machines are the only things human beings can legitimately claim to understand. The scientists and clergymen of the nineteenth century who adopted this view with enthusiasm or regret did not derive it from Kant. It was rather the legacy to Western Europe of Descartes, Galileo, Harvey, and Newton. It is indeed the total *Ghost in the Machine* view of which the camera obscura doctrine of perception and the faculty theory of psychology are merely important by-products. But what Kant did achieve, though his supporters and opponents alike paid little attention to it, was the certainty that many puzzles which worried his contemporaries and continued to worry his successors were pseudo-puzzles. The conflicts between mechanism and vitalism, free will and determinism, the laws of nature

[55] See *Preface to M.A.N.*

and miraculous intervention were all of them trivial. He never clearly stated this consequence of his thought, because it was repugnant to his Cartesian–Leibnizian upbringing, indeed he officially rejects it in the case of free will. But he is never very far away from formulating it.

In his defence throughout it must be remembered that, in view of the primitive experimental, mathematical, and logical techniques which were available to him he could not have done any better than he did. It is to his credit that he made a happier guess at what the right answers would be than many of his better-equipped successors have done. At least he realized, in the end quite clearly, that the concepts of physics were poorly adapted to the description of biological and sociological phenomena; and he tried to take time seriously.

Starting with something like his doctrine of schematism, we can now do considerably better than this by accepting something much less tidy and much less incorrigible than the simple mechanical schema which for reasons already given was all that Kant allowed himself. The best approach is probably to regard the sciences as a series (or hierarchy, if that is not too alarming a word) in which the schemata or patterns or models get more complicated as one proceeds. This entails agreeing with Kant that physics is basic; it is presupposed by and does not presuppose the other studies. But we need not claim either that it gives us the whole truth about the world or, what comes to the same thing, that the schemata of the other sciences are all reducible to those of physics. The world does not have to be as simple as that for occurrences in it to be explicable by a human understanding.

It seems to me, however, that Kant is pretty certainly justified in his claim that the higher level does depend on or presuppose the lower, though it does not have to be simply a complication of the lower in order to do this. I do not see any harm in a doctrine of logical types. Hence, except at the level of unsupported guesswork it seems to make no sense to talk of psychology except as a development of physiology. This is the reason why sociology, in spite of its manifest importance, is such a confirmed laggard in scientific development.

On the other hand Kant is certainly wrong in his addiction to all-or-nothing disjunctions in all departments. Either full self-consciousness or something less even than a dream; either tight causality or chaos; either universal law or general anarchy, are all instances. There are many more. It is quite a good rhetorical device at general elections, but a philosopher ought to manage rather finer shades of meaning than that. However, it may well be that developed or high-grade self-consciousness requires a more or less developed scientific outlook, though there are obviously states to which the term 'self-conscious' would normally be applied in ordinary or semi-technical language to which this test is not applicable. And these are not unimportant.

In the end Kant's method has much to recommend it. What he did was to study the best instances of scientific thought available, even though Stahl was a phlogiston theorist, and to offer a philosophical analysis which would make sense of it. He did his best to analyse and describe his own thinking. What else ought he to have done?

EXPOSITION OF THE SEVERAL PRINCIPLES

SUMMARY

The Principles (B 198–294)

The *Principles* correspond to the divisions of the Table of Categories as follows:

Quantity. *Axioms of Intuition.*
Quality. *Anticipations of Perception.*
Relation. *Analogies of Experience.*
Modality. *Postulates of Empirical Thought.*

They are divided into two classes, the mathematical and the dynamical, of which the former are held to possess intuitive, the latter only discursive but none the less apodeictic validity. This classification depends on the distinction between subjective representations and phenomena. The mathematical principles are valid of all appearances without reference to this distinction, the dynamical on the contrary have reference only to the latter, and cannot therefore be proved so easily. The contrast is explained[56] by a comparison of the relation between the two triangles formed by the diagonals of a square with that of the events in a causal sequence. The connexion between the triangles is merely accidental and arbitrary, while that between the events is intrinsic and

[56] B 201 n.

concerns their phenomenal existence as distinct from a chance juxtaposition for consciousness.

It is further to be observed that the first of the mathematical principles actually makes possible those axioms of mathematics which have already been considered and shown to be valid in the *Aesthetic.*

Axioms of Intuition

The principle of the understanding which makes possible the *Axioms of Intuition* is that all intuitions, empirical as well as formal, are extensive magnitudes, duration in time as well as extension in space being treated under this head. The proof is simply that space and time have been proved independently in the *Aesthetic* to be the forms of all intuition and therefore of all the immediate data of sense, and that to be either spatial or temporal implies quantitative determination. It is all one to say that *x* is an object of perception, actual or possible, and to say that it is subject to the schematized category of totality (quantity) and as such admits of numeration.

This principle has three consequences:

1. It shows that the synthetic activity of the understanding is the ultimate basis of the intuitional axioms of geometry, since the act of construction to which we attend in order to become aware of the *a priori* character of the latter actually presupposes it in that it involves the conception of adding part to part to generate a whole,[57] such as a straight line.
2. It makes evident the principle on which the number series itself is constructed, whereas the *Aesthetic* was concerned only with particular applications of that series, and the character of their intuitive certainty.
3. It renders the validity of applied mathematics more apparent by demonstrating that space and time themselves as pure intuitions are to be regarded as synthetic wholes, and consequently that events in them must conform to their conditions, and be infinitely divisible, &c.

Anticipations of Perception

In all appearances the real which is the object of perception has intensive magnitude, or degree. For if we concentrate on the

[57] Cf. A 103.

matter which is the sensuous content as distinct from the spatio-temporal form of our experience, we find that it necessarily possesses some degree of reality which, since it is not quantitative, must be qualitative or intensive in character. Now to regard a quality, e.g. heat, as having a degree of intensity, I must proceed synthetically by progressing from 0° to the degree in question, 0° being the negation of qualitative intensity which is found in the pure intuition which, as barely formal, has nò qualitative content. Thus every object of possible as well as actual intuition can be known *a priori* to possess intensity as well as extensity, that is, to have some specific and therefore numerically determinable qualitative reality. This, however, is the same as to maintain that all objects of intuition are subject to the schematized category of quality, since the synthetic activity referred to above is a process which must be conceived as temporal, though we need not maintain that the real which we are considering is itself temporally generated. Thus I need not suppose that the x which I recognize as having a temperature of $n°$ has itself passed through the continuous series of changes from 0° to $n°$ in order to reach that state, though I must myself envisage such a progression in order to conceive it as having the determinate intensity of $n°$.

The importance of this principle lies in the support which it gives to the theory of the nature of matter which Kant was anxious to maintain as a scientific hypothesis. If it can be sustained, it robs the materialist doctrine that matter is homogeneous, and that particles of it can operate on one another only by impact, of its initial plausibility. For physical reality, *qua* object of science, must be held to be an object of possible intuition or its laws could not be known *a priori*. Hence it must be subject to the categories, and therefore qualitatively as well as quantitatively determinate. Consequently its qualitative determination might perfectly well lie in its capacity to exert force, and its substantiality might ultimately be identified with this capacity.[58]

Analogies of Experience

The *Axioms* and *Anticipations* are really a digression from the central argument of the *Analytic* as developed in the *Deduction* and the section on the *Schematism* of the pure concepts. In the *Analogies of Experience* this argument is resumed and carried

[58] This is the view maintained in Kant's *Monadologia Physica*.

to its conclusion by consideration of the principles derived from the schematized categories of relation, namely substance and attribute, cause and effect, and reciprocal connexion. So far it has been maintained (1) that empirical self-consciousness is possible only as a consequence of *a priori* cognition of a world of phenomena governed by the categories, (2) that those categories must be given a temporal embodiment as schemata if they are to fulfil their function of making possible the apperception of a sensuously perceived manifold. The purpose of the analogies is to prove that awareness of the self as temporally conditioned, that is as enjoying a temporally ordered experience, requires the existence of a phenomenal world subject to the temporal rules provided by the schematized categories. More fully, Kant is here arguing that I do as a matter of fact recognize myself as having a temporal existence in a world which obeys a time order of its own, and therefore that my cognition of that order must either be derived from my awareness of the sequence of perceptions in my consciousness, or must be antecedent to such awareness and required as a condition of its possibility. But to be aware of an objective order is to be aware of an objective necessity, and this implies the formulation of a synthetic proposition *a priori*. In accordance with the main doctrine of the *Critique* this can take place only in so far as the connexion of which I become aware has been introduced into the manifold in which I discover it by a synthetic activity of mind. We have then to discover what kinds of temporal determination must exist in nature, that is, be imposed on nature by me in the act of coming to know it, in order to account for the kinds of temporal experience which introspection shows that I actually do have.

It will be generally admitted as a matter of empirical fact that I do experience objects as enduring, succeeding one another, and coexisting in time, and the purpose of the analogies is consequently to demonstrate on the one hand that these empirical distinctions are essential elements in the existence of a unitary self-consciousness and on the other that I could not possibly make them unless I implicitly recognized the existence of a world of phenomena subject to the laws given by the schematized categories.

The general principle of the *Analogies* is that the thought which makes experience possible is that of a necessary connexion of perceptions. In so far as experience is to be regarded as cognition of objects as distinct from awareness of states of myself, I must conceive my perceptions, which as such are states of myself, as standing in some real order or interrelation which is distinct from and independent of their juxtaposition in my consciousness. I must, in fact, conceive them as somehow related to objects. All events in my consciousness occur in time, since that has been shown to be the form of inner sense, and the world to which my perceptions are to be referred must also be temporal, since the unity of apperception demands that all actual and possible experience should be accommodated in a single time order. We must therefore discover what kind of temporal order must be held to exist in nature conceived as objective but none the less sensuous if we are to explain the coherent unity of our subjective consciousness. That the nature in which such order is to be conceived must be phenomenal in character is evident when we reflect that this is the essential condition of our being able to know it *a priori*; and as the schematized categories provide us with rules for such an order, we have only to show that those rules are the ones required to enable us to refer our perceptions to objects and so render experience possible.

First Analogy

In all change of appearances substance endures and the quantity of it in nature is neither increased nor diminished, for all change occurs in time and can be perceived only in relation to a permanent which itself does not change. This permanent, however, is not time itself, since time itself is not an object of perception for us. Hence substance is the perceptible permanent which we must have in order to obtain the experience of change and consequently of duration also, and since it is by definition unchangeable, its quantity cannot be subject to increase or diminution. Thus the empirical awareness of duration and change in time without which the unity of self-consciousness would be impossible is found to depend on the *a priori* cognition of an immutable permanent in nature.

Kant proceeds illegitimately to identify this permanent with matter, but the real point of the *First Analogy* is to demonstrate that if we are to discover objective coherence in our perceptions we must regard them as related necessarily to a permanent real.

This permanent is to be called substance, but the nature of it cannot be more precisely indicated *a priori*. The question 'What is substance?' must be answered experimentally by the physicist, and all that transcendental philosophy has to say in the matter is that it must be something. The *Analogies*, in fact, are, on Kant's explicit statement,[59] to be regarded as regulative, not constitutive in character, and in this connexion it is worth remarking that the details of his exposition and in particular the suggested physical applications of his principles are considerably influenced in the *Analogies* as in the *Anticipations of Perception* by his theory as to the actual nature of the physical world.

Second Analogy

Kant's argument here is so dependent for its force on his psychological doctrine of inner sense that no adequate summary is possible. I shall merely indicate the general sense of his discussion and defer serious consideration of it. His chief contention is as follows. We do actually distinguish between the temporal order of our perceptions, which is accidental and depends largely on our choice, and the temporal order of reality, which is necessary and depends on the nature of things. An instance of the former is our perception of any large object which we cannot take in all at once, and of the latter that of any moving body.

In making this empirical distinction between perceptions whose order is reversible at will and those whose order is independent of our volition we attribute to the latter succession according to an objective law or rule; and reflection shows that we are bound to do this if we are to give our sensations that objective reference which they must have if we are to regard them as constituting experience. Hence, if we concentrate on that part of our experience which consists of non-reversible perceptions, leaving the others to be dealt with in the *Third Analogy*, we find that it is a condition of experience that there should be in nature objective succession according to a rule; and this is another way of saying that changes in nature must take place in accordance with the principle of cause and effect.

The implication of this is that the unity of our self-consciousness, as defined in the *Deduction*, presupposes the existence of an objective causal order, so that empiricists are entirely deluded in

[59] B 221–2.

attempting to derive the latter from the former. The true situation is that I could not apprehend my perceptions as being mine, that is as together forming a coherent unity, which even empiricists in order to have a view at all must admit that they do, unless I knew of the existence of an objective temporal order to which those perceptions can be related. Their coherence is not intrinsic to them as such, but is derived from our *a priori* cognition of the phenomena which are their objects.

It is important to notice what this demonstration does not claim to prove. In the case of cause as in that of substance it is completely impossible to formulate any doctrine *a priori* as to the manner in which anything can operate as a natural cause or even as to the kind of thing which is capable of so operating. We can no more say *a priori* what is a cause than we can what is a substance, though Kant himself was convinced on other grounds that the essence of substance was force and that therefore nothing but a substance could actually be a cause.[60] But what we can maintain is that there is some temporal antecedent in nature which stands to any observable change whether physical or psychical in the relation of cause to effect, and this contention is untouched by the objection that in many cases cause and effect are empirically found to be simultaneous, since the order, not the lapse of time, is that with which we are concerned.

Third Analogy

All substances in so far as they can be perceived as coexistent in space are in complete reciprocal connexion, for I do perceive things as coexistent and must do so to render apperception possible. But objective coexistence can no more be inferred from the reversibility of perceptions than objective sequence can be from their irreversibility, but must be apprehended antecedently. Now to apprehend coexistence as objective, that is, as subject to a rule, I must conceive it as involving a necessary connexion between the objects which coexist, though with the same reservations which previously held of substance and causality. I cannot, in fact, determine *a priori* how any two objects are reciprocally related, but I can be certain that such relation exists in so far as the two exist at the same time.

[60] B 250.

Postulates of Empirical Thought

The contents of this chapter are of no great importance, since all that is of value in it, including the *Refutation of Idealism*, is stated elsewhere in the *Critique*. The section as a whole owes its origin to Kant's decision to include the modal notions of necessity, actuality, and possibility among the pure concepts of the understanding, which committed him to an attempt to give them the same subsequent treatment as the other categories. In the nature of the case, however, it is out of the question for him to demonstrate that the existence of the unity of self-consciousness is impossible unless they are embodied in the phenomenal world, and he makes no attempt to do this.[61] On the contrary he simply shows that for the Critical Philosophy, as contrasted with the Wolff–Leibniz position, nothing but the actual world of phenomena can strictly speaking be called possible and that all events in that world in so far as they are actual are also necessary. As regards the meaning, if any, which should be attributed to these terms outside the sphere of phenomena, that is, in relation to things in themselves, the *Analytic*, which is concerned only with the possibility of natural science, has no concern, and all consideration of this aspect of them is therefore relegated to the *Dialectic*. The whole discussion could better have been included in the section in the *Amphiboly of Concepts of Reflection* in which the contrast between the Critical Philosophy and the Leibnizian position is explicitly developed.

The *Refutation of Idealism*[61] is a condensed restatement of the main contention of the Deduction that consciousness of self depends on knowledge of objects, so that the latter cannot be doubted consistently with the retention of the former. It was included in *B* as a result of allegations of idealism made by critics of *A* and adds nothing to the fundamental doctrine.

THE DISTINCTION BETWEEN PHENOMENA AND NOUMENA

SUMMARY

(B 295–315)

§ 1

This section, and that on the *Amphiboly* which follows it,

[61] B 275–9.

between them develop fully the contrast between the Kantian and rationalist philosophical positions. Indeed, taken together they invite the criticism that Kant is here so much engaged in distinguishing his view from that of the rationalists that he fails to pay any attention to the empiricist doctrines which the *Critique* is equally concerned to supersede, and makes no mention of these except in his casual comparison between Locke and Leibniz.[62] As against this it may be urged that the form and language of the *Critique* might conceivably lead the reader to suppose that it was not really so very different from the current modifications of Leibniz, whereas its demonstration of the validity of the pure concepts clearly marked it off from all empiricist speculation. But whether this is so or not, Kant himself clearly felt that it was incumbent on him to lay down once and for all the precise point at issue between himself and the Leibnizians. He does this by expounding in the section on phenomena and noumena what he takes to be the revolutionary consequence of his own view, and exposing in the *Amphiboly* which follows what he holds to be the cardinal error of Leibniz. Neither section requires any detailed analysis since the thought in both is quite straightforward, though expressed at unnecessary length and with a great deal of repetition.

As far as phenomena and noumena are concerned, little is added to what is contained in the *Preface to B*. They are not, we are reminded, to be considered as separate entities but as a single reality viewed from different standpoints. The phenomenon is simply the noumenon as it necessarily appears to me under the conditions of sensibility, and the relation of the latter to the former may be compared with the analogous relation between the phenomenon itself and the impressions of a particular percipient under special conditions of light, perspective, &c. In the latter case, we are able by the use of the understanding to correct and amplify our private presentations so as to reach the conception of an object common to all of us. A penny which is, as we say, really round, brown, &c., appears otherwise owing to the special conditions under which we observe it. The crucial question for Kant is whether the general as well as the particular conditions of sense can be discounted so as to give us the conception of the penny as it is in itself altogether divorced from sensibility, and therefore an

[62] B 327.

object for the pure intelligence (*noumenon*). This he holds to be entirely beyond our power, since to know an object *a priori* by means of pure intelligence we should have to form judgements about it and therefore employ concepts. But it has been demonstrated that the pure concepts of the understanding possess validity only in so far as they are schematized, that is, are given a temporal embodiment, so that for us nothing can be cognizable unless it is given, or capable of being given, in sense perception. Consequently the intelligible or noumenal penny is simply beyond the reach of our knowledge altogether. To a being of a different order from ourselves whose intelligence was intuitive and not discursive in character, this limitation would not apply, but since we can know only by means of concepts combined in judgements, and since these have been shown to have validity only for objects of possible experience, the implied restriction of field is for us absolute and can never be transcended.

In these circumstances it may be asked whether the very notion of a noumenon or object in abstraction from conditions of sense is not worthless and indeed pernicious. This question can be answered only when a distinction has been drawn between two possible meanings which can be given to the term. It may in the first place be regarded as having some positive content, and this is in fact the sense in which rationalist ontology has always employed it. Such a usage is actually illegitimate and disastrous to philosophy, but the manner in which it comes about and the consequences of it are the special subject-matter of the *Dialectic*, where they are fully treated. Contrasted with this is what Kant calls the negative or regulative employment of the concept. In this sense the noumenon is valuable as indicating the limit of what with our special constitution we are in a position to know. For we can, and as rationalist philosophy shows only too clearly, we constantly do make use of unschematized categories as if thereby we could obtain knowledge of non-sensuous objects, and there is no logical objection to our behaving in this way. Thus we can conceive without contradiction the bare category of substance as that which is always subject and never predicate. As we have seen in the *First Analogy*, this category in fact only leads us to knowledge when it is schematized. Apart from such schematization it has no object and is a bare *ens rationis*. We can if we like assume that it has an object, such as the human soul considered in abstraction from spatio-temporal conditions and therefore as noumenal. If we choose to do this, our conception of all noumena as beyond the limits of our knowledge will guard us against the errors of rationalism by constantly reminding us that we must now be concerned not with knowledge but with something different, namely belief. This is a perfectly legitimate procedure which also will be further discussed in the *Dialectic*. All that is here attempted is to determine finally the difference between the two activities, since the error of the Leibnizian method lies simply in its failure to draw such a distinction. We must discriminate with the utmost care between our capacity to know phenomena, which the *Analytic* has successfully proved, and our inevitable incapacity to know noumena, remembering that this incapacity is mitigated by our competence to frame ideas which may be valid of them and in whose validity we may therefore believe if on other than purely speculative grounds we find reason to do so. Thus our ideas of things in themselves, since no objects corresponding to them can be given to sense, are problematic in character.

The criticism of the Leibnizian standpoint in the section on the *Amphiboly of Concepts of Reflection*[63] follows immediately from the exposition of Kant's Critical theory and can be dismissed very briefly, since as soon as the distinction between sense and understanding is drawn in accordance with the Critical Philosophy, the leading notions of Leibniz become evidently untenable. There is, however, no reason to follow Kant in supposing that Leibniz was unaware of this fact, though it will hardly be denied that he paid insufficient attention to the difficulties to which his own position gave rise, especially in the matter of spatial relations.

The important point which emerges from the discussion as a whole is that, on the Kantian hypothesis, the monad of Leibniz simply is the concept of a noumenon. Hence Kant's objection to it is not that it is in any way illogical or contradictory, but rather that it should properly be regarded as problematical only. In this capacity it should be rigidly kept in the metaphysical sphere, and our conception of it should have no place in the realm of physical science except as a purely regulative notion—as is explained later in the *Critique*. It is Leibniz's alleged failure to distinguish between metaphysical (or noumenal) and physical (or

[63] B 316–49.

phenomenal) reality with which Kant is at variance. With the Leibnizian idea of the former he is in almost perfect agreement.

NOTE ON NOUMENA AND THINGS IN THEMSELVES

The distinction drawn in this section between noumena and things in themselves (*Dinge an sich*) is not of any very great importance, and Kant's own use of the terms is careless. The reason for this carelessness is not difficult to discover. In the nature of the case passages in the *Critique* in which references to the distinction tend to occur are those in which the rationalist rather than the empiricist element in his thought is dominant, and for rationalism the distinction is actually non-existent. For if we grant (*a*) the existence of things independent of minds, (*b*) the capacity of minds to grasp immediately the essential nature of those things, i.e. to know them as they are in themselves, we are clearly bound to identify noumena, as objects of knowledge, with *Dinge an sich*. The *mundus intelligibilis* can therefore be described indifferently as the universe of *objects* of knowledge or as the universe of objects of *knowledge*.

But for Kant in his more critical moments this is not adequate. For, although he is prepared to maintain that we can think about noumena, that is, frame concepts of things in general or in themselves by means of the pure categories, he is equally bound to maintain that concepts so framed admit neither of deduction nor schematism. Hence it is quite impossible to assure ourselves of the actual existence of objects capable of being subsumed under them, and they must remain wholly problematical in character. Strictly speaking, therefore, the noumenon is the concept of a thing in itself, and the thing in itself is the alleged object of which the noumenon is a concept.

At this point it is easy to see that the term 'thing in itself' as distinct from noumenon is at least very near to becoming empty and meaningless. It can denote merely a 'something, I know not what', an existent with no discoverable predicates. It is from this point of view that Kant sometimes and most unfortunately slips into describing it as a transcendental object$=x$.

In these circumstances it is not surprising that many of his contemporaries and successors have urged that in the course of his own philosophical development he has really outgrown the notion altogether. It has become a mere vestigial relic which could be dispensed with to the great advantage of criticism. The noumenon would then remain as a purely intellectual concept to which nothing in experience corresponds or needs to correspond. It would be a kind of limiting notion required to give completeness to empirical investigation, an idea of reason relating solely to the activities of the understanding and having no object in *rerum natura* at all. It cannot be denied that many passages in the *Critique* lend colour to the view that this is what Kant actually did think, and many commentators have supposed on the strength of this that the final Critical position is not transcendental idealism but some form of phenomenalism.[64]

I believe Kant would have agreed that such an account did justice to his view as far as positive or constitutive thought is concerned. He might perhaps even have accepted it if pure reason had been his only interest, though he would certainly have protested against any dogmatic phenomenalism, that is, against any view which claimed to prove that belief in the existence of unknowable things in themselves was either foolish or unreasonable. But pure reason was not his only interest, and it is clear that, even if he had gone farther than he did in admitting the hypothetical character of things in themselves, it was impossible for him without utterly destroying his own theological and moral position to allow the existence of God and of the self as metaphysical realities even to be called into question. Certainly the evidence for such existence was provided by practical, not pure reason, but it was essential to maintain that the latter at least could not show the beliefs demanded by the former to be logically untenable. Now the arguments against the existence of God and the self are from Kant's point of view at least as strong as those against the existence of non-empirical objects, and it is therefore not surprising that his belief in the latter was rather more lively than strict logic required.

As we have seen already, Kant took for granted as his starting point the existence of a plurality both of selves and of objects. His inquiry in the *Critique* was into the nature and extent of the knowledge which the former could have both of the latter and of themselves. His conclusion was that knowledge was possible

[64] Cf. especially the views developed in Kemp Smith's *Commentary* and in Cohen, *Kant's Theorie der Erfahrung*.

priori, not of objects or of selves as such, but only of them as appearances in space and time. The question then becomes, 'Should he, on reaching this conclusion, have admitted that his initial assumption was incorrect?' This, after all, is what Berkeley had previously done as regards physical objects, though his notion of God as the ultimate ground of sense-data made his final position more Kantian than is sometimes recognized; and Hume had enlarged his scepticism to include the self. The difficulty to which this procedure gives rise, especially in the case of Hume, is that of seeing how, without the initial assumption, it would be possible to state a view at all. And therefore it is at least plausible to maintain that both Berkeley and Hume succeeded in destroying their own positions by arguing as they did.

As far as the case for the self is concerned this must be granted. Indeed the argument here may well be stronger than Kant's psychological view permitted him to maintain that it was. The non-empirical object, however, provides a much greater difficulty, which is actually increased by Kant's use of his own terminology. Unquestionably he maintained, as Adickes[65] and others have pointed out, that things in themselves and phenomena cannot properly be regarded as separate entities such that the existence of the one needs to be inferred from that of the other. In this sense there are no *Zwischendinge*. There is one universe only and not two or twenty. But, on the other hand, he was anxious to insist on the important difference between things as they are in themselves and things as they appear to us, because this was the essential point on which he diverged from the Leibnizian school of thought. Hence he does sometimes talk as if there really were two distinct worlds. But surely if he had anticipated the difficulties of Jacobi[66] and other later critics he might have stated his own case more or less as follows. It is not disputed that there is a distinction between subject and object. What we have to ask is, 'How much can legitimately be asserted by the former about the latter?' Hume's answer to this question is, 'Nothing except *de facto* conjunctions between sensa.' This, however, can be refuted by the argument of the *Deduction* which proves that such conjunctions never could be asserted at all without previous knowledge of a world ordered in space and time. But to assert the

[65] Adickes, *Kant und das Ding an sich.*
[66] Vaihinger, *Commentar*, ii. 36–38.

existence of such a world as ultimate can do no more than leave us in the position of Berkeley, without Berkeley's God, since the *Antinomies* preclude us from accepting the spatio-temporal as a final account of reality. Hence we are driven a stage farther and constrained to regard the object as non-spatio-temporal. But if it is that, then, by the whole argument of the *Aesthetic* and *Analytic*, no synthetic propositions can be formulated about it either *a priori* or *a posteriori*, and we can therefore have no knowledge of its properties or relations.

Can we, then, know that it exists? This must surely be an idle question, since the existence of something is a necessary assumption without which discussion cannot begin. If Hume were right and sensa with their relations were all that we could know, then these would be things in themselves in Kant's sense.

It is difficult, however, to see that Kant would have had any satisfactory answer to make to Berkeley had he understood the latter's position properly and not merely from inadequate summaries. For he could not deny that, in the light of his own conclusions, reality might be entirely spiritual in character, though he could have refuted Berkeley's case for saying that it must be so.

V

TRANSCENDENTAL DIALECTIC (B350–732)

SUMMARY OF THE GENERAL ARGUMENT

THE purpose of the *Dialectic* is to answer the remaining questions which Kant has laid down as falling within the scope of the *Critique*, namely (1) how is metaphysics possible as a natural disposition, that is, how do the transcendent ideas of God, freedom, and immortality come to be present to our minds at all? and (2) how is metaphysics possible as a science? that is, granted that we do possess such ideas, are we in a position to obtain knowledge *a priori* of the realities for which they stand? The investigation of these problems is pursued as far as possible along the lines laid down in the *Aesthetic* and the *Analytic*. The *Aesthetic* dealt with the transcendental implications of sensibility, the *Analytic* with those of the understanding regarded as the faculty by which we apprehend phenomena discursively by means of concepts connected so as to form judgements. Hence it remains for the *Dialectic* to complete the scheme by examining the transcendental implications of inference, which is the province of reason in the narrowest or purely logical sense.

Without entering again into the questions raised by Kant's addiction to architectonic, we may repeat that the division of the *Critique* which results from his attempt to distinguish between reason and understanding is extremely arbitrary. It is at once evident that the possibility of inference has in fact been one of the major points considered in the *Analytic*, and that the second of Kant's remaining questions, in the form in which he states it, has been ruled out as meaningless by the distinction between phenomena and noumena. For by demonstrating that neither the forms of sense nor the categories, by means of which alone we can conceivably have *a priori* knowledge of objects, are applicable except to phenomena, he has already proved that metaphysics, as the study of the super-sensible by pure reason, cannot possibly be scientific in character. In addition to this his metaphysical deduction of the ideas is extremely unconvincing. The ideas which are peculiar to pure reason and discovered by consideration of the syllogism, as the pure concepts were discovered by consideration of the judgement, are more dubiously connected with their counterparts in general logic than are some of the pure concepts with the logical forms from which he claims to deduce them.

Kant's general position is as follows. The syllogism, as expounded in formal logic, is, like the judgement, a form of thought, and the traditional classification of syllogisms into categorical, hypothetical, and disjunctive, like the traditional table of judgements, must be accepted as exhaustive and final. It will naturally be observed that here, as in the former case, he assumes a considerable right of adaptation as regards the traditional view by ignoring all forms of categorical syllogism except the first mode of the first figure (*Barbara*). He could, however, have defended this by reference to his early work on the *Mistaken Subtlety of the Four Syllogistic Figures*, in which he claimed to show that *Barbara* alone is the form of genuine categorical syllogisms. He further maintains that as each form of judgement implies the apprehension by us of a pure concept, so each form of syllogism implies the apprehension of a pure idea. These ideas, however, differ from the pure concepts in that they are notions not of different kinds of relation but of different kinds of totality or wholes of relations. The ideas are thus notions of totality or absolute completeness, which are concerned not directly with things but rather with the procedure by which the understanding leads us to a knowledge of things. The object of reason is thus the understanding, and the aim of reason is to provide principles or absolute starting-points for the employment of the understanding. It is only in the case of the categories of relation that such principles can be needed, and therefore we find that in respect of each of them there is a transcendental idea of totality. The categorical syllogism, corresponding to the category of substance and attribute, yields the idea of a subject, which is never a predicate, conceived as absolute unity; the hypothetical syllogism, corresponding to the category of cause and effect, that of a cause which is not itself the effect of any more ultimate cause; and the disjunctive syllogism that of an absolute unity of all conditions or unconditioned unity of an organic whole.

It is unnecessary to inquire further into this deduction which serves no purpose but to introduce confusion into Kant's subsequent inquiry into the ideas of God, freedom, and immortality. The only ideas in which he is interested are those of a first cause and a self-existent substance, and these might equally well be considered as arising from the false hypostatization of the pure concepts of cause and substance without any reference to the syllogism at all.

If, however, we grant the soundness of the method by which he derives the ideas, he may be supposed to have provided a metaphysical deduction of them parallel to that given of the pure concepts of the understanding. And if we further agree that the idea of an absolute subject which is never a predicate can be identified with that of an immortal soul, the idea of a first cause with that of a free-will, and the idea of an absolute totality of conditions determining an organic whole with that of God, then he may be said to have shown how the ideas of these realities are involved in the form of our inferential thinking. But even if these rather surprising conclusions were accepted, it would still be necessary for Kant to provide a transcendental deduction if he were to demonstrate that the ideas were necessarily ideas of things and not merely part of the machinery of the mind. In his own terms, his argument from the nature of the syllogism could never do more than show how metaphysics was possible as a natural disposition. It would remain to show how it was possible as a science, and it is precisely this which he holds to be out of the question, since the entities which can alone correspond to those ideas are by definition things in themselves and not phenomena. Consequently his treatment of the ideas falls into two sections, as anticipated in the concluding sections of the *Analytic*, namely

(1) the *Paralogisms*, *Antinomies*, and *Ideal of Pure Reason*, B 397–670;

(2) the Appendix to the *Dialectic*, B 670–97.

The former are almost entirely destructive. Kant amplifies the proof already given that noumena cannot be objects of knowledge to us by exposing the fallacies in the existing rationalist philosophy which lays claim to such knowledge. His central argument here is that men have discovered the pure ideas as part of the 'furniture of the mind' and have assumed without question or warrant that these ideas possess the same kind of objective reference as do the pure forms of space and time and the pure concepts of the understanding. They have therefore postulated the existence of objects corresponding to those ideas and treated these empty hypostatizations as facts from which valid inferences can be drawn in the phenomenal world. Such a procedure is illegitimate, since the forms of the mind can be accorded objective validity only when this is an indispensable condition of the possibility of experience. No attempt, however, has been made to show that this condition is satisfied, and indeed it evidently is not, since we have already found that unity in terms of space, time, and the categories is all that is required to render experience of objects and therefore self-consciousness possible.

Kant is not satisfied with this general attack on rationalist methods in metaphysics. He prefers a detailed refutation of the pseudo-sciences to which these methods give rise. Rational ontology has been already eliminated and replaced by the *Analytic*. Rational psychology is dealt with by the *Paralogisms*, rational cosmology by the *Antinomies*, and rational theology in the *Ideal of Pure Reason*.

This disposes of the illegitimate use of the ideas and incidentally answers completely the question, 'How is metaphysics possible as a science?' Hence Kant is constrained to deal with the proper employment of the ideas in the Appendix to the *Dialectic* as if it were a relatively unimportant afterthought. As his doctrine in this matter anticipates virtually the whole of what he has to say in the *Critique of Practical Reason* and the *Critique of Judgement*, it is unfortunate that his original formulation of his problem should have led to such an arrangement.

It is not necessary to anticipate here Kant's constructive treatment of the employment of the ideas except in so far as it is implied by his method of discovering them. Since they are on his view the necessary presupposition of our employment of syllogistic reasoning, they can hardly be regarded as mere *entia rationis* which have no purpose whatever but are simply possible sources of illusion. The clue to their legitimate use is provided by the conception that reason has as its aim the unification not of objects for consciousness but of the operation of the understanding itself. Like the concepts of the understanding they are functions of unity, but the unity which they postulate is subjective. It is an ideal unity of consciousness at which we ought to aim, and is therefore of a higher order than, though not inconsistent with, the *de facto* unity which the *Analytic* has demonstrated. Our natural desire to find in phenomena the type of unity required by the ideas is thus one which we may properly gratify only in so far as this does not involve any conflict with the unqualified validity of the forms of sense and understanding in respect of phenomena which the *Analytic* has shown to be necessary to our existence as self-conscious beings. It remains to be seen whether we can afford this gratification or not.

PARALOGISMS OF PURE REASON (B 399–432)

Rational psychology claims to expound the nature of the soul or self in so far as this can be done by pure reason alone. Its central doctrine is that we are in self-consciousness aware of the thinking self as (1) always a subject and never a mere predicate of something else; (2) simple, since if we abstract from the content of thought, the bare *I* which remains contains nothing complex; (3) self-identical in time; (4) self-existent, that is, existent independently of and in complete distinction from the things which are its objects. Now if these propositions are true they would enable us to infer the immortal nature of the soul, since a simple substance is by definition indestructible except by miraculous annihilation. Furthermore, such a demonstration if allowed to be valid would be absolutely fatal to the Critical system, since we should be then driven to admit that in one vital instance at least it is possible for the human mind to know by reason alone and without sensuous experience that something (the soul) is a substance, whereas the argument of the *Analytic* shows that nothing but experiment can ever settle such a question. It was proved in the *First Analogy* that while we know *a priori* that there is substance, the discovery of what is substance must be left to the scientist, who in any case cannot even hope to settle the matter even in respect of phenomena; but the rationalist proof claims validity of something which is not a phenomenon since it is considered without reference to the conditions under which we are conscious of it.

This claim when we consider it further serves to refute the contention of rational psychology and to restore our confidence in the *Analytic*. For rationalism in its argument is guilty of a logical fallacy or paralogism, namely that of a *quaternio terminorum* or ambiguity of one of the terms which it employs.

What it does is to take the purely formal or logical unity which certainly can be discovered in all acts of consciousness and then treat that formal unity as something given to consciousness. To do this, however, involves a natural but fallacious identification of two entities which are not properly to be regarded as identical at all, namely the subject and object selves as revealed by self-consciousness. Of these the former is indeed actual but entirely undetermined. It is barely formal in character and possesses no predicates. Just because it is the indispensable logical subject of all judgement, it cannot itself be thought in terms of the categories at all, and to say that it is substance, simple, &c., is merely a misleading way of stating a tautology. We can certainly maintain if we want to that it is not predicate, not complex, and so on, but this gets us no farther. All we are entitled to say is that it is not an object of knowledge. What deludes us is the existence of the object-self, that is, of the complex of emotions and feelings of which we do think as a unity by means of the categories. That self quite apart from the fact that it is given only in experience and has no existence apart from such experience, so that it is not the self of which rational psychology claims to treat, is essentially temporal and therefore impermanent and unsubstantial in character. Nothing but our *a priori* awareness of a world of permanent things enables us to recognize it as a unity.

Thus the attempt of rationalism to discover in the soul an object to correspond to the pure idea of an absolute subject is a failure, and we may note that even if it were a success it would commit us at least to a problematic idealism as regards the existence of objects by rendering the latter less certain than, and therefore only to be established by a doubtful inference from, the former as Descartes was constrained by his argument to do.

The whole proceeding, however, is now shown to be invalid and to depend in the end on a false hypostatization in that when we identify the purely formal or logical self with the self as object of actual consciousness we improperly endow the former with an intuitable existence in time which, if legitimate, would render it an object of experience and therefore knowable in terms of the categories. We then treat it as if it were thus knowable and formulate of it the *a priori* synthetic propositions that it is substance, simple, and so on. As soon as the fallacy is discovered it is evident that all these propositions are either tautologous or false, and that the immortality of the soul is not demonstrable *a priori*. This is not a very serious discovery, since we now see that its mortality could only be proved by an argument equally fallacious, and consequently Kant's claim that the *Critique* removes knowledge to make room for faith is so far justified.

ANTINOMIES OF PURE REASON (B 433–595)

By an antinomy Kant means a pair of propositions called Thesis and Antithesis each of which can be supported by a formally valid argument but which are none the less inconsistent with and indeed diametrically opposed to one another. 'Matter is infinitely divisible' [thesis] is opposed to 'Matter is composed of parts which are indivisible' [antithesis]. The section consists of two parts;

1. A demonstration in accordance with the architectonic of the *Critique* that there are necessarily four of these antinomies and four only, followed by a formulation with comments on each pair. The number is supposed to depend on the four headings of the categories, and the four are further divided into two groups of two each, called mathematical and dynamical. B 433–90.
2. A consideration of the origin of antinomies in human reason and of the solution of them by the Critical hypothesis. B 490–595.

1. The first of these sections is lengthy, complicated, and arbitrary. It has little but historical interest and is quite unessential to the important doctrine which follows it, but the inclusion of it in the *Critique*, and the importance which Kant obviously attached to it are easy to explain.

The mathematical antinomies and their solution by the Critical doctrine of the transcendental ideality of space and time had formed the central theme of the *Dissertation* of 1770, and the *Critique* had first been conceived as an extension of the *Dissertation*. But years before the *Dissertation* was written the existence of these contradictions, as shown by the controversies of contemporary physics, had seemed to Kant a scandal to philosophy, and was largely responsible for turning his thoughts into speculative channels. Thus it is reasonable to suppose that in course of time they came to have for him an importance which was disproportionate to their relevance to the mature Critical system. A further complication arose because of Kant's decision to combine them with the conflict between free will and universal causal necessity in the section of the *Critique* designed to refute the pseudo-science of rational cosmology, and confusion is made worse by his invention of a fourth antinomy which is nothing but an inadequate version of his subsequent treatment of the *Ideal of Pure Reason* which follows it.

In view of this it is simply not worth while to examine the arguments of the theses and antitheses in detail in order to determine whether they are actually valid or mere pretences of demonstration. It is more profitable to omit them altogether and to pass immediately to the second section, in which the general difficulty is discussed and Kant's solution of it propounded.

2. The four antinomies with which as a whole we have now to deal are as follows:

		Thesis	*Antithesis*
Mathematical	(*a*)	The world has a beginning in time, and in respect of space is enclosed within limits.	The world has no beginning, and no limits in space: it is infinite in respect both of space and time.
	(*b*)	Every composite thing in the world consists of simple parts and nothing anywhere exists except the simple or that which is formed by composition of it.	No composite thing in the world consists of simple parts and there exists nothing simple anywhere in the world.
Dynamical	(*c*)	Causality in accordance with the laws of nature is not the only causality from which the phenomena of the world as a whole can be derived. It is necessary further to accept a causality by freedom as an explanation of them.	There is no freedom, but everything in the world happens simply according to laws of nature.
	(*d*)	There belongs to the world either as part of it or as its cause an absolutely necessary being.	There exists nowhere an absolutely necessary being either in the world or outside it as its cause.

It is immediately clear that Kant considers the theses to be the *a priori* contentions of rationalist cosmology, while the antitheses represent the empiricist attack on it, and also that the truth of the theses rather than that of the antitheses is desirable both on practical and speculative grounds. For the theses, in so far as they are true, involve the existence both of God and of a moral capacity in man, both of which are by implication denied by the antitheses, and in addition they hold out the prospect of final answers being given to the problems of natural science, which equally is denied by the antitheses, since these involve us in a series of infinite regresses. Hence it is not to be wondered at that the rationalist position has a wider popular appeal than the empiricist, though this by no means implies that it is philosophically sound. Indeed, on the strength of the *Analytic* it may be argued that in this respect empiricism has the stronger prima facie claim, in that it adheres firmly to the established principles of sense and understanding and nowhere admits any argument based on the mere ideas of entities which can never be given in experience. This would indeed be the case if empiricism rested satisfied with the refutation of dogmatic rationalism, but it frequently goes far beyond this, as in the antitheses, and claims to formulate an equally dogmatic theory of its own by denying that the ideas which the rationalist has erroneously attempted to introduce into natural science can possibly have any objective reference or relevance at all.

The function of a genuine philosophy is to defend what is true in both views and to show how, by means of the Critical hypothesis, the practical merits of rationalism can be combined with the claim of empiricism that its principles are the only sound basis for natural science. It may, however, be objected that this cannot be done, since the cosmological problems involved are of such difficulty that no solution of them can be attained by human reason. This objection is invalid, and against it we may assert that the questions concerned must be answerable since they arise simply out of the nature of that reason and are not given to it from some other source, which would justify the assertion that the investigation of them is necessarily an empirical matter. They are thus on the same plane as the problems of morals and mathematics, to which it is evident that an answer must be given by reason, even though in some cases that answer consists in demonstrating that the question itself is meaningless and ought never to have been asked. That this is the case becomes apparent when we consider that what we are concerned with in the cosmological question is not something to do with an object, whether phenomenal or noumenal in character, but is simply the possibility or impossibility of completing a particular series. For this conception of completeness in the spatial, temporal, or causal series is clearly a notion which reason produces for itself and the existence of such completeness, even if it were a fact, could never be determined empirically. Equally clearly the existence or non-existence of the final terms which such completeness requires is scientifically of no interest or importance and consequently no transcendental deduction of it can even be contemplated.

Before we give a Critical solution of these cosmological questions it is as well to observe that neither the dogmatic affirmative nor negative offered by the theses or antitheses would really be tolerable even if it could be substantiated, for this will reconcile us to the necessarily inconclusive character of the Critical inquiry. Any such answer would prove to be either too large or too small to admit of reconciliation with any concept of the understanding. For it must be remembered that the empirical regresses with which the cosmological ideas deal are conceived by both parties to the dispute as being themselves objects of possible experience and therefore cognizable by the understanding. But it can be confidently asserted on the one hand that the understanding can frame no concept of an infinite series of places or events as an actual empirical object, since nothing of this nature can possibly be given in experience, and on the other that it is equally incapable of conceiving a last term in any such empirical series without falling into contradiction. The former is in fact too large and the latter too small to be reconcilable with the principles in accordance with which the understanding must conceive empirical reality. Hence there is a prima-facie case for supposing that the cosmological questions are unreal and are propounded only as the result of a misunderstanding of the proper function of the ideas of reason. That this is indeed the case becomes clear in what follows.

According to the Critical Philosophy, space and time and the substances in them which causally determine one another are all alike to be regarded as appearances and not as things existing independently of all experience, and the empirical system which they constitute is to be regarded as a representation of things in themselves, which has no existence except for consciousness. Hence the assertion that a certain object remote from me in time or space is actual can mean only that I find it as a member of a series of possible experiences which the understanding postulates as a condition of the unity of my actual present experience. The distinction between phenomena and noumena thus provides the key to the solution of the cosmological problems. Phenomena and the space and time which are their forms are not things in the absolute sense of independently real existents, but only objectively determined appearances of such things. Now the assumption made in the formulation of the cosmological problems is that if the conditioned is given, the complete series of all its conditions is given too, and as far as metaphysical substances, or noumena, are concerned, this is merely an analytical proposition; but as regards appearances the situation is entirely different. All that we can properly maintain of these is that they occur in a necessary order which is spatial, temporal, and causal, and that in those series we must always take for granted the existence of a further term which it is our task to discover. This suggests that the arguments of the antitheses are in fact justified and that the world as appearance must be regarded as infinitely divisible and extended, but the suggestion is misleading. The doctrine of the antitheses is that a part of matter consists of an actually infinite number of independently real parts, whereas the Critical doctrine is simply that the process of division can be carried on indefinitely, but that the possibility of this indefinite regress does not presuppose the actual existence of an infinite number of independent reals, since the process itself deals with phenomena, not noumena. Hence the statement that a particular member of such a series is actual means simply that it is either met with in experience or is implied by something else which is.

The error which underlies the formulation of the cosmological problems is indeed identical with that involved in the paralogisms, namely an ambiguity due to a failure to distinguish between propositions which relate to things in themselves and propositions which relate to phenomena.

As contrasted with this illegitimate or constitutive use of the notion of a totality of conditions, there is a legitimate or regulative employment of it on which the Critical Philosophy must insist. In this sense it provides a rule for the guidance of the understanding in its investigation of phenomena, forbidding it to regard any actually discovered term in an empirical regress as being actually the last of the series. Any such claim can be shown to conflict with the demand of reason for an absolute totality. This does not necessarily imply that there never can be such a last term (e.g. in the series of a given man's ancestors), but that the understanding by its very nature could never recognize any empirical member as being such a last term, and would therefore still be constrained by reason to look for a further one.

This statement of the regulative function of reason is an anticipation of the fuller formulation which is given later.

The general solution offered above is now applied in greater detail to the four antinomies, but as far as the first two, the mathematical antinomies, are concerned, nothing is thereby added to what has already been said. The regulative function of reason in demanding that investigation shall never stop short of attaining to the ideal of a totality conceived *a priori* by reason, even though this ideal can never actually be achieved, is further emphasized, and a distinction is drawn between those empirical series in which we are certain *a priori* that however far we proceed with our empirical analysis there will always be another term for us to discover, of which an example is provided by the divisibility of matter, and those in which we are bound to look for such a term even though none may exist; for even if the term which we have reached is actually the last, we can never know this and are therefore bound to search for another, as in tracing the origin of the human race. This distinction is of dubious validity and no importance. In fact these solutions of the *First* and *Second Antinomies* are included for the sake of symmetry, since they are entirely subordinate to the discussion of the *Third Antinomy* which follows them. This section of the *Critique*,[1] containing as it does all that is essential in Kant's ethical doctrine, is so fundamental to his system as a whole that it requires to be dealt with in greater detail than is desirable at this point. It is not entirely consistent with itself and involves several points which are difficult to interpret satisfactorily, but the main contention which Kant hopes to prove is clear and can be given at once.

Our conclusion in respect of the mathematical antinomies is that both sides in the dispute are correct in denying the dogmatic assertions of their opponents, but wrong in attempting to demonstrate their own counter-proposals. The position as regards the

[1] B 560–93.

dynamical antinomies is different, for here we shall find that the legitimate demands of both parties can be met as soon as we properly understand what those demands really are. The conflict in fact is between the claim of the scientist that all natural events must be explicable by natural causes and that of the moralist that unless human action is spontaneous, and therefore undetermined by natural causes, the conceptions of obligation and desert become entirely without meaning. Both these assertions are indisputably correct. The first has already been demonstrated in the *Analytic* and the second is obvious as soon as it is stated. What Critical Philosophy claims to do is to show that the conflict between them is only apparent. For this purpose it is necessary to remember that the distinction between phenomena and noumena holds of selves as well as of objects. Now the whole teaching of the *Analytic* assures us that the phenomenal self, like the phenomenal world of objects, is subject to the conditions of the categories and therefore causally determined, and from this conclusion there can be no retreat without sacrificing everything which the *Critique* maintains. The self, considered as the object of empirical psychology, must be conceived as determined in every detail, and, even where we are prevented by its complexity from empirically predicting its behaviour, we are bound to hold that such behaviour is in principle as predictable as the movements of the planets. The antithesis of the antinomy is therefore entirely correct in its assertion that human behaviour as an object of possible experience must be causally determined and admits of no spontaneity whatever. What it fails to notice is that the causal sequence in phenomena as a whole, and therefore in the empirical self as part of that whole, is a relation between appearances and not between things in themselves, and is therefore determined as as a whole by the noumena which it represents. Of these noumena (including the noumenal self) we can say nothing positive since they are *ex hypothesi* not subject to the forms of sense and understanding, but this very fact enables us to maintain that they are not subject to the causal law, or even to the limitation of time. Hence the thesis of the antinomy is also justified provided that we understand exactly what it is maintaining. There is no question of regarding the noumenal and phenomenal selves as different entities of which one can determine the other in the sense of acting causally upon it. The noumenal self is not to be conceived as interrupting or breaking in upon the chain of natural causes which determine the phenomenal self. All that is argued is that the phenomenal or observable character of anyone is what it is because of the timeless noumenal character of which it is the temporal (and therefore causally determined) representation. This being the case, we are in a position to infer, though never with certainty, the real merit or guilt of a person from his observed behaviour in a manner analogous to that in which from our private empirical representations we infer with certainty the objective though phenomenal constitution of an empirical object. Our moral judgements must always be problematical since the transcendental subject to which alone they can have any reference is not given to us as an object but is only conceived as possible by means of an idea of pure reason. To apprehend it as an object we should require that capacity of knowing by means of an intellectual intuition which we do not possess.

The solution of the *Fourth Antinomy* requires no consideration. It merely anticipates the discussion of the *Ideal of Pure Reason* and has nothing but considerations of architectonic to justify its inclusion at this stage.

THE THIRD ANTINOMY

COMMENT

§ 1

Kant's way of stating the problem of free will now looks very artificial. It is much influenced by the theological controversies of the seventeenth and eighteenth centuries which had been savage and were still quite lively when he wrote. As a matter of history it is worth remembering that the view of Leibniz as developed by Wolff on this subject had actually led to trouble with the authorities. It had indeed always been apparent that divine foreknowledge and human responsibility were not easy to reconcile with one another. By 1781, however, a new difficulty was superseding this. The type of physical theory which Kant himself had underwritten in the *Second Analogy* forced philosophers to ask themselves how freedom could be squared not with divine but with potential human omniscience. The claim of Laplace to predict, in principle without limitation, all future states of the universe made 'choice' and 'activity', except in drastically redefined senses, words for which enlightened language could have no use. They were redundant.

It has often been pointed out that to state the problem in this way is to involve oneself in unreal difficulties. The predictability of human behaviour, far from being objectionable, is an essential condition of civilized existence. What matters for morals is not the fact of prediction but the kind of evidence on which it is based. How did God know that Adam was going to be disobedient? Kant was not unaware of this. He realized that what the Critical Philosophy had to do was to produce an account of choice which would make it at once important, though inevitably unanalysable into ingredients which did not include it, and consistent with the validity of the causal axiom in the sense in which he held that the latter was a necessary condition of scientific inquiry. He meant to show that the claim of the scientist to predict occurrences in nature was not at variance with the claim of the plain man to make ethical appraisals of human conduct. This problem is awkwardly stated in the *Antinomy* thus:

Thesis. 'Causality according to the laws of nature is not the only causality from which the phenomena of the universe can one and all be derived. There is another kind of causality through freedom which must be accepted to explain them.'

Antithesis. 'There is no freedom, but everything in the universe happens simply according to the laws of nature.'

Kant's use of 'causality' here is terribly misleading. It has to be so in order to create a logical dilemma for the Critical method to resolve. What emerges is the notion that we have to decide between the intervention or non-intervention of something mysterious called 'choice' in an otherwise orderly universe. Kant explains at length that this is not what he has in mind, but it is undeniable that by his terminology he has done his best to start the reader puzzling in the wrong direction.

Although talk about two, or seventeen, kinds of causality is unnecessarily confusing, 'cause' is bound to be a slippery word for Kant to handle. The tight definition which he needs for mechanics is out of step with ordinary use which accepts 'chance' and 'fortune' as significant words. When he was speaking as an epistemologist, he generally employed *affektiren* and *Affektion* to bridge the apparent gap between his physiological and his psychological theories. A similar evasion occurs when freedom is under examination, but here he tries another two-world language and draws a Leibnizian distinction between the 'realm of nature' and the 'realm of freedom'. This is not fatally misleading if one remembers that 'realm' is strictly equivalent in his language to 'point of view'. But this is not a natural way of talking and he frequently fails to remember it himself. His claim is that 'Understanding does not admit among experiences any condition which can itself be unconditioned. But if for some conditioned in the sphere of phenomena we can conceive an intelligible condition, not belonging to the series of phenomena as one of its members, such a condition may be accepted as empirically unconditioned without prejudice to the continuity of the empirical regress.'[2] The awkward word here is 'intelligible' which is a survival from the days of the *Dissertation*. It is not quite fair to say that, on Kant's own showing, what it means is 'unintelligible', but it certainly does mean 'non-empirical' in a much more thoroughgoing way than does *a priori* in the *Analytic*. The contrast now is with what is sensible (*Mundus sensibilis atque intelligibilis*), and thus with what is scientifically discoverable, and so it looks at first sight as if we are faced abruptly with the threat of a mystical *Ding an sich* interfering with the laws of nature in a wholly unpredictable way.

This was not at all what Kant wanted. His considered view was not absurd. It can be made psychologically respectable, at least up to a point. But it is greatly over-simplified, and therefore apparently complicated, by his over-rigid disjunction between physical and psychological method which makes his problem look much more menacing and intractable than it is. What he tries to do is first to distinguish sharply between *arbitrium brutum* and *arbitrium liberum*.[3] The former is not spontaneous at all, but 'by freedom I understand the power of beginning an action spontaneously'.[4] Hence his puzzle was that at the level of mechanics all spontaneity is nonsense and therefore at this level choice is completely illusory; and this was the only level at which he admitted the existence of empirical knowledge. As we have seen, he could get no help from psychology because for him psychology was only guesswork about physics. Hence his only way out was to fall back on the notion of a different, non-empirical

[2] A 531 n. [3] A 534. [4] A 533.

level over which neither physics nor psychology has any jurisdiction. But he has ruled out the possibility of saying anything significant about events at this level by his special and restricted form of schematism. Only the physical patterns, the machines, are possible frameworks of knowledge by human beings. Hence if there are any behaviour patterns which cannot be reduced to physics patterns, we must inevitably remain ignorant of their nature and can only guess at their existence.

Sometimes when Kant is taking his scientific phenomenalism very seriously, he gets near to maintaining this, but it is not the conclusion which he wants. He is trying to say 'We have empirical characteristics or dispositions about which the psychologists can tell us something but not very much. Taken together these make up what we call our "character".' But this weakness in psychology must be regarded as temporary and accidental. Although we cannot see how the task can be carried out we have to admit on the evidence of the *Analytic* that all our acts, just because they are events in time, are in principle empirically predictable within whatever limits of accuracy we like to formulate, subject only to reservations about experimental technique. This ultimately entails strict behaviourism, since only physical bodies obeying Newtonian Laws genuinely admit of this type of prediction. Psychological prediction in itself can never be more than guesswork.

But there is no reason why we should not believe that our characters or dispositions are the phenomenal appearances of monadic substances. Of course we can never know which bits of our observable selves represent the noumenal self and which the noumenal object. It is an act of faith, though Kant is far from consistently realizing this, to maintain that both contribute. But the real self can without contradiction be regarded as wholly responsible for our empirical characters. We cannot pretend to say how this occurs, or what precisely it means, since the relation in question is not a causal one, and that is the only type of dependence we can grasp. There is, however, no good reason for refusing to believe that it does happen. Hence we are told of 'the intelligible character of which the empirical character is the sensuous schema'.[5] We can say nothing whatever about the intelligible character. 'The only resource remaining to us is the use

[5] A 553.

of analogy by which we employ the concepts of experience in order to form some sort of concept of intelligible things.'[6]

This is generally condemned as mysticism, and there can be no doubt that technically that is precisely what it is. Kant admits consistently that he cannot answer the question 'How does pure reason become practical?', that is, he cannot elucidate the relation between self as substance or moral agent and self as an object of scientific inquiry. Certainly this sounds to us a meaningless question. It is like 'What is the relation between symbols and that which they symbolize?' One does not know what 'relation between' can mean in these contexts. But Kant could not admit that it was meaningless, even though I think he was very suspicious of it.[7] In fact the root of his trouble here as in his other formulations of the problem lies in his natural but misguided disjunction between a realm of nature governed by an iron law of tight causality and a different 'realm' called the realm of freedom governed by what he called the 'causality of freedom'. Partly this is the product of any radical mind-body dualism, but quite apart from this it can be derived from a common misconception of what 'law' means in scientific inquiry.

The root of the matter is that Kant's allegiance to tight causality as an indispensable category in physics and therefore the basis of any study which could properly claim to be scientific was simply based on a mistake. Science does not depend on laws but on statistical probabilities. This does not invalidate Kant's point that regularity in some form must be taken for granted, but it does dispense with the notion that physical particles, and therefore all physical bodies, behave in accordance with simple, ascertainable 'laws that never can be broken'. We cannot indeed break the laws of nature, but to say this is not to attribute to them a unique kind of inviolability. It is because they are not that kind of law. They are descriptions and explanations of what happens, ultimately of observable regularities. To say that a law of nature is broken is merely to deny that a particular regularity is observable, and there is nothing very terrible in that.

In fact Kant has misstated his problem and therefore his solution looks psychologically more unplausible than it need have done and can be restated in a much less tiresome way. He wanted

[6] A 566.

[7] Cf. the concluding sentences of *G*.

to elucidate 'can' in 'A can do X.' At first sight one tends to say it is like 'can' in 'Fish can swim', 'Dynamite can destroy bridges.' All of them can be analysed into a number of hypotheticals or 'if ... then' sentences. In fact, they are indistinguishable from statements in biology or physics in which 'potential' or its synonyms occur. Prediction then depends on the adequacy of the analysis, and, as we are dealing with matter of fact, it would be contradictory to claim that the analysis was or ever could be complete in a particular case. On these lines we should conclude that it is true but not surprising that some predictions of the behaviour of particular human beings are better grounded than some predictions of the behaviour of animals or inanimate things. This would not commit us to asserting or denying that the reasons on which predictions are based are the same in all cases, though it does take for granted that there are reasons and that some of them are good ones. But if the only good reasons for predicting anything were reasons of a mechanical kind, which clearly they are not, the position would be quite different.

The error which vitiates the thinking of Kant and of many of his successors in this field is the unconscious metaphysical assumption that whatever can be truly asserted of a class of events can also be truly asserted of the members of that class taken separately. Because my body consists solely of physical particles, it is assumed that its behaviour must be explicable solely by the laws which apply to the behaviour of particular physical particles. This is nonsense, but Kant was right in regarding it as a basic assumption of Newtonian mechanics. It is indeed just the position which Leibniz tried without much success to escape from by introducing his principle of sufficient reason. Kant never saw how to get out of it though he clearly felt that there was something radically wrong with it. This is the basis of his faith that there would never be a Newton to explain a blade of grass on purely mechanical principles. He also recognizes, though not quite clearly and not for some time, that the notion of noumena as entities distinct from phenomena but somehow generating or 'causing' phenomena would not do, and was really groping for the right idea. He wants to maintain that physical evidence is good evidence, but it is not the only evidence we have for predicting biological, psychological, and sociological phenomena. It is indeed always valid as far as it goes, but in these departments its predictive value is not usually very great.

There is a further difficulty in personality which is not soluble on mechanical lines. Kant thought, and he was at least partly right, that we need the notion of a substantial and not merely a phenomenal self in order to be able to give an intelligible account of what occurs when A deliberately chooses to do X rather than Y. The self as a logical construct is unsatisfying, however difficult it may be to give a convincing answer to positivist criticism of any alternative view. It is inadequate both from the point of view of epistemology and from the point of view of moral appraisals.

So far I have only considered the weaknesses in Kant's approach and have not attempted to state in full his answer to his own puzzle as to the possibility of freedom. That answer really involves three levels. The levels are:

Arbitrium brutum. This is the condition attributed by Kant to animals. *Arbitrium* is misleading since what he has in mind is below the level of choosing. It is just being pushed about. Animal psychology would not now support the view that this is the whole truth about all animals.[8] But Kant had not read even the *Descent of Man,* let alone the works of Gestalt psychologists.

Arbitrium liberum. This is in the area in which there is choice as ordinarily understood. Kant restricts it to behaviour determined by maxims or general rules. In his language we are here still in the realm of nature because the principle of our willing is heteronomy and not autonomy. This analysis would include 'cool self-love' theories and indeed all teleological views.[9]

This is as far as empirical psychology can take us, and we cannot claim to prove that any other level is needed to explain our conduct. It is not a condition of possible experience that there should ever be an autonomous act, that is, an act done because it is recognized as a duty and for no other reason whatever. Kant's contention in the first part of *G.* is that the ordinary language of the plain man reveals his conviction that such acts do or at least can happen. Hence we have genuinely free action which paradoxically does not entail choice but excludes it. There are no imperatives, and therefore no choices, for the Holy Will. It is determined by pure reason alone. We can never be sure that

[8] Cf. Köhler's apes.

[9] In Prof. Broad's sense. See *Five Types of Ethical Theory.*

this has happened in a particular case, even when we are ourselves the agent concerned. We can only say that it ought to happen, which is equivalent to 'It would happen in a universe peopled by beings of which reason could approve', in a noumenal or intelligible world, and this, in the Critical Philosophy is perfectly consistent with the unrestricted admission of psychological predictability at the phenomenal level.

This doctrine is somewhat obscure because on Kant's own showing psychological, as distinct from physical, events are not *verae causae* even at the level of phenomena. He never professes to explain how, without violence to the *Principles*, even *arbitrium liberum* can be anything but illusory. Indeed this is all part of the unexplored no-man's land between physics and ethics about which he has nothing to say in detail except in *K.U.*, and there he considers only biology. I do not think he ever considered that *Anthropologie* could be extracted from the state of *bloßes Herumtappen* and set on the secure path of a science.[10] Yet he clearly held (how could he deny it?) that some psychological prediction is pretty reliable. One could predict behaviour by using psychological premisses as to a man's dispositions and probable reaction to environmental stimulus.

§ 2

THE MORAL LAW: THE LAW OF FREEDOM

On the face of it Kant's discussion and analysis of freedom in the *Third Antinomy* makes it practically impossible for him to ask sensible questions about moral appraisals at the empirical level, and that, after all, is what we are interested in. We want to know what it means to say that Jones ought not to have poisoned his wife. For Kant's position is this. The understanding imposes laws on nature, and those laws have already been expounded in the *Analytic* and will be further developed in *M.A.N.* They are *a priori*, admit of no exceptions, and the very possibility of thinking at all depends on the assumption of their universal validity for all events in time, that is, for everything of which we can obtain empirical knowledge.

But against this must be set the certainty of common sense

[10] See *Preface to M.A.N.*

supported by traditional religions and metaphysical doctrines that it simply will not do as a statement of the whole truth about human conduct. It is manifest that universal physical determinism is completely inconsistent with a belief in any sort of obligation. 'Ought' is a non-significant word if the laws of Newtonian mechanics are all the laws there are. It is significant only if these laws of nature are somehow supplemented, since they cannot be infringed, by something else to which Kant gives the name 'the Law of Freedom'. What, then, does 'the Law of Freedom' mean?

In this form, the question is hopeless. Even the desperate expedient of a two- or three- or *n*-world view will do nothing except make it more complicated and mystifying. Kant, though he certainly did not want to get involved in a plurality of worlds (a meaningless phrase anyway), had developed the language of phenomena and noumena in a way which made it very difficult for him consistently to avoid talking nonsense of this kind. He had indeed reached a point at which it was hard for him to avoid both idealism and the notion of empirical things as a kind of *Zwischendinge* half-way between reality and illusion. Plato had the same kind of difficulty. In fact Kant vacillates rather unhappily between these unpalatable alternatives whenever he gets near to facing the psycho-physical problem at all seriously. It may well be that this uneasiness occurred because he felt that he was being worried by a pseudo-problem but never succeeded in seeing just what was wrong. Sometimes, however, e.g. in the *Appendix to the Dialectic* (the *Als ob* passage), he almost recognized that *Ding an sich* referred to a verbal puzzle and not to a thing in the ordinary sense of 'thing'. Yet it was not quite that either. He did not mean 'limiting concept'. Indeed he never made up his mind as to what it was.

In view of the unsatisfactory state in which the whole idea of freedom was left in the *Critique*, in spite of the important distinction between *arbitrium brutum* and *arbitrium liberum*, it is fortunate that, when he came to discuss moral judgements as his main topic, Kant made a completely fresh start. The *Grundlegung* begins with a psychological inquiry into empirical statements on duty, and works back to the metaphysical problem of freedom. The method, as in *Proleg.*, is analytic and not synthetic. The great merit of this procedure is that it enables Kant to begin with ordinary questions about 'ought' without being embarrassed at the outset by the controversy as to the causality of nature and the causality of freedom. Free will, in the metaphysical sense, is quite a good introduction to morals provided it is recognized as a verbal or pseudo-problem. Kant unfortunately continued to suppose that it was a genuine difficulty.

The procedure of *G.* is very simple. There are three stages in the analysis of 'ought' or 'duty'. What does 'duty' mean in ordinary language? Kant claims that 'ought' statements do refer to my psychological attitude but that Hume was nevertheless mistaken in supposing that such statements assert nothing except the occurrence in me of a sentiment of approval or disapproval. The attitude to which Kant appeals is what he calls *Achtung*. This is hard to translate, but 'respect' is about the best that can be offered as an equivalent. *Achtung* is evoked solely by recognition of an act as exemplifying a law or principle. Further analysis shows that *Achtung* is ultimately felt only in respect of the principle of Law in general. It is the inherent rationality of Law which evokes it. I am moved empirically to act in accordance with rational rules just because they are rational.

This leads to the final question 'Is subordination to such a rational principle inconsistent with our subordination to natural law as demonstrated in the *Critique*?' Kant's answer is 'No, provided the Critical Philosophy is accepted. For I can hold without contradiction that, while I am determined as a phenomenon, I am spontaneously active as a substance and am therefore noumenally free. But if phenomena are taken to be *Dinge an sich*, freedom cannot be saved.'

I am not sure that Kant would have accepted my statement that this procedure is in his language analytic and not synthetic. He might have argued that it is synthetic in the same way that the development of the *Analytic* is. Thus in both cases we start with an admitted fact (Self-consciousness—the plain man's sense of obligation); we show that this fact could not be unless something else were also true (Principles—supreme principle of morals). Finally we demonstrate that the validity of these principles commits us to the Critical Philosophy (Antinomies—Empirical necessitation, noumenal freedom).

The bare outline given above now needs some filling in:

The starting-point seems to be simply a piece of introspective psychology. The 'plain man' whose views are set out so confidently is and can be no one but Kant himself, though he probably drew on his favourable recollection of his parents. The interesting point is that, while 'X is good' is taken to entail 'I approve of X', it is not at all a 'subjectivist' view. Kant sees that it might easily be mistaken for one[11] and tries to protect himself by urging that the approval he is describing is approval of a very special kind. It occurs when and only when the act under discussion is intellectually judged to possess a certain character. In Kantian language, we must distinguish between the form and the matter of an act. Moral appraisal is then distinct from all other types of approval because it rests entirely on our recognition of the formal character of an act. This, if it is granted, does enable him to draw a sharp distinction between moral approval and approval based on consequences, since the latter are by definition part of the matter and not of the form of the act. What then does Kant mean by 'formal characteristics' in this context? 'Form' as we know from the *Critique* implies a rule of some sort. So the form of an act is the rule or maxim which it exemplifies, and a free act is simply an act chosen because it satisfies a certain rule. This marks off *arbitrium liberum* from inanimate nature and also from the *arbitrium brutum* of the animal world. When fully developed it gives rise to the further line between really free (autonomous) acts and the products of *arbitrium liberum*, which are heteronomous, since their maxims, though they are rules, are still impure because related to ends.

The conclusion is that moral words are used implicitly by the plain man to designate acts which are not merely done on principle but done solely for the sake of a principle. I do not think this is true, but it is widely held, and has something to be said for it.

But even if it is accepted as true, the next move is a highly dubious development of it. The doctrine here is that, since we all do as a matter of fact feel respect for acts done on principle, there must be one supreme principle or super-maxim which dominates and explains all the others. The only rule which is sufficiently general to do this is the principle of contradiction. Hence we must scrutinize not particular acts but maxims and make sure that they can be generalized without contradiction. Only if they do can they be called strictly moral, autonomous, not heteronomous,

[11] Ak. iv. 401 n.

and therefore genuinely free. On the other hand, any which fail to come up to this standard are not truly moral. They may be observed on prudential or utilitarian grounds, but there is no moral beauty about adhering to them and they are generally speaking immoral.

The connexion of all this with the method of the *Critique* is easy to trace. The supreme principle is the moral equivalent of a category. We then have, to use Butler's terminology, (*a*) particular passions and affections; (*b*) maxims or general principles of action, self-love, and benevolence; these are forms of willing corresponding to the forms of judgement; (*c*) the supreme principle (conscience) which corresponds to the category and unifies, not particular acts but rules of action. The same type of hierarchy occurs in Kant's account of the function of Reason in regulating our scientific inquiries. 'Understanding is the faculty of rules, reason of principles.'

The upshot is that the intellectual 'foundation' of our moral appraisals is the intellectually recognized, logical principle of contradiction. It is an empirical fact that we feel *Achtung* when we contemplate the possibility of being determined to act by this recognition alone. We experience a sentiment and this sentiment produces action.

This certainly sounds very odd. As in the *Critique* I think we can best get some idea of what Kant is driving at by contrasting him with Hume. Hume in fact admits Kant's levels (*a*) and (*b*) (the calm passions) but denies that Kant's autonomy level is actual. For Hume moral appraisals do not depend at all on relations of ideas.[12] Maxims have no job to do except to codify and formalize sentiments. We can often explain the origin of a sentiment historically, but its force does not depend on this explanation. It is perfectly intelligible that we should disapprove of incest, but that is not why we disapprove. Approval is for Hume just a basic and ultimate fact. Now Kant does not profess to demonstrate the factual occurrence of acts in accordance with his supreme principle. This is quite avowedly the contrast between the *Analytic* and *G*. The reason for the difference is simply the existence of the *Schematism* in the principles of science and the absence of it in morals. All that Kant claims to do as far as his law of freedom is concerned is to show that, unless we accept it

[12] Hume, *Treatise*, III. I. I.

as being in some sense factual, the vulgar notion of responsibility is illusory and must be discarded. This is a kind of metaphysical deduction, but it is not and does not claim to be anything more than that. Hence from his point of view everything must depend on whether his formulation of the plain man view is regarded as acceptable or not. Two questions demand some attention here.

(i) Is the fact of *Achtung* as universal as Kant claims that it is? It was prevalent in Königsberg middle-class circles in 1785. But is it really universal? Nazi Germany, Communist China? The answer here is not obvious either way.

(ii) Is Kant right as against Hume? One feels that both Marx and Freud, from different points of view, should be considered here.

What has to be admitted is that, unless it is accepted as a fact, and therefore as demanding some non-empirical foundation, the whole basis of Kant's theory of morals dissolves. What he wanted to prove might be susceptible of proof by a different argument, but his actual position would be completely undermined. Even if we accept Kant's contention, however, we may still ask, as Bradley for instance did, what is the cash value of the supreme principle as Kant has formulated it? On his own showing it is a purely formal regulative principle, and since it has no schema, it is inevitably vacuous. Kant does recognize this weakness. He realizes that the supreme principle just because it has the status of a category demands a schema to link it with the empirically verifiable sentiment of *Achtung*. We do not feel much moved by the principle of contradiction. Hence we are offered in *G.* the alternative formulations (not logically derivable from the first) which provide what Kant calls 'the analogon of a schema' by introducing the notion of rational beings legislating in an ideal society or Kingdom of Ends.

§ 3

Kant's solution to his two big questions, What are the presuppositions of Newton's mechanics and what are the presuppositions of moral appraisal, involves a deadlock at precisely the point at which one can recognize that logically a deadlock is unavoidable. His initial basic assumption is that the world has to be so constructed that only two types of language can be used to give veridical descriptions of it, viz. (*a*) the tight causality language of the Newtonians, (*b*) the yes–no, right–wrong language of Pietist morals.

This lands him in a dilemma which he supposes to be factual but which is really linguistic. He puts it as 'What is the relation between the world of nature and the world of freedom?', as if this were like 'How does the way of life in the U.S.A. compare with that in the U.S.S.R.?' But there is no answer to be got here, because there are not two universes.

By working along this line Kant finds himself in a hopeless position as to what to say of biological and psychological language. These include neither 'freedom' nor 'necessity' in his own use of his terminology; so his initial basic assumption is discredited. What he wanted to do, and sometimes does do when at his best, is to ask 'Within what area of reality' or 'From what point of view' is it helpful to talk of events as the product of physical or psychological causes or as the results of choice or decision? This is an empirical question to which admittedly we do not know all the answer, but it cannot be short-circuited by assuming that the way in which ordinary or technical language works is more than a rough guide to where to look for that answer.

THE KINGDOM OF ENDS[13]

There are three different formulations of the supreme principle of morals. Kant claims that they are alternatives, though it is manifest that the second and third cannot be derived by analysis either of the first or of one another. In fact the idea of a kingdom of ends is and is admitted to be a kind of 'schema' in terms of which specific maxims can be 'subsumed under' the general principle of morality. They are exemplifications of a rule which is given in the supreme principle and schematized in the second and third formulations. To put it differently, the notion of a Kingdom of Ends provides a sort of abstract expression of non-contradiction in political terms.

It should here be noted that when Kant is discussing morals and politics, his use of 'contradiction' is extremely wide and imprecise; it means only 'incompatible'. This was characteristic

[13] Tidiness requires that this comment should be related to the *Canon of Pure Reason*. It is more convenient to insert it here.

of the Wolffian school and it explains the readiness with which they assimilated the Leibnizian 'contradiction' and 'sufficient reason'. The normal contemporary usage of 'reason' as a vague but euphemistic term is probably to blame.

To elucidate Kant's position further it is necessary to discuss his second formulation. He had a strenuous Pietist upbringing and believed firmly that the individual was extremely important. What he wants to maintain is that a wholly rational man would feel *Achtung* towards Reason as embodied in himself and in others. Hence such a man would never adopt a maxim which others, all others, could not adopt at the same time without leading to conflict; for he would have no rational ground for discriminating between their claims and his own. The rules which a society composed of such rational beings would adopt would therefore inevitably conform to the principle of suitability for universal legislation laid down as the rule of rational behaviour in the first formula.

What occurs here is a common fallacy, especially in Political Philosophy. 'Rational' slips from meaning only 'compatible with' into meaning 'coheres with', in some important but undefined sense. Kant is by no means the only philosopher who has failed to notice that something more adhesive than compatibility is required to glue his society of individualists together. Indeed the words 'Society', 'State', and 'Community' all take it for granted that some efficient glue is already there and that we are not actually discussing a bare conjunction of entirely separate individuals or substances. This is what Rousseau tried to express by his notion of a General Will, and Kant followed him. Thus the Kingdom of Ends at first sight is hardly more than a restatement of the central doctrine of the *Contrat Social.* What we need is a society in which each member is completely determined by the Law which is the General Will, but nevertheless obeys only himself and therefore remains as free as he was in a state of nature. That is why Kant compares Rousseau with Newton. Newton discovered the Law of Nature; Rousseau discovered the Law of Freedom. Kant is providing the intellectual background which combines both in a single system (the Critical distinction between phenomena and *Dinge an sich*; the realm of nature and the realm of freedom).

But Kant like many others, including Rousseau himself, failed to notice that the General Will makes sense only in a highly idealized or abstract state of things; and like Rousseau, when he gets to grips with actual laws (in the *Rechtslehre*, which corresponds to *M.A.N.*) he adopts a fairly straightforward organic political theory without clearly recognizing its implications. He has to do this because his second and third formulations of the Law, like the Constitution of the United States, are far too vague and abstract to produce a definite answer to any precisely formulated political problem. For what does 'Treat as ends in themselves' really mean? What does 'Life, liberty and pursuit of happiness' mean? What indeed does 'person' mean? Such questions can be answered only by the judges of the Supreme Court and their answers will depend more on their political prejudices (in a neutral, not a dyslogistic sense) than on their *Achtung* for the principle of contradiction.

Thus the second and third formulae are in the end no more useful than the first. They do indeed provide rough practical guides to conduct, but it is idle to expect more than this of them. They have not the same logical power as the mathematical schemata expounded in the *Analytic*. We might indeed call them empirical schemata, though implying that we need judgement to use them; Kant, however, tries to make them absolute and incorrigible by making his definitions of 'self', 'end', &c., localized in time and space.

Fundamentally his trouble is that he is mistaken as to the job which moral philosophy is required to do. He wants it to expound the same kind of systematic theory as he wrongly supposed that geometry and mechanics were concerned to establish, i.e. a system prescribing universal laws. He recognizes that, as far as phenomena are concerned, this cannot be done, or rather, it has been done and done completely by the geometers and physicists, since he has given physics complete legislative control over the realm of nature. So he is driven to assert that moral legislation is effective in another realm, in a non-empirical noumenal world.

The relation of moral law to actual conduct now becomes a sheer bewilderment. For, granting that moral conduct somehow represents or is analogous to real character, which is timeless and therefore cannot significantly be said to change or develop, it has to be admitted that I cannot formulate a single statement about this real character. Hence, as Kant himself admits,[14] I can never pass a reliable moral judgement on the actual past conduct of anyone, including myself. This may conceivably be true. But if it is, then future conduct is in just the same position and I can never know what I ought to do, quite apart from inevitable ignorance or uncertainty as to the facts.

The schema of the Rousseau state indeed looks as if it might help at this point. It does at least suggest a line of possible behaviour which is factually relevant. But the promise turns out to be illusory. When it comes to the point, Kant, like Rousseau, can do nothing but fall back on authority, divine or human, to interpret his principle for him in a particular case. Interest indeed can give him plenty of maxims, but, as everyone has pointed out, any maxim can be generalized without fear of contradiction if no account is taken of the consequences of generalizing it. There is nothing contradictory in the state of nature described by Hobbes.

The substantial self, as Kant introduces it, is thus completely useless to him. It will indeed solve his pseudo-problem of freedom *versus* necessity, but only at the cost of admitting scepticism in all practical moral decisions. It enables the unscrupulous to parade high-sounding moral 'principles' and then to hire a clever corporation lawyer to see that the practical consequences are not at all embarrassing. The supreme principle, far from being as some writers have claimed, too rigid, is completely vacuous (as Bradley saw).[15] The notion of humanity as an end in itself and that of society as a kingdom of ends are also useless except as empirical generalizations as to what most Americans and a great many West Europeans appraise favourably. They solve no moral problems except under ideal conditions in which by definition no moral difficulty could ever be found.

In spite of this I think it is a mistake to dismiss Kant's ethical writings as mere metaphysical moonshine. His view can be developed in the language of reasons (instead of Reason) so as to omit the notion of substantial selves altogether; and I think it may make sense to go further than this and to argue that, even when the remodelling is completed, we may still require a concept recognizably like Kant's 'noumenal self' in order completely to eludicate our moral appraisals. What stops Kant from talking

[14] Ak. iv. 406–7.

[15] *Ethical Studies. Duty for Duty's Sake.*

helpfully at this point is not his lack of insight into moral judgements but his mistaken theory of natural law.

As regards the first point a good deal has already been said. Kant clearly overstates the disjunction between mechanics and mysticism as well as that between nature and freedom. This leads to some sort of two-world theory with an unintelligible *Ding an sich*. To maintain the supposed incorrigibility of both moral and physical laws he is driven to postulate a physical and a moral realm for them to govern. But there are no such realms in the sense in which Kant is compelled to postulate them. There is only one world, and Kant knew that there was only one world. All the same he was stating an important truth when he identified 'free acts' with 'acts done on principle'. There is a distinction, which hardly anybody seriously disputes, between deliberate choice and reaction to stimulus, whether 'psychological' or 'physical', and the best test for deliberate choice is that I can give a reason for it. Up to the level of maxims Kant seems to me to be on very good ground. But it is much less clear that in any actual system all maxims could be or ought to be consistent with one another. It was part of the faith of Kant and later of the philosophical radicals that they ought to be, but I can see no logical or empirical justification of this faith, except the jurists' objection to a conflict of laws for which his judicial system can provide no remedy. And is not irritation at this lack of consistency one of the main arguments in favour of a *Führerprinzip*, the avoidance of principles?

The most helpful method of evading Kant's dilemma seems to me to lie in the study of patterns or types of behaviour at different empirical levels. They do vary with environment and it may therefore well be the case that the notion of a Kingdom of Ends as a kind of *focus imaginarius* is not nonsense though it is misconceived. The trouble arises when we try to identify this ideal abstraction with any actual state of affairs. Kant saw this point when he was discussing epistemology in the *Dialectic* but forgot it when he was discussing politics in the *Rechtslehre*. There are in fact plenty of societies which are not at all like a Kingdom of Ends, however it is interpreted, and their actual and probable behaviour is just what we want to know about. In fact the patterns or schemata of political organization are far more numerous and complex than Kant supposed. There is no one

diagram or model that will meet the case. There is, however, n
particular difficulty in accepting choice as a fact, explaining it i
terms of observable human situations and claiming that it pre
supposes but is not presupposed by observable physical regulari
ties. The need for a realm of freedom and a noumenal self ca
thereby be removed. This point can be developed further by con
sideration of the major gap in the Critical Philosophy caused b
Kant's omission of all studies except mechanics on the one han
and *a priori* moral psychology on the other. He attempted thi
himself in *K.U.* without any great success.

Finally, what is one to say about Kant's work in relation to tha
of the British Empiricist School, Hume, and a good deal of Butler
Shaftesbury, Hutcheson on morals and aesthetics?

1. Kant correctly noted a large gap in Hume's analysis of 'self
or 'person'; for Hume can offer no account of activity
nobody does anything. This precludes any satisfactor
account of 'discovery', 'trying', 'researching' in epistemolog
and of 'rights', 'duties', &c., in sociology.
2. He tried to fill the gap by *a priori* or non-empirical specula
lation. I do not think this was wholly mistaken, but it di
(historically) encourage reactionary Hegelian talk. In par
ticular it directed philosophers' attention away from Hume'
salutary attempt in the *Treatise* to apply empirical method
to moral subjects, and led them to waste a lot more time o
the kind of *a priori* sociology which has been called 'Politi
cal Philosophy'.

IDEAL OF PURE REASON (B 595–620)

The section on the *Ideal of Pure Reason* resembles that on th
Paralogisms in that it begins with a complicated but unimportan
piece of architectonic. The aim of this is to demonstrate that Go
the subject of study in the third great rationalist science o
rational theology, is to be identified with the *ens realissimum* o
absolute first cause of all existence, and further that the idea o
such a first cause can be shown to arise naturally in our minds a
being the presupposition of our employment of the disjunctiv
syllogism. This leads to the consideration of the traditiona
proofs of God's existence which can be represented as attempt
to deduce or provide an object corresponding to the idea of pur

reason, though such examination is really quite unnecessary in view of the preceding proofs that all attempts to provide objects for such ideas are void *ab initio* owing to the restriction of our knowledge to the sphere of phenomena. Kant, however, aware that he had something important, though not very original, to say in respect of these proofs, decided to include this in the *Critique* in spite of the fact that he had already shown all discussion of such proofs to be superfluous.

RATIONALIST PROOFS OF THE EXISTENCE OF GOD

(B 620–70)

The Ontological Proof

The ontological argument is too well known to require stating in any detail. With unimportant variations in different writers it depends ultimately on the proposition that in the case of God only it is legitimate for us to argue from our possession of a concept to the existence of an object corresponding to that concept. For God is conceived in Cartesian terminology as the absolutely perfect being, and by Kant, following Leibniz and Wolff, as combining in himself all positive predicates. In either case it may be argued that as such he possesses existence as part of his essence and that therefore he exists of necessity. Kant's refutation is as follows:

The nerve of the ontological argument is its contention that existence, in so far as it belongs necessarily to the concept of God's essence, cannot be denied of him without a violation of the principle of contradiction. To deny it would be as illogical as to deny that a triangle has three angles or that body is extended. This was certainly a plausible view, but it failed to take note of a vital distinction between the two cases. Certainly it must be admitted that it belongs to the essence of a triangle to have three angles and of body to be extended, and therefore these predicates cannot be denied of them without contradiction; but equally clearly it is possible for me to deny the existence of any object corresponding to the concept under consideration, and if I do this, I annihilate at the same time the reality of that concept's implications. If 'triangle' and 'body' are empty, then analytical propositions derived from them are likewise empty. This amounts to a denial of what is assumed in the ontological argument, namely, that existence can be called a predicate or form part of my concept of something in the same way that extension does. This assumption alone justifies the view that denial of existence which is logically possible in respect of bodies and triangles is impossible without contradiction in the case of God. But Kant does deny, as on the Critical hypothesis he is bound to do, that existence can conceivably form part of my concept of anything; for he is committed to the view that for us at least existence or actuality has no determinate meaning except in relation to possible experience, that is ultimately to sense perception. Hence to assert of anything that it exists is for him to formulate a synthetic proposition. To establish this view more firmly, though it has already been proved in the *Postulates* and tacitly assumed throughout the *Dialectic,* he points out that existence cannot be regarded as a predicate since it adds no new determination to any concept. There is no difference whatever as far as predicates are concerned between a hundred real thalers and a hundred imagined thalers, and to suggest that there is implies merely that the concept is imperfect. The 'reality' of the real thalers lies in their synthetic connexion with actual or possible experience, not with anything which can be discovered by analysis of concepts.

Thus if the existence of God is to be proved at all, it must be shown to be a condition of possible experience, that is as synthetically connected with our actual perception of phenomena. It can never be demonstrated by pure reason alone.

The Cosmological Proof

The cosmological proof is the scholastic offspring of Aristotle's demonstration of the existence of a necessary first cause, and is otherwise known as the proof *a contingentia mundi*. It argues from the conditioned and therefore contingent character of all observed phenomena to the existence of an absolute or uncaused cause, and is not distinguishable from the argument contained in the thesis of the *Fourth Antinomy*.

It has a prima facie advantage over the ontological proof in that it takes its start from an admitted fact, namely the contingency of the given, but Kant finds no difficulty in demonstrating that this advantage is superficial. His refutation is an application of what he holds that the section on the *Antinomies* has already demonstrated, namely that the concept of a first cause as itself a term in the phenomenal series is not required by and is even inconsistent with the demands of the understanding; whereas the postulation of it as outside the series is the postulation of the existence of a determinate thing in itself. But the thing in itself cannot be known, since it cannot be given in sense perception, and therefore its existence can never be demonstrated synthetically. Hence the demonstration of the existence of a transcendent first cause can be achieved only by pure reason, that is by falling back on the ontological argument which has already been discredited.

The Physico-Theological Proof

This demonstration, which is better known as the teleological proof, had always made a great appeal to Kant and he treats it with far more respect than he does the ontological and cosmological arguments. It is actually the common argument from design, and maintains that the observed fact of orderliness and purpose in nature proves the existence of a divine artificer. But although Kant regards it as persuasive and practically valuable, since it appeals to the plain man to an enormously greater extent than the scholastic arguments already disposed of, he has no difficulty in showing that as a demonstration it suffers from exactly the same defect as they do. For even if it is allowed that observation of the wonders of nature tends to generate in me the concept of an omnipotent architect of the universe, it is still necessary to show that this concept has an object; and this I cannot do without surreptitiously introducing the discredited ontological argument from concept to existence. I can never demonstrate that the order and apparent purposiveness of nature could not be the result of ordinary causal laws, or alternatively that they do not represent noumenal agencies which are unknown to me and which cannot be identified with my concept of an omnipotent deity.

In conclusion Kant again points out that this refutation of the ambitious claim of dogmatic theology to demonstrate the existence of its object has no tendency when properly considered to upset man's faith in the existence of God. On the contrary, the Critical Philosophy renders such belief obligatory on moral grounds, though it must be admitted that speculative proof is out of the question. The function of our idea of God as an object of speculative inquiry is to be regarded like that of freedom as regulative and not constitutive in character, and we are thus led to consider more carefully in the following sections the character of this regulative employment.

REGULATIVE EMPLOYMENT OF THE IDEAS (B 670–732)

SUMMARY

§ 1

To complete the *Dialectic* it is necessary to develop further what has already been said of the legitimate or regulative employment of the ideas. That such employment is possible can hardly be doubted when we consider that they arise in us from the very nature of our capacity to reason and therefore it would be intolerable to suppose that they are necessarily empty and misleading.

We must first remember that reason is not, as concepts are, related directly to objects, but that its function is rather to order those concepts themselves and connect them by its inferential process with one another. By so doing it introduces unity into a manifold not of things but of concepts, and its final objective may be regarded as the complete unification of the processes of the understanding. The unity at which reason aims, however, differs in a vital respect from that which is effected by the understanding. The latter is an immanent unity brought about in our experience, whereas the former is ideal and transcends experience. It is rather to be conceived as an imaginary point on which actual lines of investigation converge but which they never reach,[16] and the fallacies which have been considered in the *Dialectic* are then due to the mistaken assumption that the convergence is completed. Reason indeed aims always at complete systematization; it seeks to make explicit the interrelation of parts in conformity with a single principle, and thus presupposes the ideal form of a completed whole of knowledge which precedes a determinate knowledge of the parts. It demands that knowledge gained by the understanding should be perfectly unified so as to constitute a system, not a mere aggregate of propositions. On the other hand, this systematic unity must never be conceived as given prior to detailed knowledge of the parts which constitute it, but simply as a project to be carried out or a

[16] Described as a *focus imaginarius*. B 672.

problem to be solved. Thus it is proper for empirical investigation in the light of reason to aim at the conclusion that all mental processes are ultimately to be regarded as manifestations of a single fundamental power, e.g. the *vis representativa* of Baumgarten, but it is fallacious to posit such a power as actually existing. It is to be treated as the aim of our empirical inquiry, not as a datum for use in that inquiry. It must not, however, be supposed that such ideas when conceived as regulative are mere luxuries from the point of view of empirical investigation. On the contrary, they are essential to the effective employment of the understanding. For if we consider the three fundamental heuristic maxims formulated by logic for the direction of empirical research, we find that each of them postulates something about the phenomenal world, and that such postulation, while required for the proper functioning of the understanding, is necessarily ideal since transcendent in character.

The first of these principles is that of the reduction of genera in the direction of ultimate unity (*entia praeter necessitatem non esse multiplicanda*). This maxim sets before us as a goal the continued search for unity underlying diversity, and forbids us to stop before complete unification is achieved. Obviously such complete unification is not something given, but is conceived as purely ideal. But even to aim at it presupposes an essential homogeneity in apparently disparate phenomena, and, apart from such presupposition, the understanding could not come into operation at all, since the formation of concepts takes for granted the legitimacy of the search for unity in diversity.

The second principle is the converse of the first, namely that of the multiplication of species (*entium varietates non temere esse minuendas*). The implication of this maxim is that there can be no limit to the search for variety in nature any more than to that for unity. Here again it is clear on the one hand that no empirical grounds can be given for the postulation of variety which transcends all possible experience, and on the other that the existence of such variety is as essential for the formation of empirical concepts and therefore for the employment of the understanding as is the unity postulated by the first principle.

The third principle which completes and depends on the other two is that of continuity (*non datur vacuum formarum*). This asserts the affinity of all concepts, by forbidding us to admit that there are species or sub-species which reason can admit to be as close as possible to one another, and requiring us always to prosecute the search for further intervening forms. Such a presupposition must like the others be regarded as purely ideal, since species in nature are really discrete from one another so that there can be no actual infinity of species intervening between any two of them.

Thus these ideas have genuine objective validity as heuristic principles, but we should nevertheless be mistaken in attributing to them the same kind of validity as the categories of the understanding, since the transcendent nature of their objects makes any strict deduction of them wholly impracticable. They refer to unities beyond all experience, to which our systematization is necessarily asymptotic. The unification required by the pure ideas is different from that brought about by the pure concepts in that no intuitional schema for the systematic unity of all concepts of the understanding can be given. All that we possess here is what might be called the analogon of a schema, namely, the notion of a maximum expressed by the ideas themselves. In this sense an idea of reason may be regarded as comparable with the sensuous schema; but it must be clearly recognized that the application of the concepts of the understanding to the schemata of reason yields no knowledge of objects, as does the application of the categories to their sensuous schemata, but simply provides us with rules for the direction of the understanding with a view to the maximization of systematic unity. Hence it relates to the object of experience only in an indirect manner, since it determines nothing in that object but shows the way in which the procedure of the understanding, which does determine something in the object, can be made completely coherent. Furthermore, the rules or maxims which reason gives to understanding, just because they do not determine objects, cannot conceivably conflict with one another. If we were to assert at the same time the actual existence of complete unity and infinite diversity in the real world, such conflict would be inevitable, but the maxim that we must never cease looking for such unity and diversity among phenomena involves no contradiction whatever and is indispensable to the advance of scientific knowledge.

We must now consider the application of this discussion to the three ideas of pure reason, the self, the world, and God. Although no deduction of these in the strict sense can be contemplated, we should be able to show that they are at least genuine ideas in that they do really contribute to the unification of our conceptual knowledge of phenomena. We thus regard them not as objects absolutely but as objects in the idea, that is as schemata for which not even an hypothetical object can be directly given. As a result of the argument which has preceded, it is clear that we must regard them as heuristic, not constitutive notions. They are to be regarded as analoga of real things or schemata of the regulative principle of the systematic unity of all knowledge of nature. In spite of this limitation, however, we may hypostatize at least the ideas of the self and God without error provided we realize that in so doing we have not extended our conceptual knowledge to the super-sensible. In each case we assume the existence of something which we do not know in itself at all, but to which as a ground of systematic unity we ascribe properties analogous to those required by the understanding in the empirical sphere. We may then legitimately represent phenomenal connexions as the ordinances of a supreme reason of which our own is merely a faint copy. By so doing we only think of our relation to a being itself completely unknown to us and employ that thought as the schema of a regulative principle. Indeed, reason cannot think of the systematic unity which is its goal except by giving an object to the idea of such unity, though it must leave quite undetermined the character of this transcendent object which our concepts cannot grasp. This must be conceived simply as the point of view from which that unity which is so necessary to reason and so advantageous to understanding can best be extended.

§ 2

The notion of reason as regulative requires us to proceed in our empirical inquiries *as if* the ideas of pure reason were actually realized in experience.

In respect of the self this means that reason must substitute for the psychological notion of what the soul actually is, which is of no use to ethics, the rational notion of the unity which underlies the whole consciousness of the individual, and, by thinking this unity as unconditioned or original, form from it the idea of reason which is that of a simple substance immutable in itself and standing in relation to other real things independent of it. In respect of the world reason must maintain that in the explanation of phenomena we must consider the series to which understanding gives rise *as if* they were themselves infinite, that is, it must assume the possibility in every case of a progress or regress *in indefinitum*. But when, on the other hand, reason is regarded, as in ethics, as a determining cause, we must proceed *as if* we were dealing with an object not of sense but of pure understanding. Finally, as regards God, we must treat the connexions discoverable among phenomena *as if* they had as their source a single intelligent being as their supreme and all-sufficient cause. We thus regard phenomena as connected in a purposive whole and ourselves as bound to look for connexions among them which reflect this purposiveness; we are actually enjoined by reason to do so, though only as a supplement to, not as a substitute for mechanical causes, and we can never fare worse than by discovering a pure mechanical nexus where we had hoped, in addition, to find a teleological one. To sum up, we may say that the whole function of reason is to perfect the use of the understanding by arming it against two errors to which it is essentially liable and which may be named respectively the faults of *ignava ratio* and *perversa ratio*. The first consists in the liability of the understanding to regard its analysis of experience as complete at some point and to resent the demand for further inquiry; the second is the error of false hypostatization which leads us to treat the hypostatized ideas of reason as premisses for arguments about phenomena instead of notions to assist us in our empirical investigation of them.

Natural science must pursue its investigations into nature in the light of natural necessity alone. It may entertain the idea of an intelligent originator of the universe, but never with a view to deducing from that idea the purposiveness in nature which it must seek to discover; and whether it discovers such purposiveness or not, the notion remains as an ideal which is both valid and necessary in its regulative employment.

THE REGULATIVE EMPLOYMENT OF THE IDEAS OF PURE REASON

COMMENT

§ 1

The constructive doctrine of the *Dialectic* is of fundamental importance to the Critical Philosophy. It contains a preliminary discussion of the doctrine which Kant later developed in *K.U.*, and is in several respects more important than the *Analytic*, despite the more intricate reasoning of the latter; but, partly because it is awkwardly placed and inconspicuous, it has seldom been given the prominence which it deserves. It has, in addition, been the subject of some misunderstanding, particularly as regards its terminology.

Much of this misunderstanding arises from the distinction which Kant draws in the *Critique* between reason and understanding. The fact that he describes both as 'faculties' is largely responsible, since it has led many of his interpreters to suppose that what he has in mind are two specifically different kinds of mental activity. This would give rise to insoluble problems, since if it were the case we should have to inquire whether, since what Kant calls the understanding is obviously concerned with what we commonly call thinking, reason is occupied with (*a*) a special kind of thinking, or (*b*) some mental activity which is not thinking. Inquiries of this nature are, however, pure waste of time, and the problem they are intended to solve is imaginary, since the distinction between reason and understanding is in the first instance one of architectonic and nothing else. Kant is writing a transcendental logic whose main divisions are laid down for him in advance by those of the general logic which they are required to amplify. General logic distinguishes between concepts, judgements, and reasonings considered as connexions of judgements, therefore transcendental logic must do the same. On the face of it the distinction here is purely formal. No one supposes that the logical activities of judging and reasoning are to be ascribed to different 'faculties' in the sense in which seeing and hearing are different faculties. They are distinguishable activities of a single faculty, thinking or *Vernunft* in the widest sense. It is from this starting-point that Kant's differentiation should be approached, and it is certain that he did regard the distinction between the kinds of thinking activity treated in the *Analytic* and in the *Dialectic* as being of great importance. The distinction, however, as in the case of transcendental and general logic, is emphatically not between one kind of thinking and another, but between one kind of object of thought and another. More precisely, the object of the reason, as distinct from the understanding, is the activity of thought itself. It is essentially reflexive in character.[17]

Against this it might be maintained that transcendental logic as such is reflexive in character, and that therefore this is no genuine differentiation between understanding and reason. Up to a point this contention is correct, since the *Analytic* is already dealing 'not so much with objects as with my thought about them in so far as this is possible *a priori*', indeed, this is simply the definition of transcendental philosophy. It is better, therefore, to say that the function of reason as treated in the *Dialectic* is doubly reflexive, it is thought concerning itself with its own limitations as expounded in the *Analytic*. More accurately it is thought about the efforts of thought to transcend those limitations of its own activity which it has already discovered. In the *Analytic* we have considered, by means of thought, the claim of thought to know phenomena. In the *Dialectic* we consider its claim to transcend phenomena. The object of the reason is thus the understanding.

At this stage it is as well to recall the character of the limitation which the *Analytic* disclosed. It was there maintained that we can obtain *a priori* knowledge of connexions between real existences if and only if those real existences appear to us under the sensuous forms of space and time. It was also suggested, though this point is not properly brought out till we reach the *Dialectic*, that even in our empirical or scientific investigations as to the ultimate nature of material things and conscious minds we aim quite inevitably at transcending the limitation implied by this condition of our knowledge. Indeed, it is only the belief that investigations of this character do somehow bring us nearer to understanding the self and the material universe as they are in their own right, without any reference to the conditions of their being apprehended, which seems to give anything more

[17] B 709.

than a practical or pragmatic importance to them. Inasmuch then as critical reflection on the activity of the understanding in its scientific use leads us to doubt the validity of these ideas of an absolute self and a real world, though as far as Kant himself was concerned, this doubt was purely academic, we must inquire further into the origin and true function of such ideas.

With Kant's account of the origin of the *Ideas of Reason* we have dealt already. It is not very satisfactory and was to some extent dictated by his view of the necessary completeness of the classifications of formal logic. It may save trouble to point out at once that he does not in fact adhere to his statement that the only ideas of reason are God, the self, and the universe as a whole. Indeed, as he goes on (especially in *K.U.*), it becomes obvious that what he really understands by 'idea' is the concept of any kind of organic whole as contrasted with a mere aggregate or mechanism. This concept is in no way inconsistent with his official doctrine, since God, the self, and the universe are obvious instances of what he has in mind. But his method of deriving the ideas from the three types of syllogism is not the best way of making his view clear. Nor is it quite safe to say without qualification that the object of an idea is always an organism since he held that the idea of space (since it was a whole the concept of which preceded that of its parts) was an idea of pure reason. All that can be said without misrepresentation is that the concept of an organic whole is often helpful in elucidating his account of the function of the ideas.

This leads to a further consideration of the distinction between the constitutive and the purely regulative employment of such ideas. The employment of such a notion as a fact from which inferences can be drawn as to the actual nature of phenomena is illegitimate and fallacious; this is the constitutive employment of the idea. As contrasted with it the employment of the same idea as a guide to our investigation of phenomena on strictly empirical lines is both fruitful and necessary if we are to avoid a complete relativism in which no sequence of phenomena is more interesting or important than any other.[18]

An instance (not his own) of what he has in mind may further elucidate his meaning. Take the conception of the political State as an organic unity which precedes and alone makes possible the

[18] The idea provides a *focus imaginarius* for our empirical investigations.

conception of its members. In its abstract form this is just a pure idea. It is what Kant himself regards as the idea of a kingdom of ends, and is a purely intellectual conception, which does not admit of any deduction in the sense in which the concepts of the understanding were found to admit of one. It cannot be maintained (at least Kant thinks it cannot) that our existence as self-conscious beings is inexplicable except on the admission that such an idea is in fact actualized in our spatio-temporal experience.

Suppose, now, that in spite of this absence of deduction we assume that this idea is actualized in experience and that some particular state or community is an instance of it. If we do this we are naturally entitled to draw inferences from it as a fact, and maintain, for instance, that the individual can have no rights against the State because his relation to it is admittedly of a certain kind, e.g. that of mode to substance or member to body. To do this is simply to commit the fallacy of false hypostatization which Kant regards as the perpetual tendency of human reason unless checked by criticism, and he would certainly have regarded conclusions reached in this way as a particularly pernicious result of muddled thinking. It is peculiarly the perquisite of the less reputable followers of Hegel. The view with which it must be contrasted is that of Rousseau (in his better moments), namely, that the aim of political philosophy is to discover a form of association in which both the organic unity of the whole and the reality of the individual are preserved. Admittedly Rousseau does not always hold this but transforms his 'general will', which can be discovered by analysis of the idea, into an actual entity or real existent located in a general assembly, a piece of confusion which has given rise to a good deal of disastrous theorizing by his successors. But at least he had the merit of recognizing in principle that the organic state was a problem to be solved, not a fact to be discovered by simple inspection of any existing institution. The contrast between the two methods is simply this. The first treats the realization of the idea in the phenomenal world as a fact and proceeds to explain that world on the assumption that it is a fact. The second regards it simply as a guide to empirical investigation, not necessarily as an ideal or goal to be aimed at in the moral sense, though in certain cases it may be this also. The situation is rather that, in so far as we have an idea of a whole or unity of this kind, it is perfectly legitimate to examine existing institutions with a view to discovering elements in them which are consistent with it, or *as if* they conformed to our idea. But the maximum result which we can hope to achieve by this procedure is to confirm our belief that the idea is not a mere fiction. We can never by this or by any other means pass from belief to strictly scientific knowledge since this is barred by the *Analytic*. No possible deduction could give the kind of certainty we require.

It may well be argued that so far the procedure suggested by Kant, though perhaps legitimate enough, is of very little use to political theory. I am inclined to agree that this is so, but should draw from it the conclusion not that the method is valueless but that no existing political institution is sufficiently far removed from being a mere aggregate to give it much chance of success. A better example from this point of view is provided if we turn for a moment to the studies which deal with entities of a more promising character from the organic point of view, namely, the biological sciences. Here the difficulty under modern conditions is rather to see the other case, and to find instances of the abuse of the idea of pure reason which political theory so adequately provides. An instance of such an argument, though it is improbable that it has ever been used in quite such a crude form, would be something of this kind. The human, or any other, body is an organism, that is, it is a totality or whole whose notion is antecedent to that of its parts. Hence *x*, which is an organ in the body, must have a function relative to that body. The only function which it could perform, so far as we can see, is A. Therefore the *ratio essendi* of *x*, the ground of its being there at all, is the performance of A. Possibly if Leibniz had been quite consistent as to the organic and 'windowless' character of the monad he would have been forced to accept this as a valid scientific method. The point to be noted is that it is always possible, even if nobody does it, to regard a special kind of totality as being actualized in experience and then to maintain that, *qua* actual, it literally determines the 'parts' or phenomena in which it is so actualized.

It is rather in respect of the regulative use of the idea that biological science is helpful, since here it may be argued that

(1) we do not and cannot know that anything is an organism as defined by the idea;

(2) we suspect that some things, e.g. living bodies, are at least to some extent embodiments of the idea, and possess a kind of unity which is not that of a simple aggregate or mechanical construction;

(3) in view of this suspicion we are at liberty and indeed are bound to seek such mechanical sequences as are consistent with an organic or teleological interpretation of the phenomenon under investigation.

What is being looked for throughout, and all that can be looked for, is mechanical sequences of phenomena, but the clue in looking for them must be provided by the conception of a teleological nexus, even though the actual existence of such a nexus can in no circumstances be demonstrated.

§ 2

This necessarily raises the further problem, whether such a nexus is strictly possible, let alone actual, if the results of the *Analytic* are to hold good. What Kant is aiming at appears to be, and in fact is, the reconciliation of mechanism with final causes, whereas the two notions are, on the face of it, incompatible with one another. Here again his solution drives him back on his conception of the thing in itself as the ground of the appearances which our faculties enable us to know.

Both the problem[19] and his solution of it are expounded in *K.U.*, and as might be expected, Kant formulates it as a logical antinomy. *Thesis*: All production of material things is possible in accordance with merely mechanical laws. *Antithesis*: Some production of material things is not possible according to merely mechanical laws.

At first sight it would seem that one of these propositions at least must be false. This, however, is the case only if we seek to regard them as true of things in themselves. But, says Kant, we have no warrant for doing this. If, on the contrary, we regard them simply as indicative of regulative maxims for our investigation of phenomena, there is no conflict or contradiction between them.

For if I say, I must *judge* according to merely mechanical laws, of the possibility of all events in material nature, and consequently of all

[19] § 70, Bernard trans., pp. 294 ff. Ak. v. 386.

forms regarded as its products, I do not therefore say: they are *possible* in this way alone (apart from any other kind of causality). All that is implied is: I *must* always reflect on them according to the principle of the mere mechanism of nature, and consequently investigate this as far as I can: because unless this lies at the basis of investigation, there can be no proper knowledge of nature at all. But this does not prevent us, if occasion offers, from following out the second maxim in the case of certain natural forms—in order to reflect on them according to the principle of final causes, which is quite a different thing from explaining them according to the mechanism of nature. Reflection in accordance with the first maxim is thus not abrogated. On the contrary we are told to follow it as far as we can. Nor is it said that these forms would not be possible in accordance with the mechanism of nature. It only asserts that Human Reason in following up this [teleological] maxim . . . could never find the least ground for that which constitutes the specific nature of a natural purpose. . . .

Thus it is left undecided whether or not in the unknown inner ground of nature mechanical and purposive unity may belong to the same things in a single principle: we say only that our reason is not competent so to unite them. . . .

Kant goes on to develop this view further and points out that we clearly cannot prove the impossibility of the production of organized wholes by purely mechanical processes since 'we cannot see into the first inner ground of the infinite multiplicity of the particular laws of nature which are contingent for us since they are only empirically known'; and continues with a remark, which recalls the view of Locke,[20] that

Whether the productive faculty of nature is sufficient for that which we judge to be formed in accordance with the idea of purpose or whether there lies at the basis of things which we must judge as natural purposes a quite different kind of original causality which cannot be contained in material nature or the understanding—this is a question which our reason, very narrowly limited in respect of the concept of causality if it is to be specified *a priori* can give no answer whatever.[21]

We can never rule out mechanism as a possible sufficient ground for apparently teleological phenomena because we cannot prove *a priori* that the latter cannot be mechanically produced. But equally we are not entitled to assert mechanism as the

[20] On sensitive knowledge see Locke, *Essay*, bk. iv, chap. 3, § 26.
[21] Ak. v. 388.

only explanation since our ground for doing so would be simply that it is the only kind of causal nexus that we can understand *a priori*.

Thus Kant does not abandon or qualify in any way the contention of the *Aesthetic* and *Analytic* that objects of experience *qua* spatio-temporal must admit of indefinite analysis in terms of efficient or mechanical causality. That doctrine is and remains absolutely central to the Critical system and establishes the limit of *a priori* cognition. But he asserts in addition that investigations of this kind will never really satisfy us. It is absolutely certain *a priori* that even if organic nature is generated mechanically, and he agrees that we can never prove that it is not, we can never understand the method of this generation. This is really obvious, though frequently forgotten by primitive mechanists. Hence his suggestion, which depends on faith and not knowledge, is that the real, intelligible, or noumenal character of things is through and through organic and that these things appearing under the forms of space and time preserve discoverable traces of their organic nature. But this organic nature is in no sense constitutive of their essence as phenomena, though, if the Critical view is accepted, it is definitely more than a vague intimation of a noumenal character. It provides, in fact, an indispensable indication of the lines along which investigation of mechanical causes must proceed if it is to have any hope of providing a systematic account of the physical world. There can be little doubt that Kant's belief in analogy to some extent determined his doctrine of teleology and also that of beauty as *Zweckmäßigkeit ohne Zweck* which precedes it in *K.U.* The statue is not itself purposive or organic, but derives its form from the fact that the original is organic. Similarly we cannot prove that mechanical forces are inadequate to produce a statue or that sufficient monkeys armed with typewriters would not ultimately produce *Hamlet*, but if we take the statue and *Hamlet* as finished products it is quite legitimate to hold that in some way, which admittedly cannot be understood, non-mechanical forces are involved in their production. But we must not treat the two kinds of cause as being on the same level and suggest that either can interfere with the other.

The relation of reality to appearance is therefore that of archetype to ectype. But the archetype, or thing in abstraction from the conditions of sensibility, is the necessarily unattainable goal of empirical investigation. We can think organic connexion *in abstracto*, but we cannot reconcile our thought of it with the conditions of sensibility, simply because the idea of an organism is *ex hypothesi* the idea of a totality, and the idea of a totality cannot be fully realized in space-time. This is Kant's final answer to the question 'How is metaphysics possible as a science?' The remaining sections of the *Critique* add nothing to it, though they clarify his position on some points.

VI

THE DISCIPLINE AND CANON OF PURE REASON

DISCIPLINE OF PURE REASON (B 735–822)

EVEN the architectonic justification for the inclusion of this chapter is rather weak. Ordinary logic, as expounded for instance by Meier, always contains a section on the practical employment of logic, and therefore transcendental logic must have something to correspond to this. All that can be offered, however, is a summary of the use and abuse of reason which in fact is exactly what the *Critique* as a whole has provided. Consequently it is not surprising to find that the 'discipline' is simply a brief recapitulation of the principal Critical doctrines. The subsections into which it is divided should be read in connexion with the parts of the *Critique* to which they refer and which they do to some extent elucidate. Easily the most important is the first (the *Discipline of Pure Reason in its Dogmatic Employment*, B 741–66), which is a really excellent summary of the Kantian doctrine as to the peculiar nature of mathematical truth. It adds nothing indeed to what is contained in the *Preface* and *Introduction*, but it is the nearest approach in the *Critique* to a clear account of the 'schematic' character of the figures by means of which the geometer is held to 'construct his concepts in pure intuition'. It also offers an interesting contrast between the meanings of the terms definition, axiom, and demonstration in mathematics and natural science. As it was presumably one of the earlier parts of the *Critique* to be written, it possesses some historical interest as a link between the view of the *Analytic* and that of the *Essay on the Fundamental Principles of Mathematics as contrasted with those of Morality and Religion.*

The remaining subsections do no more than re-emphasize the doctrine of the *Dialectic* by insisting that the limitation of reason to the sphere of experience is a two-edged weapon since, though it prevents us from hoping for any extension of our own knowledge to the super-sensible, it gives us complete confidence that no materialist efforts to prove the non-existence of God, freedom, and immortality have the slightest chance of success. The *Discipline of Pure Reason in respect to its Hypotheses*[1] develops slightly the conception of the regulative employment of reason by insisting that hypotheses for the explanation of phenomena are illegitimate if they involve the postulation of noumena as actual agents in the physical world. Such postulation may be used only controversially to confute equally empty noumenal assumptions by an opponent.

CANON OF PURE REASON (B 822–58)

It may seem that in restricting pure reason to merely regulative use we have unduly limited its powers. This would be the case if our reason admitted of nothing but speculative employment, but this is far from being so. On the contrary it is in the sphere of moral action that reason comes into its own and justifies us in asserting on moral grounds the existence of God and the immortality of the soul which, as the *Dialectic* has shown, could never be regarded as more than probable from the point of view of pure speculation. For if we accept as valid the notion of duty or obligation, we find that it implies the notion of desert. That is to say, we know that a person who does his duty deserves to be happy. It is evident, however, that in the phenomenal world the results of his actions are determined by purely natural causes and that there is no synthetic connexion between moral action and consequences beneficial to the agent. Now the demand of reason that the universe as a whole should be conceived as a rational totality forbids us to accept the notion that duty and interest ultimately conflict with one another, though even in such a case our duty would be unaffected, and we are therefore entitled to posit the existence of God and the immortality of the soul in order to produce a moral theory which reason can accept. These assumptions, however, are based on our conviction of obligation, so that it is quite inadmissible to attempt to base the latter on the former, and we must admit further that our rational belief in God and immortality will be proportionate to the extent to which we accept the existence of obligation as a fact. As against anyone who rejects this fact all that can be argued is that, since as a result

[1] B 798–810.

of the *Dialectic* he cannot rationally refute the existence of God, he would be well advised on prudential grounds to behave as if he accepted it.

The argument of the Canon in fact anticipates completely the position of *G.* and *K.P.V.*, but is too condensed and incomplete to deserve any careful study apart from them.

The sections on *Architectonic* and *History* (B 860–84) are merely footnotes which add nothing to what has been stated or implied elsewhere in the *Critique*.

PART III

INNER SENSE AND TRANSCENDENTAL SYNTHESIS

I

INTRODUCTION TO PART III

MY aim in Part II was mainly to elucidate Kant's general position by linking up what he says with questions which are now generally regarded as philosophically respectable. I hope I have not misrepresented his views, but I have certainly changed his emphasis; indeed I have followed all British and a good many German commentators in substituting for what he regarded as one of the two cardinal problems of the *Critique* a different though closely related difficulty. Kant's question was 'How is pure physics possible?'; I have concentrated on 'What non-empirical assumptions are made in our ordinary talk about the world?', or 'in our normal material object language?'

This method has considerable advantages from the point of view of exposition since it postpones consideration of the highly technical problems in which Kant became involved in his attempt to resolve his own difficulty. It is also the case, as I tried to show in discussing his argument in *Preface B*, that 'How is pure physics possible?' in the sense in which Kant asked himself the question, is not generally regarded as an askable question at all. Hence much of what he has to say in attempting to answer it is inevitably considered to be of historical rather than of philosophical interest. I think this view does less than justice to his contribution to our understanding of the presuppositions both of Newtonian and of modern physical theories, though I agree that, as far as epistemology and scientific methodology are concerned, most of what needs to be said about Kant's general position has already been covered in Part II. What was left out may be summarized as follows.

Kant's avowed aim in the *Analytic* was to prove that the

objects about which true synthetic *a priori* statements can be made are, strictly speaking, objects as they are conceived in Newtonian physical theory. This is manifest when we notice that the categories when schematized give us more or less exactly the characteristics which Newtonian bodies have to possess. Although this was an ambitious aim, it was really no more strange than the attempt to prove in the *Aesthetic* that the conclusions of Euclidean geometry are 'necessarily valid of objects'.

What is really astonishing is that Kant, having set himself a problem of which nobody denies the difficulty though many would assert that it is a pseudo-problem and therefore insoluble, appears to go out of his way to make things harder for himself by accepting at the outset a peculiar psychological theory of inner sense. This appears to be both arbitrary and complicated. It handicaps him throughout in his attempt to show that his *Transcendental Idealism* is a completely different view from those advocated by Descartes and Berkeley; and, to make things worse, he never states explicitly what it is; but it is fairly obviously bound up with his causal or quasi-causal theory of perception, which also is never clearly expounded and was recognized by his earliest critics as raising much more serious problems than Kant himself had recognized.[1]

I shall therefore begin by reconsidering Kant's theory of perception, perhaps one should rather say, his unanalysed assumptions about seeing, hearing, &c., and pass from this to a fairly lengthy examination of the doctrine of inner sense. From this it appears that inner sense, whether we consider it a psychological monstrosity or not, is no mere whim of Kant's but is an essential ingredient in the philosophy of science as he conceived it. Acceptance of it is imposed on him by his basic conviction of the importance of experimental method propounded in *Preface B*.

Turning now to the specific question posed in the *Analytic*, we find that Kant's attempted answer to it is to a great extent dictated by the same psychological assumptions. In the end his fundamental problem is always that of time, the form of inner sense. He must not say 'Time, like space is intuitively recognised as a characteristic of experience', for this would be inconsistent both with his psychological and his metaphysical presupposi-

[1] See above, Kant's Epistemological Embarrassment, I and II in Part II, and Vaihinger, *Kommentar*, ii. 1–123.

tions, since he would then have to admit that immediate awareness of my own existence is at least possible; and this would undermine Transcendental Idealism by again opening the door to the Problematic Idealism which he believed himself to have finally refuted.[2] None the less he needs to maintain that physical objects have a time order of their own, distinct from the time order of my perceptions; for, unless this can be shown to be the case, the Newtonian view which he is underwriting, and in particular, the causal theory of perception, would become, he believes, untenable.

The *Analytic* claims to overcome this difficulty. More precisely, Kant accepts the central theses of contemporary psychologists as sound and then argues that they must be supplemented by specific *a priori* principles if, in his terminology, experience is to be possible. It is not enough to establish a non-empirical background vaguely related to the categories. Hence the argument of the *Deductions,* though necessary, is incomplete. What is still lacking is a set of precisely formulated principles which can be elucidated only by careful analysis of the notion of time itself. This line of thought is developed simultaneously with the more general argument we have already discussed. It is the central theme in the technical case for *Transcendental Idealism.*

From this point of view the *Metaphysical Deduction* prepares the ground by differentiating between general and transcendental logic, which are distinguished not in themselves but in their objects. Transcendental logic has as its subject-matter the pure manifold of space and time. The *Transcendental Deduction* proves that empirical thought processes depend on transcendental operations, and the latter presuppose a transcendental unity of apperception. Thus our ordinary thinking about things presupposes the validity of the categories. The *Transcendental Schematism* explains how the categories are realized in a pure space-time manifold by the activity of transcendental imagination, while the *Principles* enunciate the specific *a priori* synthetic propositions which depend on this embodiment. Throughout all this Kant's guiding thought is that physical things must have and be known to have those properties which are required to establish time as an order in them and not merely an order in my perceptions.

[2] Especially in the *Refutation of Idealism* in B 274–9.

II

PERCEPTION AND PHYSICAL OBJECTS

§ 1

THE distinction between phenomena and noumena, as we have already seen, was first put forward by Kant after a long period of uncertainty to deal with a particular difficulty, namely that of space. He had indeed been previously troubled by problems concerning God and causality, but these were not uppermost in his mind at the time of the composition of the *Dissertation*. But Euclid and Newton could not be kept indefinitely in separate compartments, and he was inevitably led in the years before the publication of the *Critique* to assign substance and causality as well as space and time to the phenomenal realm. Noumena, however, though denuded of their spatial and physical character, still remained as real. They could not do otherwise, since Kant was above all else convinced that, if we once allowed ourselves to treat the universe of space, time, substance, and causality as real without qualification, we must thereby be committed to all the fallacies exposed in the *Antinomies* and confess the incompetence of reason to solve its own problems.

This being the case, there were inescapable difficulties of causal interaction for Kant to solve, and the nature, though not the solution of them, is revealed by even a superficial study of the opening section of the *Aesthetic*. Perhaps in the end they may all be fairly said to resolve themselves into the general question of how the term 'phenomenon' is to be interpreted without doing violence either to the reality of physical objects or to that of non-empirical or noumenal objects.[1] The problem is as follows:

1. Kant held a physiological theory of perception and maintained unequivocally that physical atoms affect our physical sense organs and produce the psychological data of consciousness so far as their matter is concerned. The spatio-temporal form is contributed by our sensibility, but the

[1] See above, p. 125.

empirical sensa of colour, hardness, &c. (the secondary qualities) are generated by physical stimuli.

2. He also held that causation was a relation valid only of objects as spatio-temporal, that is, of phenomena. Hence it seems clear that both the self affected and the objects affecting it (in 1) must be phenomena.

But 3. Phenomena are themselves in the last resort only representations. They seem to have no existence save as the result of a synthetic operation performed by the self on a given manifold of sense.

Hence it would appear that for Kant there must be perception to give material for synthesis before there can be perception caused by synthesized objects. In other words something must happen before it happens, which is certainly rather peculiar.

A suggested solution[2] is that Kant must be supposing a kind of 'double affection' of the self. The account would then run:

(*a*) The non-empirical object 'affects' the non-empirical self. This relation of affecting must itself be conceived as non-empirical, and the employment of any term in ordinary use to describe it is therefore misleading.

(*b*) The non-empirical self performs the synthetic activity which transforms the result of this 'affection' into the complex of empirical self and empirical object.

(*c*) The empirical object *causes* empirical sensa in the empirical self. Thus

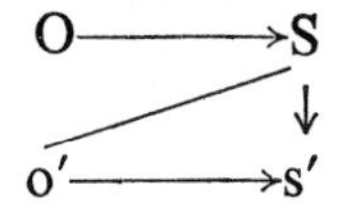

Although this view of Kant's position is clumsy and still seems to involve something happening before it happens, though less blatantly than the account which it claims to supersede, it is not far from being correct.

It can, however, be better stated if Kant's general doctrine of representation and of the distinction between things in themselves and phenomena as one of viewpoint only is borne in mind throughout. 'Representing' is conceived by Kant as the funda-

[2] For a fuller discussion of this problem see Adickes, *Kant's Lehre von der doppelten Affektion unseres Ich*, 1929.

mental intellectual activity of the self. It covers all forms of awareness by the self both of objects and of itself. It takes place at different levels (or from different points of view), and these distinctions are not, as Leibniz had supposed, merely those of relative clearness or confusedness, but distinctions in kind, so that representations are no longer homogeneous; and since reason demands a completely coherent system, we find that (*a*) within each level of representations, (*b*) between the different levels, there must be systematic connexion.

Kant holds that there are actually three levels with which we are concerned, namely (*a*) things in themselves, (*b*) phenomena, (*c*) 'mere representations'; i.e. empirical perception. The manifold of (*c*) is connected by association only. This is shown in the *Analytic* to be made possible only by the causal connexions of (*b*). It is, however, strictly inaccurate to say that the causal interactions of physical bodies (in *b*) cause the modifications of sensa (in *c*). The latter represent the former at a different level and are therefore dependent on them, but the dependence is not to be confused with that of bodies operating on one another. Association is analogous to causality, and the connexion of ideas by association as a whole depends on the causal interaction of physical reality as a whole.

Similarly the causally connected world of phenomena as a whole may be believed to depend on a systematically connected but unknowable world of things in themselves and to be in fact our representation of that world and its relations under the forms of sense and understanding. Indeed 'affection' of the non-empirical self by the non-empirical object and the 'affection' of my empirical sense by the phenomenal object are actually the same event viewed from different standpoints. There is no numerically multiple affection of the self, though the relation of self to objects has to be conceived at different levels.

It would certainly be more satisfactory if levels (*b*) and (*c*) could be made to coalesce into a single whole bound together by complete causal interaction, and many commentators would maintain that this was in fact Kant's view. I believe that in this respect his doctrine is not really complete or consistent since it is fatally handicapped by his failure to provide any really satisfactory analysis of the self. Apart from this his position is at least intelligible. We may sum it up as follows:

1. Physical particles stimulate the nervous system and are somehow responsible for the occurrence of ideas in a vague Lockean sense. This is an empirically established truth discovered by the employment of the experimental method underwritten in the *Principles*.
2. There is a non-empirical but real self which underlies the synthetic unity of apperception and whose 'affection' by similarly non-empirical but real objects is the real basis of the causal relation between physical objects and our sense organs. This is indeed a metaphysical proposition which cannot be proved but which is a legitimate object of belief provided that it makes possible the unification of our general philosophical proposition.

Difficulties begin to multiply as soon as the distinction between space as the form of outer sense and time as the form of inner sense is taken seriously. In the *Dissertation*, and most of the *Aesthetic*, Kant had noticeably failed to do this and, in Part II, I followed him. Now, however, very little consideration is needed to reveal the embarrassments to which the distinction gives rise. Why should the distinction between outer and inner sense be made at all? Why, if it is, should time be connected with the one rather than the other? Prima facie Kant's requirements would be better met by the doctrine that all knowledge requires sensuous as well as intellectual ingredients. The question whether spatial or temporal order or both of them are involved in a particular instance of knowing seems to be a purely empirical one and to raise no special philosophical problems.

It might be possible to restate Kant's philosophy of science along these lines, but the result would be one which he could hardly have accepted. For what he is pledged to maintain in the interests of freedom as well as of scientific knowledge is

(*a*) that the self is less well known than physical objects are (against Descartes);
(*b*) that some truths about physical objects are known *a priori* (against Hume);
(*c*) that the self is a possible object of thought but not of knowledge (against Sceptics and Dogmatists alike).

None of these claims can in his final view be substantiated unless both the distinction between inner and outer sense as well as that between things in themselves and phenomena can be upheld. The doctrine of inner sense is therefore essential to his view if it is to get beyond generalities and detailed consideration of it is essential if he is to be treated seriously.

III

INNER SENSE

§ 1

It is a commonplace to assert that much of Kant's metaphysical thinking was dominated by psychological assumptions whose validity he never questioned and to which much of what we find in his view that is either unattractive or unintelligible may safely be attributed. Up to a point this seems to me to be sound enough. It is undeniable, though somewhat surprising, that Kant accepted much of the empirical psychology of Locke and his successors in Germany, particularly Tetens, as having the same kind of essential rightness as he held to belong to the logic of Aristotle. In neither case did this commit him to a detailed adherence to the views of the master, but his allusion to Locke as the great physiologist of the human understanding[1] is certainly to be taken as seriously as his assertion that logic was in principle completed by Aristotle[2] and has since required no modification except in its details.

It is not, however, easy to discover exactly what his psychological doctrine actually was. That it was Lockean in principle though not in detail is generally held to be the case, but it is precisely that difference which is of vital importance when we attempt to consider the character of his doctrine of inner sense.

It is all very well to say of a crucial passage that 'this, like everything else which Kant wrote about inner sense is profoundly unsatisfactory'[3] and to allude in passing to Tetens's *Philosophische Versuche*, but it is not very helpful. Few readers would deny that a whole section of the *Deduction* in *B* (§ 24) which Kant obviously thought was extremely important to his argument is as it stands completely unintelligible, and this is the section which contains his considered account of what is to be understood by inner sense in relation to apperception.

I shall first explain what I take Kant's psychological position

[1] A iii.

[2] B viii.

[3] Kemp Smith, *Commentary*, p. 148. See also p. 294.

to have been. Although this account is largely non-controversial and capable of being established beyond doubt from his own writings, that part of it which relates to inner sense is necessarily conjectural. The conjecture seems to me, however, at least highly probable in the light of the additions introduced in *B*, which are designed very largely to elucidate difficulties in the doctrine of inner sense which had already given rise to serious criticism.

The first psychological doctrine to which attention has already been drawn is the division of the faculties of the mind into cognition, volition, and feeling. This is never questioned by Kant, though he gives no grounds for maintaining it. It forms the basis of the division of his own lectures on empirical psychology or anthropology, and appears to have been accepted as intuitively certain and in need of no discussion or elaboration, though it has important consequences for his view. All that it gives rise to in the first instance is the division of the Critical Philosophy into the three *Critiques* dealing respectively with these three faculties, and the implied limitation of the first of them to cognition to the exclusion of conation and feeling.

We must next attempt to discover Kant's doctrine of the psychology of cognition from the *Critique* and the *Anthropology*;[4] and for the time being at least, the investigation may be restricted to the sphere of sensibility. This, as has already been observed in other connexions, was for Kant, as for his contemporaries, essentially representative in character. The image in consciousness while not conceived as a literal copy of an independent real was at least analogous to it.

That Kant held a view of this kind is clear from the account which he gives in the *Anthropology* of the psychology of sense perception. Each of the special senses is there dealt with in turn, and it is carefully pointed out that they differ considerably from one another in respect of their representative character. Thus sight,[5] which he here and throughout his work regards as the most 'objective' sense, represents primarily the character of the object and only minimally, except in special cases of bad light or bad eyesight, the character of the nervous system; whereas in taste, which is the most subjective, the situation is reversed. The

[4] *Anthropologie in pragmatischer Hinsicht*. Ak. vii: also *Menschenkunde oder philosophische Anthropologie*.

[5] *Anthr.*, § 16.

other senses fall between these extremes. Kant's view of the nature of the special senses is therefore as follows. The content of consciousness in so far as it consists of data provided by these senses is a representation partly of an object in space outside my body and partly of the receptive apparatus of my body itself.

Now the five special senses, as again he states explicitly[6] in the *Anthropology*, constitute between them the outer sense, and from this the inner sense has somehow to be distinguished. The difficulty which at once presents itself is that the immediate data of consciousness are already exhausted and therefore there is in fact nothing left for inner sense to do. We might at first suppose that, in so far as it is clearly regarded as being cognizant of my own states, it could have as its content the non-cognitive states of the self. It seems plausible to suggest that outer sense makes me aware of tables and pictures whereas inner sense provides my consciousness of toothache or aesthetic satisfaction. But this interpretation is quite un-Kantian and cuts clean across both the division[7] of faculties and the doctrine that sense *qua* cognitive is representative. My toothache and my pleasure are for Kant both 'feelings' which are non-representative and therefore not to be attributed to sensibility. Clearly this was not consistent of him since toothache at least could be as plausibly regarded as representative of my physical body as the taste of wine, but I can find no evidence that he ever considered this point.[8] If, however, we do eliminate all data of the special senses and all volitional and emotional states, the problem of finding any content for inner sense seems insuperable. Yet Kant obviously believes that such a content is provided, and that it is representative of the self in the same way that the outer sense is representative of objects in space. This is certainly a sufficiently hard saying to deserve some elucidation, but it would be unfair to expect such an elucidation except by accident in the *Critique*, since on Kant's view the cataloguing of the faculties of the mind and the explanation of their manner of operating is the province of anthropology and not of transcendental philosophy. Unfortunately, however, the reference to inner sense in the *Anthropology* is as brief and obscure as the account of outer sense is prolonged and detailed. None the less some

[6] Ibid., § 16.

[7] Ibid., § 15.

[8] He distinguishes between *sensus internus* and *sensus interior*, but not in any very satisfactory manner. Ibid., § 15.

valuable information can be extracted from it. Kant asserts[9] (1) that inner sense must be distinguished from pure apperception; the latter is a man's consciousness of himself as active, which belongs to the faculty of thought, whereas the former is his consciousness of himself as passive, that is as being affected by the play of his own thoughts; (2) that this doctrine is not barely anthropological but rather psychological (in Kant's sense), that is, it presupposes that man has a soul; (3) that the soul should really be regarded as the organ of inner sense; (4) that inner sense is subject to illusions inasmuch as the data of purely subjective origin may present themselves to me either as representations of real things or as divine revelations. In such cases there is a disease of the organ, i.e. the soul, comparable to diseases of the organs of outer sense.

At first sight this is not particularly encouraging. In so far as it suggests any meaning at all, it might lead us to suppose that Kant, in despair of finding any other content for inner sense, has made it responsible for the apprehension of illusions or hallucinations. This cannot be the correct interpretation since, whatever precisely the term inner sense may mean, Kant is at least consistent in maintaining that what I apprehend by means of it is my own self. Furthermore, it is his invariable practice both in the *Critique* and the *Anthropology* to regard inner and outer sense as parallel to one another, and, since this is the case, it is as well to attempt an interpretation of the former on the analogy of the latter. Now outer sense is defined as the faculty by which I represent to myself outer objects through the medium of specific organs, eyes, ears, &c. If these organs are diseased or imperfect, the result of such imperfection is a misrepresentation of the object. If the parallel between outer and inner is to be maintained, we should therefore expect that the account of the latter would run as follows. Inner sense is the faculty by which I represent to myself not external objects but my own self, through the medium of a specific organ termed the soul. If this organ is diseased, the result is a misrepresentation of myself.

Now while there is no difficulty in reconciling this form of statement with what Kant actually says, it is far from easy to attribute any positive meaning to the view, and it is at this stage that a certain amount of conjecture is unavoidable. It seems not unreasonable to suppose that he is here taking for granted a con-

[9] *Anthr.*, § 24.

temporary theory without troubling to make explicit what exactly that theory is, and it happens that there is evidence in his correspondence to show us whose theory it was most likely to be. It is safe to say that there were only three of his contemporaries to whose philosophical judgement he attached any great importance, and one of these was the philosophical psychologist Tetens whose chief work[10] appeared shortly before the publication of the *Critique*, and which is distinguished among other things by a curious and novel doctrine of the nature of inner sense.

§ 2

The essence of this view was as follows.[11] It is thoroughly psychophysical in character and takes for granted that the occurrence in consciousness of any representation of outer sense presupposes the occurrence of a physical modification in the cortex as a result of the stimulation of a sense organ by an object. It is, however, by no means behaviourist or epiphenomenalist in character, since the author is equally convinced that the self can originate changes in consciousness and that these are necessarily accompanied by modifications in the cortex. This he holds to be perfectly consistent with either pre-established harmony or *influxus physicus* as an account of the relation between mind and body, and therefore he is not called on to decide between these. His difficulty is to see how, on such a view, the representational character of inner sense is to be explained, though as regards the existence and function of such a sense, he is never in the least uncertain. Its function is to provide immediate awareness of awareness, and its existence is obvious to introspection. Tetens also maintains on introspective grounds that awareness and awareness of awareness are never in fact simultaneous. It is never true to say 'I know that I am thinking' but only 'I know that I have thought', and this is ultimately his ground for maintaining the representative character of inner sense.

The solution is that the mind in the act of thinking modifies its ideas (by abstraction, concentration, &c.). This modification is accompanied by a corresponding modification of the *ideae materiales* in the cortex,[12] and to this physical modification

[10] Tetens, *Philosophische Versuche über die menschliche Natur und ihre Entwicklung*, Leipzig, 1777.

[11] Tetens, op. cit., § 7.

[12] Cf. Ak. ii. 345.

corresponds the event in consciousness which I describe as awareness of awareness and which constitutes the content of my inner sense. To put the matter in a sentence, what I am aware of by means of inner sense is my own past acts of awareness. Tetens himself was prepared to take a similar view of my awareness of volitional and, with reservations, even of emotional experience, but he paid little attention to these.

If we now revert to Kant's statement in the *Anthropology*, it seems possible to attribute a fairly intelligible meaning to it assuming that he had Tetens's doctrine in mind. He would be bound to begin, as in fact he does, by dissociating himself from the view that inner sense provides me with immediate awareness of the mind's activity since that would confuse it with pure apperception and obliterate the sharp distinction which Kant draws between the receptivity of sense and the spontaneity of understanding. None the less, provided this point is made clear, inner sense might still be awareness of awareness, or awareness of a past act of perceiving, since Kant seems to have entirely agreed as to the distinction between any cognitive act and my awareness of its occurrence. Furthermore, such an interpretation is perfectly consistent with his belief in illusions of inner sense, since the illusion, due to disease of the relevant organ, would lie in taking a past event as a perception when it was a hallucination. In such a case there would be a misrepresentation of a state of myself which could reasonably be regarded as parallel to the illusions of outer sense in relation to objects.

The upshot of all this is a psychological theory of perception which is both odd in itself and difficult to harmonize with Kant's theory of knowledge. Nevertheless it does seem to be consistent with what he says both in the *Aesthetic* and the *Analytic*. The view is simply that the content of immediate awareness is (*a*) non-cognitive states with which we are here not concerned; (*b*) intuitions which are representations of objects (including my own body); (*c*) intuitions which are representations of myself as perceiving. These are literally scattered about among my perceptions of things and are entirely separate both from one another and from those perceptions.

If, now, we assume that this was Kant's view, it is not hard to explain his formulation of it in the *Aesthetic* in the light of his contention that space and time are forms of sensibility and not attributes or containers of things in themselves. The doctrine of space in relation to outer sense presents little difficulty and would have presented even less if Kant had been more careful at the outset to distinguish between representations which are objective or independent of the particular perceptual peculiarities of the individual and those which are mainly or wholly dependent on such peculiarities. All he needs to maintain is that representations of outer sense are as such spatial in character. Admittedly illusion and obscurity are possible, so that I am liable to judge falsely if I exercise insufficient care in ascertaining what the data of outer sense really are; I may take a representation of an occurrence in my body for a representation of something at a distance from it, or vice versa. But this seems to present no insuperable obstacle to the doctrine that all data of the five senses are spatial or have space as their form. Equally it seems simple to say that the data of inner sense are essentially temporal, though it soon becomes apparent that grave difficulties are involved in doing so. The argument in favour of such a course is evident. If the data of inner sense are actually awarenesses of past perceptual awarenesses interspersed among such perceptual awarenesses, the only form or order which they possess is that of succession in time, and they must share this order with the acts or passions of perceptions by outer sense among which they occur. Time thus becomes the form of inner sense without qualification, and also the form of outer sense in so far as the latter is looked at from the side of the subject perceiving and not of the content perceived. It is at this point that the real problem emerges, for the inevitable conclusion of such a doctrine is that awareness of succession is always and only awareness of succession of activities of representing, and can never be awareness of succession as inherent in the content represented. To put it differently, the data of the five senses must always have space, not time, as their form. The only temporal element in them is that they occur successively for me.

§ 3

This is certainly a queer and paradoxical view, but Kant was led to adopt it, not by any old-world attachment to a distinction between inner and outer sense or even by the representation view in the special form in which he happened to hold it, but simply because he saw more clearly than many of his successors have done what is really implied by the acceptance of any causal theory of perception.

That he did adopt it is established beyond reasonable doubt by some of the passages added in *B*. I will cite only one of these from the elucidation of the *Aesthetic*. 'Since time', he says, 'does not represent anything save in so far as something is posited in the mind, it can be nothing but the mode in which the mind is affected by its own activity (namely through its positing of its representation) and so is affected by itself; in other words, it is nothing but an inner sense in respect of the form of that sense.'[13]

That he was also conscious of the implication of the view which I have mentioned above is clear from the remark on time which occurs in both editions: 'time is nothing but the form of inner sense, that is, of the intuition of ourselves and of our inner state. It cannot be a determination of outer appearances; it has to do neither with shape nor position, but with the relation of representations in our inner state.'[14]

Kant, then, appears to have been clear as to the difficulty in which his view involved him and to have recognized that by adopting it he was committed to maintaining that succession in time was always of, not in, appearances, so that a central problem for him was bound to be 'How do we come to apprehend objective succession, since it is now *ex hypothesi* impossible do so by means of sense?'

That this awkward situation does not arise because of any prejudice or lack of consideration on Kant's part, but is really inherent in any theory of perception which attaches importance to what are normally regarded as physiological facts, is well illustrated by the discussion on space and time perception in Professor Koffka's book on the *Principles of Gestalt Psychology*.[15] The fundamental hypothesis of this view is very similar to that of Tetens, namely that there is analogy or as the moderns prefer to call it, isomorphism, between events in the cortex and events in consciousness, and this notion is capable of being developed with what, for the layman at least, is considerable plausibility as long as space perception alone is in question. The difficulty arises when an attempt is made to produce a cerebral occurrence which can

[13] B 68. [14] A 33, B 50.

[15] Koffka, op. cit., pp. 438 ff.

make possible any discrimination between a succession of apprehension and an apprehension of succession. It will not do simply to say that successive stimuli give rise to consciousness of succession, for successive stimuli must in any case be called in to explain my continued perception of what is in fact static. Hence Koffka is led to say that, whereas successive stimuli on the same part of the cortex produce succession of consciousness, stimuli on different though neighbouring parts of it produce consciousness of succession. Whether this account is physiologically tenable or not is of no importance here. The question is whether any conceivable physiology could do it any better, and I do not at the moment see that this is possible. For if we posit an organ of sensation, the cortex, which possesses a temporal as well as a spatial order of its own, there is no particular difficulty in supposing that the psychical occurrences which are correlated with it are also temporal in character. But I cannot conceive any mechanism which would automatically differentiate psychical data into representations of succession as distinct from successions of representations. This difficulty can easily be disposed of by those who maintain that physiological difficulties have nothing to do with philosophy, and commentators who wish to set Kant on the road to absolute idealism may find here considerable encouragement. All that is necessary is to drop the notion of things existing independently of the percipient subject, give the self an intellectual intuition of its own operations, and the problem is solved. To do this, however, is not to interpret Kant but to deny out of hand practically everything which he believed to be true. If we take this line we certainly need trouble no more about his problems as to the physical universe since all of them become irrelevant.

§ 4

As an alternative we may consider the manner in which he attempted to supplement his doctrine of sensibility by his conception of thought as a spontaneous synthesizing activity. Before proceeding to this, however, it is as well to notice that his account of perception differs sharply from that of some other empiricists in that it is not atomic, it is cinematographic. His view is not that bare sensibility provides a mere manifold which has somehow to be poured into the moulds of space and time, but that it provides a number of three-dimensional representations, discrete from one another, and related in a temporal series which is the order of their apprehension by the perceiving subject.

We must now consider what I have already mentioned as a crucial passage in relation to Kant's psychology, namely § 24[16] in the *Deduction* in *B*, which is mainly devoted to a difficult discussion of the doctrine of inner sense in relation to apperception. As a preliminary to this it is necessary to emphasize a further Kantian assumption which we should probably regard as psychological in character, though he himself would not have admitted this. The doctrine in question is simply that, whereas in perception the mind apprehends something which happens to it, in thinking it exercises a synthesizing activity which is absolutely spontaneous and therefore in itself non-empirical in nature. This does not imply that there can be thought about thought as such or in itself, for this would involve an intellectual intuition of which we are not possessed. On the contrary, it means that understanding or apperception as distinct from sensibility can never of itself provide a manifold or content either pure or empirical as a content for thought.

The purpose of § 24 is twofold. It aims in the first place at distinguishing between inner sense and apperception and in the second at elucidating what is meant by the contention that inner sense provides me with a mediate or representational acquaintance with myself. These problems are not considered separately, but answers to them emerge, or rather can be disinterred from the general discussion of apperception, imagination, and inner sense. It seems to me that the following is a fair though somewhat condensed account of the position which Kant wishes to defend.

Inner sense and apperception tend to be assimilated (wrongly) by psychological writers. The explanation of this is the difficulty which these writers find in the assertion that we are affected by ourselves in such a way as to provide the representational element essential to sense perception. This difficulty disappears when we consider that apperception is based on the spontaneity of the understanding. This spontaneity consists, not merely in the ordering of the actually presented data of sense in accordance with the categories, but in the activity of the imagination by which those data must be supplemented in order to make possible an experience which is unitary or coherent for thought as distinct from

[16] B 152–6.

mere association. This synthetic activity is not inner sense, but is the reality which affects that sense, just as objects are the reality which affect outer sense; the understanding by its activity affects or determines inner sense, but this determination of inner sense by understanding does not mean, what superficially it might be taken to mean, that inner sense is a something which is determined by the understanding in the sense of being understood by it. On the contrary, affection is used in its ordinary literal sense. At a later stage the data of inner sense like those of outer sense may be 'understood', but that is not yet the question.

The result of inner sense is to impose on the synthesizing activity of the understanding (which in itself is non-sensuous and therefore non-temporal in nature) a temporal form, so that the timeless thinking which is the real self is represented as a series of discrete activities located in time, just as by outer sense the non-extended thing in itself appears as located in space.

The function of the understanding assisted by the productive imagination is then to introduce intelligible order into both these manifolds, and the difficulty with which it is presented is (*a*) that such order can be introduced into the manifold of inner sense only after and not before it has been introduced into that of outer sense; (*b*) that such order can never be introduced into inner sense unless time can first be postulated as a condition of the phenomena of outer sense, as distinguished from timeless things in themselves. Kant's attempt to tackle these problems in the section dealing with the *Schematism* and in the *Principles* throws further light on his position and will be considered in greater detail later. It will, however, be generally conceded that he did regard them as fundamental and spent a great deal of time and energy in trying to solve them. Hence all that I am here concerned to show is that they are the inevitable consequences of the psychological theory which I suggest that he held.

For suppose that by outer sense I am provided with a series of pictures, none of which contains any temporal sequence in itself and each of which vanishes completely on being perceived, and also that by inner sense I am aware simply of acts of synthesis which follow one another but have no content other than the activity of the subject. It is at once evident that the latter do not by themselves present any material on which thought can work so as to produce the conception of an object (in this case the empirical self) of which they can be called representations. 'For all inner perceptions we must derive the determination of lengths of time or of points of time from the changes which are exhibited to us in outward things, and the determinations of inner sense have therefore to be arranged as appearances in time in precisely the same manner as we arrange those of outer sense in space.'[17] We cannot even date these affections of inner sense unless we commence operations by considering the contents of the acts of synthesis by which acts alone the inner sense is affected. Hence the understanding must first project time into the empirical objects of which the data of outer sense are representations. Only after it has done this can it proceed to the further task of constructing an empirical self. If this is a correct account, then the *Schematism* becomes the procedure by which time is postulated by the understanding as a condition not of the representations of outer sense but of the empirical and therefore phenomenal objects to which those data are to be 'referred', that is, of the objects of pure physics, and this incidentally accounts for the fact, to which attention has frequently been drawn, that Kant in the later part of the *Analytic* almost wholly neglects space in favour of time. For if the spatio-temporal objects of my representations (i.e. phenomena) are in fact represented as spatial by outer sense, no special difficulty in respect of space is thereby presented to the understanding. But if they are presented as non-temporal but are none the less known to be really temporal, which physics evidently claims that they are, then some account of how this knowledge can be attained is essential.

Kant is here involved in a difficulty which is not of his own making but which must be faced by any view which pretends to take seriously the investigations of physics and physiology. For physics has no more interest or importance than a peculiarly intricate crossword puzzle unless we maintain, as Kant undoubtedly did, against empirical idealism, that there is a universe of events in space-time which is objectively real in the sense of being independent of any and every percipient mind; and physiology has at any rate a good prima facie case for maintaining that psychical data are determined by occurrences in the physical world. But if we admit the validity of these assumptions, Kant is surely quite correct in holding that our admission is something

[17] B 156.

which requires philosophical examination. The difficulty is that, if the physicist is right, it is *a priori* impossible for the physiologist to invent a mechanism which will enable us to know that he is, and consequently the assumptions of physics, if they are to be justified on grounds other than those of revelation, require to be established or at least rendered intelligible by the concept which itself may perhaps be only an assumption, of a spontaneous synthesizing understanding.

Kant was aware of this difficulty, and the theory of knowledge put forward in the *Critique* is largely an attempt to overcome it. Hence it is natural that the psychological background of the theory should be determined by the peculiar character of the problem and that the comparatively straightforward empiricist view of Tetens should be developed into the intricate doctrine of transcendental apperception and productive imagination. It seems a fair guess, though admittedly nothing more, that something like what follows is what took place in Kant's mind during the development of the Critical view.

'The physical theory of Newton', he might have said, 'is undoubtedly sound, but if we are to establish its *a priori* character, and also that of Euclid's geometry, we must hold that space and time are both forms imposed by the mind and also objective conditions of the realities with which physics has to deal. This leads to the conclusion that those realities are representations, not things in themselves.

'But the physiological theory of perception, whose validity is also unquestioned, assures us that the data of sense are produced by the operation of physical bodies on our nervous system and are therefore representational in character. Now consideration of what we are told of the nature of those processes shows that the data obtained by means of them cannot by themselves be adequate to give us awareness of the truth of what the physicist asserts, since they cannot provide any means of distinguishing between a succession of apprehension and an apprehension of succession. Therefore we cannot say that time as a form of phenomena is capable of being given immediately to sense, as we are able to do in the case of space. Time, therefore, must be regarded as essentially the form not of outer but of inner sense. This being the case, we must, in the interest of Newtonian physics, devise a means whereby time can be projected, not into representations, which remain purely spatial, but into the phenomena which are the objects of representations, and to do this we must introduce the notion of apperception and also that of productive imagination.'

The resulting view is that apprehension of the Newtonian universe, of space, time, substance, and causality is in fact the presupposition or precondition of my awareness of the representations of outer sense as being in a temporal order from which alone the determinate order of the representations of inner sense can be deduced. Empirical self-consciousness presupposes the apprehension of an objective world of phenomena.

§ 5

At this point a reservation must be made. Kant's use of 'inner sense' was developed concurrently with his use of 'synthesis'. In a very early and semi-critical employment, both can be found in the *Dissertation* and in the correspondence with Herz; and the psychological theory of Tetens was adopted by Kant before the publication of *A*. There are, however, plenty of passages both in Kant's other works and in the *Critique* itself in which 'inner sense' is employed in a casual, Lockean, way as equivalent to 'introspection'; it is what enables us to study the operations of our minds, just as our sense organs are what enable us to study what is outside us. This need cause no confusion. It is only in the sections of the *Analytic* which are explicitly concerned with 'How is pure physics possible?' that the relation between 'inner sense' (in the technical use I have just considered) and 'apperception' has to be made and pressed.

IV

TRANSCENDENTAL KNOWLEDGE: THE METAPHYSICAL DEDUCTION

§ 1

'TRANSCENDENTAL' has a long and complicated history going back as far as Plato and Aristotle. The outline of it is clearly set out by Martin[1] and I shall not go into it here. The essential point is that some words (*ens unum, verum,* and *bonum* are those most frequently treated in this connexion) can be used in all the categories without the commission of a category mistake. Hence it was natural enough to suppose that the entities to which these words referred, the *transcendentalia,* enjoyed a very exalted ontological status, and these entities were commonly held to be the subject-matter of transcendental philosophy or metaphysics. Now Kant's achievement, though it was not his original aim, was to show that this linguistic framework was unusable. No answer to his question 'How are synthetic *a priori* propositions . . . ?' could be found along this road; indeed in discussing his own table of categories[2] he speaks in very slighting terms of the traditional *transcendentalia.* All the same he retains 'transcendental' just as he does 'metaphysics' and is by no means careful to say when he is using either of them in the customary and in his own special way. Generally speaking this uncertainty is not confusing, but, as will appear, the phrase 'transcendental object' has led and is still capable of leading to unnecessary obscurity.

Officially Kant gives two definitions of 'transcendental'. In the *Introduction to A,*[3] 'I call all knowledge transcendental which occupies itself not primarily with objects but with our non-empirical concepts of objects in general.' This is revised in *B*[4] to read, 'I call all knowledge transcendental which occupies itself not primarily with objects but with our way of achieving knowledge of objects in so far as this is possible non-empirically.'[5] Taking Kant's references together, we can have no doubt that his

[1] op. cit., §§ 16 and 17.

[2] B 113.

[3] A 11.

[4] B 25.

[5] For further references see Ratke, *Handlexikon, Begriff der transcendentalen Erkenntniss.*

considered use is one which emphasizes his crucial move from 'What is . . . ?' to 'What do we know about . . . without an appeal to empirical evidence?' Now it was not immediately obvious to Kant, and it is certainly not at all obvious to his readers, that this switch, momentous as it turns out to be, has any special relevance to his doctrine that time is the form of inner sense. The difficulty is masked by his method of presentation in the *Aesthetic*, it is more apparent in the *Metaphysical Deduction*, but it becomes crucial only in the *Transcendental Deduction* and the *Analytic of Principles*.

What emerges in the *Aesthetic* is that the parallelism between 'space' and 'time' which Kant takes for granted is a radical error and also that it is one which Kant on his own premisses can hardly avoid; for, in Newtonian mechanics, x, y, z, and t have to occur in the same formulae and to be operated with by ordinary algebraic methods. Hence it is to be expected that space and time, which they symbolize, can properly be conceived as entities of the same type, and Kant originally thought that this was an unexceptionable method of going to work.

Now as far as space is concerned, the notion that it is a form of sensibility, and not a substance, accident, or relation, seems to work quite well and to escape the difficulties to which the doctrines of Newton and Leibniz are exposed. Time, however, as we have already seen, is an unruly member. In the first place, it is at least plausible to say that I can intuit or imagine empty space. After all, I know what it means to talk about a stage with no scenery and no actors on it, and the difference between furnished and unfurnished rooms is not at all mysterious. Empty time is a very different proposition, and although Kant does claim that 'we can quite well think time as void of appearances'[6] he does not stand by this claim. In B 49 he is already in effect admitting that it cannot be substantiated.

> Time is nothing but the form of inner sense, that is, of the intuition of ourselves and of our inner state. It cannot be a determination of outer phenomena; it has to do neither with shape nor position, but with the relation of ideas in our consciousness. And just because this inner intuition yields no shape we endeavour to make up for this want by analogies. We represent the time sequence by a line progressing to infinity etc.

[6] B 46.

Clearly this is very awkward, for we were told on B 40 that 'I understand by a transcendental exposition the explanation of a concept as a principle from which the possibility of other *a priori* synthetic knowledge can be understood.' The concept of space is transcendental because it 'makes geometry possible'. By contrast, though Kant tries to escape this conclusion, the concept of time does not make any science possible. It has to be given and is given entirely different treatment in the *Analytic* when it is taken seriously and construed in the light of the fully developed doctrine of inner sense.

§ 2

Kant shared with his contemporaries the basic assumption that our thinking about physical objects fitted into two logically separate compartments called 'geometry' and 'physics'. It was not doubted that the axioms of Euclid were invulnerable or that the laws of Newton were additional to but logically independent of the Euclidean system. The revolution in physics at the beginning of the twentieth century, generally attributed to Einstein and Planck, consisted to a great extent in the overthrowing of this conviction. As Max Born put it in his Inaugural Lecture in 1936:

> I doubt whether Kant would have maintained this view if he had lived a little longer. The discovery of non-Euclidean geometry . . . shook the *a priori* standpoint. Gauss has frankly expressed his opinion that the axioms of geometry have no superior position as compared with the laws of physics, both being formulations of experience, the former stating the general rules of the mobility of rigid bodies and giving the conditions for measurements in space. Gradually most of the physicists have been converted to the empirical standpoint. I do not think that there is any objection to this form of empiricism. . . . It has not only doubted the *a priori* validity of Euclidean geometry . . . it has even made geometry depend on physical forces, gravitation, and it has revolutionized in the same way nearly all categories *a priori* concerning time, substance and causality.[7]

This is manifestly right. Kant could not have talked like that. All the same it seems to me clear that difficulties in talking about physics sprang largely from his genius in realizing, however, incompletely, that he ought to talk like that. He tries to make a

[7] *Physics in my Generation*, p. 39.

rigid distinction between geometry and physics—and it breaks down. In the *Principles* he admits that it has broken down. His notion of synthesis, which only emerges in the *Metaphysical Deduction*, is stronger than his belief that Euclid can be elucidated without reference to Newton. In the same way, the parallelism of time and space, also a traditional tenet, has to give way to his complicated doctrine of inner sense—and this, too, is basically dependent on the notion of synthesis.

What survives of the original over-simplified doctrines of the *Dissertation*, not merely in the *Aesthetic* but all through his philosophical life, is the doctrine of pure intuition, and this emerges clearly in the *Metaphysical Deduction* and combined with the notion of synthesis, is the foundation of what is strictly his *Transcendental Philosophy*, immanent metaphysics, or philosophy of science.

§ 3

Apart from the section, B 80–82, in which the second-order reflexive character of Transcendental Philosophy in general and Transcendental Logic in particular is emphasized, the opening sections of the *Analytic* are devoted to a general statement of Kant's view of the limitations of formal logic, which is concerned simply with the form of our statements (*Erkenntnisse*) and has nothing to do with the subject-matter to which they refer.

It is only in § 10[8] that the special job of Transcendental Logic is expounded. This section is usually referred to as the *Metaphysical Deduction*. The general drift of it is not particularly obscure and has already been dealt with in Part II; the precise meaning is one of the most difficult to unravel in the *Critique*. To avoid constant references to what has already been maintained, I shall restate what I take to be Kant's general position as regards judgements and synthesis and then attempt to throw some light on the detailed argument of § 10.

The *Metaphysical Deduction* depends on two distinctions of which Kant claims to be the first philosopher to appreciate the importance, namely, that between sense and understanding and that between general and transcendental logic.

The first requires no further explanation. The vital point about

[8] B 102–6.

it is that, whereas sense is receptive, thought is spontaneous; this explains the distinction between the forms of sense and those of thought. A receptive form, such as a mould, can easily be conceived as capable of becoming itself an object of apprehension in abstraction from content; the forms of spontaneity, on the other hand, are bare functions of unity, that is, capacities of imposing unity of a specific kind on a manifold provided from elsewhere. They can be apprehended only as embodied in contents, and contents, except for an intuitive understanding, which ours is not, can be provided only by intuition.

The distinction between general and transcendental logic is more difficult. It certainly does not involve the notion of a special kind of philosophical or speculative thinking on Hegelian lines. Kant admits one set of rules and one only, valid of all thought whatever, namely the standard rules of logic set out in contemporary handbooks and expounded in his own lectures on that subject. There is not the slightest ground for holding that transcendental logic involves the discovery of rules valid for 'synthetic' as distinct from 'analytic' thinking.

It must, however, be remembered that the handbooks[9] contained a good deal more than the formal rules of syllogistic logic. They set out to give instruction as to the precautions to be taken to see that those rules were observed in different branches of inquiry where special difficulties, mainly psychological in character, were to be expected, and issued warnings against the types of fallacy prevalent in arguments concerned with special kinds of subject-matter. This practice gives rise to the bad habit of describing practical rules for the guidance of the understanding in relation to a special subject as the logic of that subject. Now Kant claims to demonstrate in the *Metaphysical Deduction* that our employment of the forms of thought in general implies acquaintance with specific rules of synthesis or ways of combining concepts which he calls 'pure concepts of the understanding'. The discovery of these requires a transcendental investigation or reflexive investigation into the nature of our thinking with which general logic is not at all concerned, and for this reason alone he is prepared to describe the section of the *Critique* which makes this discovery the first section of the *Transcendental Logic*. The remainder of the *Analytic* deals with the employment of these

[9] e.g. Meier. See above, pp. 49 ff.

pure concepts in relation to the pure manifold of space and time in the production of valid synthetic *a priori* propositions. His statement here, as in the *Aesthetic*, is handicapped and rendered unnecessarily obscure by his initial failure to recognize the full implications of the notion of synthesis, especially in relation to inner sense, so that the section which deals with synthesis requires to be supplemented by what is only explained later in the *Critique*. This section is not, indeed, indispensable to a prima-facie understanding of Kant's general purpose, though his full view cannot be comprehended without it.

Kant's argument is as follows:

1. Understanding is the activity of thinking as distinct from perceiving.
2. To think is to enunciate propositions. (Kant held that these were always reducible to the subject-predicate form, but his view does not depend on this assumption.)
3. All propositions can be classified by reference to the kind of relation in which the predicate stands to the subject.
4. This classification reveals the pure concepts.
5. The pure concepts are therefore functions of synthetic unity in propositions. Without their use thought is impossible.
6. Therefore propositions can give knowledge of reality if and only if it can be shown that the pure concepts are the necessary grounds of synthetic unity in reality as well as in propositions.

Kant's practical difficulty is that the sections which develop (5) and (6) are the *Transcendental Deduction* and the *Principles*, yet the point of the *Metaphysical Deduction* remains obscure unless (5) at least is established. He therefore compromises, not very successfully, by inserting the passage on synthesis,[10] whose chief importance lies in the attempt which it makes to reveal the connexion between the synthesizing activity of thought and the pure intuitions of space and time as the basis of pure physics. It already becomes clear that the notion of those pure intuitions as a kind of mould or container of phenomena formulated in the Aesthetic will not do. They are now regarded not as given wholes but as pure manifolds to be organized by the understanding through the pure concepts, and this process is analogous to the activity of

[10] B 102–5.

thought in general in conceptualizing the manifold presented by (empirical) sensibility. Transcendental logic is thus mainly concerned with the possibility of applying the pure concepts to a pure manifold of space and time, general logic with the application of empirical concepts to the empirical manifold of sense. Indeed, all thinking is the introduction of a peculiar kind of unity into a given diversity in accordance with a rule, and all thinking, even that which is concerned with the analysis of concepts, presupposes synthesis.

All synthesis, however, is not thinking. Before concepts can be formed, the imagination (conceived as intermediate between sense and thought) must perform a preliminary synthetic act in the absence of which the prima-facie unity required for the formation of concepts will not be discoverable in the presented manifold at all. If we now concentrate on the kind of synthesis in which transcendental logic is particularly interested, we find an instance of it in counting. Counting has three characteristics:

(*a*) necessity—which precludes any *a posteriori* explanation of it;

(*b*) synthesis—it is a procedure according to a rule;

(*c*) a basis of unity—the character of the rule is determined by a single underlying conception, that of the decad.

The pure concepts are extreme forms of (*c*), and it should be noted that (*a*) depends on (*b*) and (*c*).

The aim of transcendental logic may now be stated:

1. It is concerned with pure, i.e. non-empirical, thought.
2. The object of such thought can be nothing but the pure manifold of space and time.
3. This multiplicity must first be synthesized by imagination.
4. The result of this synthesis must then be further synthesized by understanding by means of the pure concepts.

It is the function of the *Transcendental Deduction* and the *Principles* to develop (3) and (4), and to show that the possibility of empirical thinking depends on the preliminary performance of these two syntheses, whether or not we are actually aware of performing them.

The true relation of the *Aesthetic* to the *Analytic* now remains to be stated. In the former, space and time are conceived as exhibiting a kind of synthetic unity. They are neither mere multiplicity nor complete synthetic unity intellectually apprehended.

They have, in fact, sufficient unity for the purposes of mathematics. Pure physics, however, demands the higher, that is, more abstract level of synthesis contemplated for the first time in the *Metaphysical Deduction* and which the remainder of the *Analytic* is devoted to expounding and justifying in detail. From this point of view the contribution of the *Metaphysical Deduction* is simply to prove that the empirical processes of judging and conceptualizing have transcendental presuppositions, namely the categories as functions of unity in judging and conceiving. So far, however, the relation of categories to objects is not considered and therefore the special problem of the temporal character of phenomena does not arise. The *a priori* structure of thought and intuition has been examined, not that of things.

§ 4

We can now consider § 10, and it should be noted that Kant's title for it is 'Of the pure concepts of the understanding or categories', and the section of the *Critique* in which it is a crucial passage is called the *Analytic of Concepts*, with which the succeeding section, the *Analytic of Principles* is contrasted. I mention these obvious points because a good deal of the apparent mystification of § 10 springs from the fact that Kant assumed in his readers complete familiarity with the standard textbooks on general logic, especially with those of Wolff and Meier. His own lectures were not published in 1782, but Jäsche, with Kant's approval, edited them for publication in 1800.[11] Unfortunately for us, Kant here, as elsewhere in the *Critique*, does not give any indication of the points in his exposition at which he is simply referring to what was then, but is not now, non-controversial common knowledge, and the points at which he is introducing his novel doctrine of the distinction between general and transcendental logic. As regards the former, his logical terminology and his view as to the way in which empirical concepts are formed are set out clearly in Ak. ix. 91–96. He treats the process as one of progressive abstraction, and regards abstraction as one of leaving out more and more of the characteristics in respect of which things differ from one another, not as one of taking out the characteristics in respect of which they resemble one another. Hence the

[11] See Ak. ix. 1–150 and 503–5.

connotation (*Inhalt*) and denotation (*Umfang*) of concepts vary inversely with one another. Sometimes, however, he rather carelessly uses *Inhalt* in a different way as equivalent to *Materie*, and contrasts it with *Form*. This happens mostly in the phrase *Inhalt einer Erkenntniß* which is approximately equivalent to 'what a statement is about'. This ambiguity of *Inhalt* is sometimes confusing, but there is nothing to be done about it but to consider the context. In the same way, in considering § 10 the ambiguity of 'synthesis' and 'synthetic' must be constantly borne in mind.

Kant now proceeds to tell us that, whereas general logic is purely formal,

> transcendental logic has lying before it a manifold of *a priori* sensibility, presented by transcendental aesthetic, as material (*Stoff*) for the concepts of pure understanding. In the absence of this material those concepts would be without any content (*Inhalt*), therefore entirely empty. Space and time contain a manifold of pure *a priori* intuition, but are also conditions of the receptivity of our mind, conditions under which alone it can receive ideas (*Vorstellungen*) of objects, and which therefore must always affect the concepts of those objects. But the spontaneity of our thought requires that this manifold be gone through in a specific way, taken up and connected if a proposition is to be made out of it. This act I name synthesis.[12]

What this means is certainly not immediately obvious. To begin with, however, we learn from Kant's Logic[13] that empirical and pure concepts are distinguished thus: 'A pure concept is one which is not derived from experience (*Erfahrung*), but its content (*Inhalt*) originates from the understanding.' This is elaborated in a footnote:

> The empirical concept comes from the senses through the comparison of objects of experience with one another. All it derives from the understanding is the form of generality. The reality of these concepts rests on the actual experience from which as far as their content (*Inhalt*) is concerned, they are generated. But whether or not there are pure concepts which as such come simply from the understanding independently of all experience is something which metaphysics (i.e. transcendental philosophy) must investigate.

So far, Kant's doctrine is this. Starting from our perceptual acquaintance with oaks, elms, cedars, &c., we proceed by leaving

[12] B 102.

[13] Ak. ix. 92.

out differences of size, shape, colour, &c., to construct the general idea (later called the empirical schema) 'tree'. Parallel with this process, pure concepts which we do not make but which are part of our equipment as human beings are conceived as referring to a 'pure manifold'.

I do not think that 'pure concept' or 'pure manifold' can be clarified at this point, but some of their meaning at any rate can be extracted from the ensuing passage on 'synthesis'. The first paragraph, Ich verstehe aber . . . urteilen wollen,[14] is concerned only with general logic. It is a little difficult to follow because Kant's use of *Erkenntniß* here, and indeed throughout his work, is rather like Plato's use of ἐπιστ μ and Leibniz's *cognitio*. It has no single word in English to correspond to it except 'cognition', and 'cognition' is in this context a word made up by philosophers to translate 'Erkenntniss', &c.[15] We cannot, fortunately, talk in English of 'having a knowledge'—or 'a number of knowledges' about something; and 'distinct' and 'confused knowledges' are impossible. Kant, however, does not regard any of these locutions as even peculiar. He has, too, a distinction between *die Erkenntniß* and *das Erkenntniß* which is not of great importance though it adds a further complication.[16] In these circumstances, to translate *Erkenntniß* by 'cognition' confuses rather than clarifies his view, though it sometimes saves trouble and I must admit that I have used it myself. Sometimes 'knowledge' will do, more frequently 'proposition' or 'statement' is to be preferred.

In the light of this the paragraph under consideration may be paraphrased: '"Synthesis" means combining ideas (words)[17] so as to comprehend the complex of entities for which they stand in a single statement. Such synthesis is pure when the subject-matter is grasped *a priori* and not empirically (e.g. spatio-temporal patterns). We cannot begin to analyse our ideas (*Vorstellungen*) unless these are first given, and no concepts can arise analytically as far as their content (connotation) is concerned. It is synthesis of a given collection (trees, houses, triangles, cones) which first gives rise to statements. Such statements may be rough and confused, and therefore in need of analysis. But it is synthesis which

[14] B 103.

[15] *N.E.D.* Cognition 2 (b).

[16] Mellin, *Philosophisches Wörterbuch. Erkenntniss.*

[17] Cf. Ak. vii. 192. 'Denken ist reden mit sich selbst.'

reduces our complex perceptions to linguistic form and provides some usable reference for our statements. Synthesis is therefore the first item to consider if we wish to understand the origin of our scientific knowledge.'

All that Kant is doing is to refer in terms much too condensed for our comfort to the position set out at greater length in his Logic, namely that we acquire general words (*a*) by abstraction from what we see, hear, &c., (*b*) by using 'pure intuitions'.[18] Mellin explains thus:

> *A priori* propositions (*Erkenntnisse*) do 'have an object', but this 'object' is so called in virtue of a presupposition that there are things to be exhibited which have the form of this object. These 'objects' of pure knowledge are simply the *a priori* shapes of real things. The mathematician's triangle is the object of *a priori* knowledge but it is not a real or actual thing but simply the shape of a wooden or brass triangle, that is of every triangle which can be experienced.[19]

The short answer, then, to 'What is synthesis?' is 'It is what we do (*a*) when we construct significant sentences, (*b*) when we go through the process of organizing what we see, hear, &c., in such a way that the construction of significant sentences, however imprecise and confused, becomes a practical operation.'[20] This is repeated and slightly expanded in the next paragraph, *Die Synthesis überhaupt . . . verschafft*. Synthesis as such, or in general, we are now told is the bare or basic operation of the imagination. Now we have already seen that 'imagination' is an awkward word for Kant to handle. It fits badly with his treasured disjunction between 'sense' and 'understanding', yet it is needed, he thinks, as a bridge-builder between them. At this point, and still at the level of general logic, it clearly stands for the mental operations specified in (*a*) and (*b*) above, the developing of primitive talk to the stage of the articulated table of judgements is the job of the understanding. This is a further and more difficult synthetic operation, but it is still supposed to occur without our knowing what we are doing. 'We are seldom or never conscious of it.'

It is only in the next three paragraphs (*Die reine Synthesis . . . nicht leisten kann.* B 104) that Kant introduces the idea of pure

[18] Ak. ix. 141.
[19] Mellin, loc. cit. Cf. *K.U.* 454.
[20] Cf. J. Z. Young, *Doubt and Certainty in Science.* Fourth Lecture.

synthesis and transcendental logic seriously. Even now his remarks are anticipatory of what is coming in the *Transcendental Deduction*[21] rather than explanatory by themselves.

§ 5

It is the general idea of pure synthesis which provides us with the pure concept of the understanding; and Kant elucidates this by setting out his criteria for calling an activity 'synthetic'. These, together with his notion of counting as the paradigm of all developed thinking, have been discussed in Part II. He then goes on:

> But how to arrive at concepts, not of ideas, but of the pure synthesis of ideas is what transcendental logic has to teach. The first thing which has to be given us to fill the requirements of all *a priori* knowledge of objects is *the manifold of pure intuition*; the *synthesis* of this manifold by the imagination is the second, but this still does not yield any knowledge. The concepts which give *unity* to this pure synthesis, and which consist solely in the idea of this necessary synthetic unity are the third factor which contributes to the formulation of *a priori* propositions about a given object, and these rest on the understanding.[22]

Evidently this is a crucial passage in Kant's exposition of the nature of transcendental logic; equally evidently it is extremely hard to interpret with any precision. The general idea of the 'pure concepts or categories', whether it is sound or not, is unmysterious. The point here, however, is that Kant obviously means something important (*a*) by his contrast between general and transcendental logic, (*b*) by his assertion that the latter has 'lying before it a manifold of sensibility *a priori*, which the transcendental aesthetic provides to give material to the pure concepts of the understanding without which they would be without any reference (*Inhalt*) and therefore completely empty', (c) by his further reference to this manifold of pure intuition and the synthesis of it by imagination.

What, then, does 'the manifold of pure intuition' mean? The temptingly simple answer is 'space and time are pure intuitions, and therefore these are what Kant had in mind in these references'. But this will not do as a complete answer, though it be-

[21] A 119. [22] B 104.

comes clear enough as Kant goes on that he did attach meaning and importance to the idea that space and time themselves as well as spatio-temporally determined things were synthetic in character. But to suggest that this is what he has primarily in mind in the passages before us seems to me to strain the meaning of *das Mannigfaltige* very hard; for it is not a technical word, but is roughly equivalent to 'a variety of . . . ', or 'an assortment'. A box of mixed chocolates could be said to 'contain a manifold', but space and time could hardly be said to contain or to consist of a lot of little spaces and times, though Kant sometimes talks as if they were. It is much more natural to take Kant's references here to be to the figures with which plane and solid geometry are concerned and with the diagrams which represent the movements of solid bodies in Newtonian mechanics. The *a priori* science derived from these is what Kant calls 'Phoronomy', and he deals with it in the first section of *M.A.N.* It is contrasted with *Dynamic*, which is concerned with the physical properties of matter, impenetrability, elasticity, &c. The distinction corresponds to that between 'mathematical' and 'dynamical' in the *Analytic of Principles.* It is not a very good one, but to deal with it in any detail requires a study of eighteenth-century physics which would be out of place here.[23] The reason why Kant's references are so enigmatic is simply that for him 'mobility' is an empirical concept and as such cannot find any place in the *Critique.* It must be relegated to *M.A.N.*

The upshot is that the pure concepts, quantity, quality, relation, and modality, or, in their expanded form, unity, plurality, &c., are explicitly tied to bodies in the Newtonian technical sense; and this commits Kant from this point in his exposition onwards to an awkward use of 'transcendental'. For to say that an argument or a proof is transcendental commits us at least to the assertions (*a*) that it is not based on empirical evidence, (*b*) that it deals, not with things but with our knowledge of things in so far as this is *a priori,* and (*c*) that it is the foundation of an actual *a priori* science. Now in one sense the categories clearly fulfil these requirements since they are the concepts on which pure physics, as expounded in *M.A.N.*, is founded; but in another, as the concepts on which all judgements of experience as distinct from mere judgements of perception rest, their validity is assumed by all

[23] See Adickes, *Kant als Naturforscher*, especially vol. i, pp. 271–92.

empirically grounded statements whatever. The second claim is obviously wider than the first and might be taken as including it, but Kant's view is that the first claim must be established in order to justify the second. Hence in the *Transcendental Deduction* both claims are put forward. Transcendental synthesis and transcendental knowledge are now regarded as the essential precondition of, or counterpart to, empirically discoverable psychological processes which Kant maintains could not occur unless their transcendental support could be guaranteed.

V

TRANSCENDENTAL KNOWLEDGE: THE TRANSCENDENTAL DEDUCTION IN A

INTRODUCTION

IT is in the *Transcendental Deduction* that the problem of time which Kant's doctrine of inner sense involves first obtrudes itself seriously into his solution of 'How is pure physics possible?' So far, with reservations to which attention has already been drawn, he has taken it for granted that 'space and time provide a manifold of pure intuition' which can be 'brought to concepts' by the understanding; but it becomes increasingly clear that this is much too simple to be just asserted when the implications of the Tetens view of the way in which mental processes work are accepted. For this view does give rise to an intractable 'How possible?' question, namely, 'How can we explain the fact that creatures whose mental equipment is what ours is taken to be can have any knowledge of a temporal order of events which is independent of the order in which events are perceived by us?'

This is a lot more difficult than the problem presented in the *Aesthetic*, for there, when once it is granted that space and time are the forms of all our immediate awareness, the validity of Euclidean geometry is *ipso facto* demonstrated, since whatever is perceived must be spatio-temporal, and therefore subject to the laws of geometry. But the admission that the pure concepts are forms of thought does not entail the conclusion that phenomena must be subject to them. It is possible that our perceptual experience might not conform to them. Perception of succession does not obviously commit us to the causal axiom, and 'fate' and 'chance' are used in our language.

THE TRANSCENDENTAL DEDUCTION IN A

§ 1

The Meaning of 'Objective'

The *Transcendental Deductions* in *A* and *B* are rather like variations on a theme. Sometimes Kant finds a variation so interesting and important in itself that the theme is superficially forgotten, but it is always there if one listens carefully. This is more evidently the case in *A* than it is in *B*, and that is why the analyses of Vaihinger, Adickes, and Kemp Smith enjoyed at one time considerable popularity. It is quite clear that Kant is not consistent in his employment of 'sense', 'imagination', 'synopsis', 'recognition', and so on. But the geological analogy of 'strata' is not a happy one for explaining his thought in these sections of the *Critique*.

Kant's theme throughout both *A* and *B* is synthesis. The variations fall into two groups, transcendental synthesis and empirical synthesis, and within these into syntheses of sense, imagination, and understanding. The question to be asked is, 'For what recognizable mental processes do these revolting technical phrases stand?' I have tried to answer a good deal of this question in Part II. What remains is the central distinction between 'empirical' and 'transcendental'.

Now it is undisputed that Kant's 'revolution' in philosophical thinking about thought in general and scientific thought in particular lies in his insistent repetition that thinking is an activity; it is something we do, not something that happens to us, and to describe it as a kind of contemplation is to misrepresent it. This is the nerve of his criticism both of Leibniz and of Hume. More specifically and in a different idiom, what Kant really tries to drive home is that what we do when we come to know for certain that a proposition is true is much more like what we do when we build a house or fight a campaign in accordance with a preconceived plan than it is like what happens to us when we go round a corner and get a first view of the Jungfrau or the Matterhorn.

We must be careful, however, not to press this distinction to the point of maintaining that looking at things and making true generalizations about things are completely distinct from one another. It is not the case that we can describe either fully without reference to the other; 'without sensibility, no object would be given to us, without understanding, no object would be thought. Thoughts without content are empty, intuitions without concepts are blind.'[1] Hence substances in the traditional sense, or things in themselves in Kant's terminology, are not the kind of entities about which human beings can know for certain that any pro-

[1] B 75.

position is true, and what we have to ask is 'What objects are there about which we can obtain certain knowledge?'

The general position which Kant seeks to establish is strikingly like that maintained by many modern physicists. As Max Born puts it:

> The root of the matter is a very simple logical distinction which seems to be obvious to anyone not biased by a solipsistic metaphysics, namely this; that often a measurable quantity is not a thing, but a property of its relations to other things. To give an example; Cut out a figure, say a circle, of a piece of cardboard and observe its shadow thrown by a distant lamp on a plane wall. The shadow of the circle will appear in general as an ellipse, and by turning your cardboard figure you can give to the length of the axis of the elliptical shadow any value between almost zero and a maximum. That is the exact analogue of the behaviour of length in relativity which in different states of motion may have any value between zero and a maximum. . . . It is evident that the simultaneous observation of the shadows on several different planes suffices to ascertain the fact that the original cardboard figure is a circle and to determine uniquely its radius. This radius is what mathematicians call an invariant for the projections produced by parallel projection.[2]

Unfortunately Kant was handicapped in his attempt to state his position along this line by the doctrine of inner sense. For it looked to him, rightly or wrongly, as if his fundamental difficulty was, 'How, since all my perceptions are successive and independent of one another, can I ever come by the idea of anything constant or invariant in nature at all?' It is in his search for an answer to this question that he commences his operations in *A* by scrutinizing the 'empirical syntheses' of apprehension, imagination, and recognition, for he is convinced that these, which are admitted and psychologically verifiable facts, could not happen in the absence of what he calls 'transcendental syntheses' which are their foundation.

So far the going is fairly easy. The combined effect of the doctrine that what we know about for certain are phenomena and not things in themselves, and of the special theory of inner sense is that Kant has to postulate transcendental synthesis of some sort. The difficulty is now to say just what these processes are. I do not think that Kant ever solved this to his own satisfaction; he

[2] Born, op. cit., pp. 48–53. See also pp. 104–6.

returned to it in the *Opus Postumum*, but by then he was too old to make any progress. I suspect, too, that the question was wrongly posed and therefore insoluble anyway. His line in both *A* and *B*, however, was that, since we are in possession of pure forms of intuition and pure concepts of the understanding, the combination of these must be assumed to provide the background of non-empirical certainty which is needed to explain our empirical knowledge of phenomena. This, as it stands, is not very informative, and a good deal of the hard work involved in understanding the *Deductions* and the *Principles* consists in the elucidation of it.

The fundamental conception which holds Kant's doctrine together is that of the 'original, transcendental, synthetic unity of apperception', on which as he emphasizes throughout, the possibility of experience depends. It is fruitless to attempt any simple exposition of Kant's argument here except in very general terms. It may help to understand what he has in mind if we start by looking at a different approach to what I think is basically the same difficulty. It is indeed the approach adopted by Kant himself in his very sketchy deduction in *Proleg.*, §§ 18–20.

Any experience, however hallucinatory, which admits of being described at all, has a spatio-temporal setting. It is a series of events in the autobiography of someone, and therefore possesses a kind of unity. But this unity and the space-time order which it includes are private. This formulation is too abstract to be convincing, but a good instance of what I have in mind is provided by the erotic phantasmagoria in the brothel episode in *Ulysses*.[3] There is a sort of lunatic coherence about it, but it could not be maintained that the episodes had to follow one another in the order in which they occur, or even that any of them had to happen at all. Nothing connects them but the fact that they are all episodes in the life of Mr. Leopold Bloom. In Kantian language we have here an (imaginary) instance of the synthesizing activity of the subjective unity of apperception.

Suppose now that a biographer or historian records that at midnight on 16 June 1904 Mr. L. Bloom entered a house in Tyrone Street, Dublin, what is asserted is a public, checkable fact. It has a definite position in a common world of space, time, and material things. The record could, if the evidence survived, be proved or disproved. It belongs to objective apperception. This,

[3] James Joyce, *Ulysses*, Bodley Head edition, pp. 410 ff.

however, is still empirical. What is transcendental is the analysis of 'space', 'time', and 'material thing' or 'phenomenon' which Kant holds is necessary in order to give the vital distinction between subjective and objective apperception any significance.

To put it differently, the technical concepts which the Newtonian physicist finds indispensable for the description of phenomena are the foundation of the ordinary language words, 'before', 'after', 'behind, 'because', &c., which the plain man has to use to recount even to himself his very private experiences. At this point it should be noted that Kant would deprecate the use of 'experience' here if it is to be used as a translation of his word *Erfahrung*. The latter belongs exclusively to the vocabulary of objective apperception, that is, to the vocabulary of the scientist and the historian. The patient relating his 'experiences' to the psychiatrist does not need it. He is a patient because he does not need it.

All this goes a good deal beyond the specific purpose Kant had in mind in *Deduction A*. I claim no more for it than that it seems to me to illustrate the kind of job he was trying to do. There certainly is, he claims, experience in his sense of the word; and he does not see how there could be, consistently with the doctrine of inner sense, unless we were possessed of some specifiable *a priori* knowledge of phenomena. Pure science of nature is an indispensable prerequisite of objective apperception.

§ 2

The Threefold Synthesis (A 95–114)

Kant's aim is therefore to show the *a priori* conditions on which the possibility of experience rests. His method is to take the results of empirical analysis for granted and show in every case the necessity for parallel *a priori* synthesis on which empirical syntheses depend. This process eventually reveals the necessary objective validity of the categories as well as the synthetic character of the physical world.

Two points especially require to be noticed to make the argument clear:

1. It is taken for granted that our apprehension is subject to time in the sense previously noted. Perception is supposed to consist of a temporal series of spatial (but non-temporal) images, that is, to be cinematographic. The spatial unity is

given by synopsis (identical, I think, with what is called imagination in the *Metaphysical Deduction*).

2. The three syntheses are not independent. The third presupposes the second and the second presupposes the first. Together they are an account of the activity of the understanding in the production both of the empirical and *a priori* knowledge.

The synthesis of apprehension in intuition

(*a*) General Remark (see 1 above), paragraph 1.
(*b*) Empirical Synthesis, paragraph 2.
(*c*) Transcendental Synthesis, paragraph 3.

The empirical point is the familiar one that to perceive a large object as *one* I must somehow combine in a single whole data which I apprehend successively. The transcendental counterpart is that the ideas of space and time demand a similar act.

Both acts are plainly synthetic in character.

The synthesis of reproduction in imagination

(*a*) Empirical Synthesis, paragraph 1.
(*b*) Transcendental Synthesis, paragraph 2.
(*c*) Relation of reproduction to apprehension, paragraph 3.

This is explicitly only a development of the previous synthesis. The association of ideas is here accepted as a fact, from the existence of which Kant infers that there must be some regularity in our impressions to make association possible. The transcendental argument is that we can maintain *a priori* the impossibility of any knowledge, even of the characteristics of space and time, apart from the admission of an *a priori* synthesis corresponding to the empirical faculty of association.

The synthesis of recognition in a concept

The first two syntheses are in themselves relatively unimportant. The third is vital to Kant's whole view of objectivity and is so difficult to follow that it must be analysed in greater detail. We may observe in advance:

(i) That here also there is first an empirical (A 103–6, end of 1st para.) and then a transcendental argument (to the end of § 3, A 110).

(ii) That the aim of the whole section is to connect the empirical activities with the *a priori* synthesis of the pure understanding, and to show that the possibility of the former depends wholly on the performance of the latter. That this will be the case is already to be expected as a result of the first two syntheses.

(iii) That the central theme of the *Analytic* and also the general character of the *Deduction* begin to emerge at this point with the introduction of the notion of experience as involving objects and not merely perceptions.

Empirical synthesis (A 103–6)

First paragraph (A 103). No serial process, such as counting, can possibly be performed except by an agent who recognizes at least implicitly the character of the act of synthesis which it involves. Reproduction alone will not give an explanation of any such process.

Second paragraph (A 103–4). Reflection shows that all formation of concepts really, though not obviously, involves an act of just this kind. For general ideas, house, dog, &c., are formed by abstraction from particulars which are apprehended successively. For this, apprehension, reproduction, and recognition are all necessary, but the essential point is that the complete process involves, though covertly, an awareness by the agent of his own act which is essentially of the same kind as that required for counting. Concepts therefore presuppose synthesis, and they are presupposed by all knowledge.

Third paragraph (A 104). The last statement requires development. It is evident that we do 'refer ideas to objects' in asserting that colours, tastes, &c., belong to things, and are not just states of our consciousness. But when we ask what the 'object of ideas' can be, the only possible answer seems to be a Lockean substance, a 'something, I know not what' or unknown *x*, since by definition it does not correspond to any ingredient in our knowledge.

Fourth paragraph (A 104). The function of this unknown is to unify our sensa. Apart from it they would be quite haphazard and disconnected. Data of sight, taste, smell, &c., are combined in the concept of an orange, and the combination is conceived as objective, or necessary.

Fifth and sixth paragraphs (A 105–6). The ground for this

unification cannot be discovered in *x*, since we have, as already stated, no immediate acquaintance with *x*. Hence it must be looked for in our own consciousness, and we must admit that we are constrained to consider data as combined in objects by a necessity which is internal to ourselves. We produce synthetic unity in our own experience, though of course we could not do so unless that experience were of such a kind as to make the synthesis possible. Further, we produce this unity by a process of combination according to a rule. The nature of that rule is not yet known, but the general idea of it is given by consideration of something which we undoubtedly construct, such as a triangle. Here it is not difficult to see that the awareness of the unity of the object depends on awareness of the synthetic character of the act required for its construction. Apart from this, it disintegrates into three straight lines, or any other possible analysis of the data contained in it. A similar argument holds of the notion of body. Thus it appears that all empirical thought presupposes a unity of apperception, or self-conscious unity of the thinker, apart from which there could be no concepts and therefore no thought at all.

Transcendental Synthesis (A 106–10)

Paragraphs 1–4 (A 106–8). Empirical thought has now been shown to depend on the self-conscious unity of the subject. But this consciousness of unity cannot be empirical or immediate. Mere observation or inner sense, however defined, can give no awareness of a necessary unity either of self or of anything else, and I cannot possibly discover the ultimate ground of synthetic unity by simple inspection. I can discover it only inferentially, by realizing that the possibility of any experience depends on the existence of it.

We are thus brought to the doctrine of a transcendental unity of apperception which is the only possible explanation of that empirical unity of self-consciousness which has already been proved necessary for all empirical thought. That such a transcendental unity is required to make possible even our ideas of space and time can easily be seen by reference to the preceding sections.

Pure self-conscious synthetic activity is thus the *a priori* ground of all concepts, just as pure intuitions of space and time are the ground of empirical intuitions.

In fact the existence of an active self-conscious subject synthesizing its experience in accordance with *a priori* laws which spring from its own nature is the only possible basis for the activity of empirical thinking which admittedly does happen.

Paragraph 5 (A 108–9). The ground for maintaining the existence of a transcendental unity of apperception is that only thus can the reference of our thought to objects be made possible. We may now again ask exactly what 'object' is to mean, and we can now answer that it is the correlate of this transcendental unity, namely the transcendental object. For the moment this can only be described as non-empirical and $= x$, i.e. unknown. It 'refers only to that unity which is to be met with in any manifold of knowledge which stands in relation to an object'. What it is can be specified only when we have discovered what are the principles of synthetic unity in accordance with which self-consciousness operates.

A great deal has been made of the fact that the chief passages in *A* in which mention is made of the transcendental object were omitted by Kant in his revision for *B*. On the strength of this it is sometimes argued:

1. That in the section on the *Paralogisms* in *A*, the transcendental object is explicitly identified with the thing in itself. (This passage is actually retained in *B*.)
2. Almost all mention of the transcendental object is suppressed in *B*.
3. This shows that by 1787 Kant was losing his faith in the existence of things in themselves and was attempting to replace his pre-Critical subjectivism by a thoroughgoing phenomenalism.

This seems to me to be inconceivable. It is true that Kant's theory of knowledge admitted of a development in which the doctrine of the thing in itself would have been superfluous, but the whole argument of the Second and Third *Critiques*, to say nothing of the *Opus Postumum*, makes it perfectly clear that Kant himself remained faithful to it to the end. He could not do otherwise without making nonsense of the entire Critical Philosophy. This, however, does not mean that the term itself or Kant's employment of it can be regarded as felicitous.

The difficulty in respect of it arises mainly from the account which he gives in the first and leaves intact in the second edition section on the *Paralogisms* of the Transcendental Employment of Concepts. He wishes to distinguish (quite unnecessarily) between two methods of employing the pure categories, both of which must be condemned by Criticism as illegitimate.

The first is their employment in relation to objects of experience beyond the limits which experience itself can justify (e.g. the assertion or denial of the infinite divisibility of matter). This is transcendental. The second is their employment in relation to non-empirical objects as such (e.g. God). This is transcendent. Having made this distinction, he tends, not unnaturally, to describe the real but non-empirical substratum of physical objects as a transcendental object. In fact, in terms of this distinction it might equally be described as transcendental or transcendent, which in itself demonstrates the futility of the distinction.

This tiresome use of the phrase in the *Paralogisms* is connected with, but distinct from, Kant's employment of it in the *Deduction* and the passage on *Phenomena and Noumena* (both in *A* only). There it stands for the 'bare correlate of the synthetic unity of apperception'. It is the *a priori* element in phenomena viewed in abstraction from their material content. This is in accordance with his original account of transcendental knowledge as concerned not with objects but with our knowledge of them in so far as this is possible *a priori*.

In this sense, too, the transcendental object is not in itself a possible object of knowledge. It denotes simply the formal characteristics which render intelligible the manifold of pure or empirical sensibility, the ground of synthetic unity in phenomena.

What happens in the illegitimate employment of reason is that this purely formal ground of synthetic unity is hypostatized as if it were something efficacious and substantial though non-empirical in character, and we thus come to credit ourselves with constitutive knowledge by means of pure reason (i.e. knowledge of the thing in itself, now identified with the transcendental object).

This hypostatization is especially unfortunate in the case of the idea of the self with which Kant in the *Paralogisms* was mainly concerned. For it is only too easy to confuse the real self with the transcendental unity of apperception, and to suppose that acquaintance with the wholly formal unity of synthetic activity implied by the 'I think', which accompanies all my ideas, constitutes awareness of a transcendent self.

The Categories (A 110–14)

The principles, or functions of unity, are in fact the categories, for they are required for thought in general and are therefore the indispensable conditions of knowledge. But it is now clear that they must also be embodied in objects, since these are to be regarded as synthetic unities. Hence it follows that the transcendental or non-empirical objects of our thought must be subject to the categories, and the deduction of them is thereby accomplished; it has been proved that the categories must be valid of phenomena and the remainder of the *Analytic* shows how this is possible. Phenomena are non-empirical in the sense that they are not empirically intuited but known, as we find later, by imagination operating through the categories and the pure forms of intuition.

§ 3

The relation of the understanding to objects and the possibility of non-empirical knowledge about them (A 115–30)

Kant's argument in this section is not too difficult to follow as long as we are content with a general statement and do not press the distinction between 'transcendental' and 'empirical' very hard. Superficially he is trying to escape from an 'egocentric predicament' and to put forward a kind of logical construct view to do the job for him. To suppose this, however, is to stand his whole argument on its head. His case is that we could not even talk significantly about 'private experiences' or 'inner lives' except by contrast with publicly verifiable statements (*Erkenntnisse*) referring to a common world; indeed his general line is very much more like that of Ryle than it is like that of Ayer. 'Not only is it false that ideally we should talk, not in the vocabulary of gateposts, but only in the vocabulary of sensations, but we cannot describe sensations themselves without employing the vocabulary of common objects.'[4] Now Kant's argument might run like this: it is a mistake to suppose, as empiricists do, that any number of statements of the form 'It looks to me . . .' are logically equivalent to 'There is a . . . .'[5] Unless we realize the force of 'There is a . . .' statements, 'It looks to me . . .' statements have no force at all. But to get the point of 'There is a . . .' we need both the concept of a

[4] Ryle, *Concept of Mind*, p. 237. Cf. Kant, A 120–1.
[5] Warnock, *Berkeley*, pp. 176 ff.

thing, which commits us to the concept of an order in nature independent of particular percipients, and the concept of a self or perceiving subject. 'It looks to me...' makes sense only because it involves the idea both of a real order and of a spectator regarding this order from a specifiable point of view. In Kant's language the unity of the manifold in a subject is synthetic. Hence pure apperception provides a principle of the synthetic unity of the manifold in any possible intuition (*Anschauung*).[6]

But while the general line here seems clearly to be defensible and indeed correct as far as ordinary material object language is concerned, Kant's detailed argument is questionable. For it is not obvious what the objective correlate of the synthetic unity of apperception is supposed to be. Yet this is just what we have to know if this section is to contribute anything to answering the question, 'How is pure physics possible?'

There seem to be three possible lines for Kant to take: (1) The correlate of the synthetic unity of apperception is the transcendental object, whose character is expounded in the synthesis of recognition in a concept. (2) It is the intuition *a priori* of space and time as synthetic wholes. (3) It is the recognition by us *a priori* of spatio-temporal connexions between perceptual data. Actually, he uses all three. (2) is the nerve of the transcendental arguments on the synthesis of apprehension in intuition and the synthesis of reproduction in imagination; (1) is used in the synthesis of recognition in a concept; (3) is the mainstay of his contention (in the passage under consideration here) that the understanding prescribes laws to nature. Hence, unless we are prepared to fall back on the patchwork theory, there is no alternative to supposing that he regarded all three lines as the same, and so that he could use whichever of them was convenient. I believe that he did take this for granted, relying on his general doctrine that all recognition of connexion is the work of the understanding, and that the rules for connecting, all connecting, are provided once and for all by the categories.

Now, if this were the case, it would follow that the language of Newtonian mechanics and the language of everyday life differed from one another only in detail, if at all, and that all significant speech was built on the Newtonian categories. But this, though Kant never noticed it, is not obviously true; and when the cate-

[6] A 116.

gories of quantum physics replace those of Newton, there is at least a case for saying that it is obviously false. So Kant's belief that 'synthesis' in his very general use of it will open all the philosophical doors for him, was at least over-optimistic. Probably he was uneasily aware of this when he tried to bring in Transcendental Imagination to ease the transition from the *Deduction*, which is almost wholly concerned with ordinary speech, to the *Principles* which are mainly concerned with the language of Newtonian mechanics; but the link is a very brittle one.

VI

TRANSCENDENTAL SCHEMATISM

§ 1

In discussing Kant's idea of schematism in general, I have already explained that 'schema' as commonly employed in the philosophy of the seventeenth and eighteenth centuries is not at all a difficult or mysterious word. A schema (or scheme) is simply a plan or diagram, such as the ground plan or elevation of a building or the diagrammatic presentation of the positions of the heavenly bodies. It may thus without difficulty be thought of as standing midway between the general idea 'house' and a particular construction of bricks and mortar. It is general, in that the number of houses which can be built to a single plan is infinite, yet, as contrasted with the notion 'house', it is particular. Furthermore, and this is important to Kant's argument, while it is itself an intuitable particular inscribed on paper it also provides a rule or principle in accordance with which the builders must act. To explain how we produce such schemata is, he believes, impossible, at any rate he has no account to offer of it. They must be conceived as products of imagination which is here productive and not merely reproductive of past experiences. It is clearly a synthetic activity, and we may therefore expect to find that the empirical use of it, which is all that we have so far considered, is ultimately dependent on a transcendental synthetic activity, and this turns out to be the case. In fact Kant's starting-point is that if we start with any general notion and aim at producing a concrete instance of it, we are bound to evolve a schema to mediate between the two. If we now apply this notion to general logic, we find that the middle term in the syllogism may plausibly be regarded as the schema which mediates between the major and minor, and hence the faculty of 'judging', that is, of discovering the appropriate middle term, is directly connected with imagination regarded as a natural gift which can never be taught.

To this it may well be objected that no real distinction between concepts and schemata can be drawn on these lines. There are no general ideas which are foreordained to be always middle and never major or minor terms. To argue thus, however, would be to miss Kant's point. His conception of the schema is essentially functional. A plan to a person who does not know what it is for is not a plan at all but a picture, and the whole doctrine of the syllogism takes it for granted that the minor is not subsumable under the major without the intervention of a middle term. It is possible to use plans or maps as decorations, but that is not to use them as plans or maps. They are then no longer employed as schemata but as ornaments.

§ 2

After this preliminary comment we must consider the special problem raised by the character of the pure concepts of the understanding. It is at once clear that if these are to have any application to reality it must be possible to group particulars under them. A concept with no concrete instances is for Kant empty. We must therefore ask how such grouping is possible, since it clearly presents a difficulty which the bringing of particulars under empirical concepts does not. This difficulty arises from the complete absence of homogeneity between pure concept and concrete particular. Whether Kant's argument here is sound is exceedingly dubious, but in fact it depends on his theory of the formation of empirical concepts and cannot properly be considered apart from this. Such concepts, e.g. house, are, he believes, all formed by abstraction from particulars. They are thus never purely intellectual, but have always a sensuous element which makes the bringing of particulars under them possible. They are thus potential schemata, and he would, perhaps rightly, have regarded 'house-ness' and 'horse-ness' as mere monstrosities. Pure concepts, on the other hand, are wholly intellectual, since they are bare forms of thought and utterly different from sensible particulars. How then can the latter conceivably provide instances of them? That they must somehow do so is already proved by the *Deduction* since, in the absence of such categorial determination of experience, all knowledge of objects and therefore all thought has been shown to be impossible. Thus the problem is not, 'Do the pure concepts require schematization?' but rather, 'Since the pure concepts must be schematized, what are the schemata which must be employed to make their employment possible?'

Clearly this is a problem for transcendental logic, since the whole possibility of physical knowledge *a priori* depends upon the answer to it. The argument of the *Deduction* should convince us that an answer is to be found and has also given a clear indication of where to look for it, but that is all. We may expect to discover that there are transcendental as well as empirical schemata, that the former are products of transcendental as distinct from empirical productive imagination, and that the material for them is provided by the pure intuitions of space and time. It must also be noted that here as elsewhere there is a sharp contrast between the situation for general and for transcendental logic. The former, since it takes no account of content, can never determine *a priori* what the schema of any given concept must be. This, as we have seen, is a matter for empirical judgement only. Transcendental logic, however, is wholly *a priori* and must therefore say of its pure concepts that there is one way and one only in which their schematization is possible. It must in fact determine not merely that but also how their application to phenomena is possible.

§ 3

In the *Aesthetic* space and time are conceived as given. It is assumed that they are formal intuitions as well as forms of intuition, and that their essentially synthetic character needs no discussion at that stage. In the course of the *Deductions*, however, it has become apparent that this account is too simple to serve the purposes of transcendental logic, and in particular the problem raised by the nature of time is by now clearly fundamental to the whole Critical view. We are in fact compelled to ask how space and time are themselves constructed, though it must be remembered that this inquiry is logical and not historical in character and is therefore in no way inconsistent with their givenness in the *Aesthetic*.

Now time is the form of inner sense. All our awareness is temporal, and anything which can be an object to us must be capable of being apprehended in a specific way. In fact the physical world, if we are to know it, must be temporal, since, if it were not, it would be no object of possible experience for us and could therefore have no valid synthetic *a priori* propositions formulated about it. A timeless real could be for us an object of thought, since it involves no contradiction. It could never be an object of knowledge, since it would lack the intuitional element on which the possibility of knowledge, as distinct from belief, must for us always depend.

But the pure concepts are wholly intellectual and therefore completely divorced from time, which is a form of sense. They must therefore somehow be brought into relation with it to render the subsumption of phenomena possible. Hence the function of the transcendental schemata is to mediate between temporal phenomena and timeless categories and thereby exhibit the necessary realization of the latter in the former.

Time itself is synthetic as well as intuitional. Hence what is required is an exposition of its nature designed to show that all the categories are in fact involved in it, and that therefore they are necessarily valid of all phenomena which are subject to it, i.e. of all objects of possible experience. The transcendental schemata are therefore ideas produced by the faculty of transcendental productive imagination which provide a rule in accordance with which time itself and phenomena *qua* temporal admit of being imaginatively constructed.

We must now return to the categories set out in the metaphysical deduction. There are twelve of them, but each group of three can properly be considered as a whole, since the units which compose it are not independent of one another. We are left, therefore, with quantity, quality, relation, and modality as the concepts which require schematization. It is understood that the articulation of these (unity, plurality, &c.) will be apparent in the corresponding schemata, and we find that in the case of the categories of relation these articulations are so important and difficult to appreciate that they receive in the *Principles* separate and lengthy consideration (*Analogies of Experience*).

The schemata which mediate between these categories and phenomena are set out in the following table; the last column indicates the section in the *Principles* in which each is fully treated.

A full explanation of this table would anticipate the argument of the *Principles* which follows, but some preliminary elucidation may be useful.

		Schema	Treated in
1. Categories of Quantity	Unity Plurality Totality	Number	Axioms of Intuition
2. Categories of Quality[1]	Reality Negation Limitation	Degree	Anticipations of Perception
3. Categories of Relation	Subject and predicate Ground and consequent Reciprocity	Permanence Cause Necessary simultaneity	Analogies of Experience
4. Categories of Modality	Possibility Actuality Necessity	These are not strictly categories at all and have no schemata	Postulates of Empirical Thought

1. *Quantity.* Space and time (and therefore all phenomena *qua* temporal) are what Kant calls extensive magnitudes, that is wholes formed by the successive addition of parts. They therefore require for their apprehension the concept of number, which Kant conceived as involving an intuitive element. As such it can be regarded as the schema which mediates between the pure concept of extensive magnitude and the concrete notion of a physical body as a whole consisting of extended parts.

2. *Quality.* Anything real must possess degree as well as extension. This is obvious in the case of secondary qualities. Any shade of red has an intensity which could always be greater or less than it actually is, and which may therefore be conceived as lying between complete reality and complete negation. The application of this idea to time and phenomena is complicated.

3. *Relation.* The connexion between schemata and categories needs no special explanation. It would have been more helpful if Kant had not substituted the names of the schematized categories for those of the pure categories of the *Metaphysical Deduction*, but his meaning is not in doubt. The first category gives the bare idea of something which is essentially subject and not predicate. To actualize this we must conceive a physical substance permanent

[1] Kant is not here depending on the arbitrary description of the positive and negative character of judgements as their 'Quality' in the traditional Logic. His point is that the notion of intensive quantity (degree) really does express the combined categories of being, not-being, and limitation, and that these actually do correspond to the positive, negative, and infinite judgement forms. The term 'quality' is accidental and unimportant.

in time, &c. The complete interdependence of the three relational categories becomes clear in the course of the *Analogies of Experience*.

4. *Modality*. The categories of modality are, in Kant's view, categories only by courtesy. They deserve far more careful treatment than he was in a position to give them.

§ 4

As we have already noted, Kant himself gives no satisfactory analysis of imagination in spite of its extremely important function both in the schematism of concepts and indeed throughout the *Critique*. In the absence of any such authoritative pronouncement, however, some attempt must be made to find out what his position actually was. At the level of empirical psychology the situation is easily understood. Imagination is simply the faculty by which we create images for ourselves in the absence of objects. It is thus naturally differentiated into (*a*) reproductive imagination, which recreates impressions which have been perceived previously (this, when accompanied by self-consciousness, is practically indistinguishable from memory) (*b*) productive imagination which creates impressions. This faculty is active

(i) in the amplification of actual impressions;[2]
(ii) in fantasy and day-dreaming;
(iii) in deliberate artistic creation.

Corresponding to this empirical faculty, we have also transcendental imagination which differs from it not in the manner of its operations but simply in the subject-matter with which it works, which is the pure manifold of space and time as distinct from empirical data of sense. The precise nature of this operation is exceedingly difficult to follow, but Kant believes that he has expounded it in the *Schematism* and *Principles* and has proved (*a*) that it provides an indispensable link between pure concepts and pure intuitions, (*b*) that in the absence of these transcendental elements empirical thought and empirical self-consciousness would be impossible.

Up to this point what he wants to maintain is clear enough, though the arguments by which he supports his view are far from easy. But there is a more serious difficulty than that of mere

[2] e.g. Hume's missing shade of blue (*Treatise*, I. 1) and many other instances cited in works on Gestalt psychology.

complexity in the doctrine of transcendental imagination which arises from the dual function which the faculty has to perform. Imagination, we are told, is a faculty distinct from sense on the one hand and thought on the other. By its schematizing activity it provides a necessary link between them. Further, it is capable of doing this because as a faculty it partakes of the character both of thought and of sense. Its products are both synthetic and intuitable.

At this point Kant really ceases to speculate about it, although the resulting situation is clearly unsatisfactory. It admits of development in two directions, each of which is inconsistent with Kant's claim to have produced a view which avoids the errors of both rationalism and empiricism.

A. It may be argued that Kant's doctrine of imagination really amounts to an admission that the hard-and-fast distinction between sense as receptivity and thought as spontaneity has broken down. The third faculty is nothing more than a *deus ex machina*, and, while it is supposed to create a bridge between the other two, it in fact supersedes them. If this is the case, the Critical Philosophy needs drastic reconstruction. It should properly set out from the notion of a self capable of generating its own objects by a fundamental synthetic process and show how the Kantian machinery of cognition arises necessarily in the course of the self's development. It is evident that such a process, if it could be carried out, would vastly increase the rationalist as against the empiricist element in the view. It would also explain, as Kant himself was never able to do, the articulation of the fundamental activity of synthesis into specific forms of thought and sense, and we may argue that he himself foreshadowed it in much of his mature work. There is, however, no evidence to show that he accepted it, and he could not have done so without completely revising his views both on science and on ethics.

B. It may be maintained, on more or less positivist lines, that the whole doctrine of imagination is in the end simply a psychological hypothesis. The multiplicity of forms of both sense and thought is then a purely empirical matter, and any *a priori* account of their nature and origin must itself be hypothetical.

This may be the case, but it is certainly not what Kant himself believed.

§ 5

To clarify Kant's references to transcendental imagination or to reconstruct it in such a way as to support his claim that 'we have a pure imagination as a fundamental faculty of the human soul which lies at the base of all *a priori* knowledge and by means of which we bring the manifold of intuition on the one hand into connexion with the necessary unity of apperception on the other'[3] are not operations which can be carried out satisfactorily. It is possible, however, to throw some light on what Kant was worried about and what produced the cramps which occurred when he tried to expound his view; for he was not just muddled, he had something important to say.

The root of his embarrassment was his addiction to contemporary psychological theory, especially the notion of inner sense. This led him to pose his questions in the 'How possible?' idiom and to suppose that observable psychological processes must be as it were underpinned by unobservable processes before they could be regarded as epistemologically respectable. What he was really asking was the perfectly sensible question, 'Where do the accounts offered by Locke and Hume of the way in which we come to know truths about the world break down?' He was sure that both left out something important, and jumped to the conclusion that this something had to be a piece of unobservable psychological clockwork. There had to be a transcendental faculty whose activity 'made possible' empirical perception, memory, imagination, and so on. As we have already seen, the doctrine of inner sense which he accepted did not leave it open to him to analyse scientific theory-making except along this line.

It was, as things turned out, a bad line. His successors, confronted with the dichotomy stated in the last section tended, under the leadership of Hegel, to opt firmly for alternative A and it was a good many years before serious consideration of the possibilities offered by alternative B took place.

Now, however, the logic of the inductive sciences has been considerably straightened out and we can see more clearly the kind of thing which Kant was aiming at. As usual his mistakes contributed a good deal to the more defensible positions occupied by his successors.

[3] A 124.

The most illuminating discussion of the real point at issue in the schematism is Prof. Braithwaite's analysis of the relation of models to theories.[4] This is already highly condensed and cannot be summarized without distortion. I will merely mention two important points in it which are highly relevant to what I take to have been Kant's central position. In the first place, models are in some sense *like* reality. They are intuitable. And in the second, the essential characteristic of a good model is that conclusions reached by the study of it conform to the conclusions reached by straight theorizing. At the same time it is not necessary, as Kant, developing Locke's theory of abstract ideas, believed that it was, to regard the spatio-temporal model provided by Newtonian mechanics as 'making possible' or standing behind our theorizing about physical reality; nor is anything gained by calling such models 'transcendental schemata' and attributing their creation to a special faculty named 'transcendental imagination'. It is their function in scientific theorizing, not their origin or their alleged resemblance to products of empirical imagination which is philosophically interesting, and Kant, because of his preoccupation with empirical psychology, attends too little to this.

[4] Braithwaite, *Scientific Explanation*, chap. iv.

VII

THE ANALYTIC OF PRINCIPLES

§ I

AXIOMS AND ANTICIPATIONS

THE idea of schematism underlies the whole of Kant's discussion of the *Principles*. The application of it to the doctrines of the *Axioms* and the *Anticipations* is, on the whole, straightforward. Number is the schema of quantity. It brings the pure category of quantity into relation with the pure manifold of space and time, and thus makes possible the realization of the former in the latter. In the first place, this application is to space and time as such, and in the second to all representations *qua* spatio-temporal. The *Axioms* elucidate this.

Any spatial whole, Kant maintains, must be capable of generation by the successive addition of part to part; so can any extent of time. Indeed, one of the essential characteristics of space and time considered as objects of thought is that they admit of this kind of generation. It has already been observed that they are synthetic in character and this fact of numerability is the first kind of synthesis which is realized in them, corresponding to the first group of categories (quantity).

Presumably what Kant has in mind is that any solid can be conceived as a synthetic whole composed of an indefinite number of very thin layers, and its volume can be determined by regarding it in this manner. Space (and also time) regarded as objects of thought are therefore *tota synthetica*, or wholes of parts. This is not really inconsistent with the teaching of the *Aesthetic*, which maintains that as objects of sense they are *tota analytica* or wholes which are antecedent to their parts. It is meaningless to ask what they are really or in themselves, for in themselves they are nothing.

The argument of the *Anticipations* is identical in principle with that of the *Axioms*, though it is slightly harder to follow. The categories here are those of existence, non-existence, and limitation, grouped together perhaps not very fortunately under the title 'quality'. The schema which mediates between these and the pure manifold of time is that of degree. Kant's point appears to be that any degree of intensity may be regarded as a synthetic whole of intensities, just as any extensive magnitude may be regarded as a synthetic whole of quantities. This applies to time itself in the sense that empty time is a bare abstraction or limiting concept. The filling of time with events is something essential to its very existence, and the quality of this filling is the degree of reality which those events possess.

This argument is not very plausible or even intelligible apart from Kant's detailed view of the nature of the physical universe. He did in fact hold (1) that there was no empty space, (2) that matter occupied space intensively as well as extensively, (3) that the essence of physical things consisted in their being centres of force.[1]

Certainly it seems odd to maintain that time itself, and therefore all phenomena in it, is synthetically intensive as well as extensive in character, but this is what Kant's argument obviously requires, and he does actually claim that it is true.

§ 2

The distinction between the *Axioms* and *Anticipations* on the one hand and the *Analogies* on the other is of some importance. Briefly it is that phenomena, as far as the categories of quantity and quality are concerned, are themselves static. The fact that as wholes they have a temporal duration of their own is disregarded and we are concerned simply with their synthetic character as wholes. It is only in the *Analogies* that they are considered as wholes in time. Thus when a billiard ball is described as a synthetic whole, what is meant is that it possesses a specific character in virtue of which we are able to formulate propositions about it. Nothing happens to the billiard ball when we do this. The process occurs wholly in us. Suppose, however, that the ball is in motion, we have at once a different and more complex situation to deal with. The relations of the ball to other objects, and for that matter to its own qualities, have now to be conceived as synthetic in

[1] See above, p. 62, on the *Monadologia Physica*. There is no reason to suppose that Kant retracted the physical view which it contained, and indeed the illustrations in the *Anticipations* are themselves good evidence for maintaining that he continued to hold it.

character in spite of the fact that they are independent of our awareness in a sense in which the syntheses already considered are not. The problem of the *Analogies* arises from our concern with an objective as well as with a subjective time-sequence, whereas in the earlier categories the sequence was subjective only; and for this reason, Kant maintains, the principles expounded in the former differ in two important respects from those of the latter. In the first place they require a discursive as distinct from an intuitive proof, and in the second they are regulative and not constitutive in character. The point here is that the argument of the *Axioms* and *Anticipations* holds without qualification of all data of sense whether pure or empirical. Secondary as well as primary qualities necessarily possess some temporal extension and some degree of intensity. They cannot, however, properly be conceived either as substances or causes. Hence the distinction between mere impressions and physical objects now becomes of vital importance since the latter only are subject to the principles of the *Analogies*. The problem of physical science is to discover the detailed character of phenomena, and this can be done only experimentally. All that the principles claim to do is to establish purely general rules which make such experimentation valid. Furthermore, the proof of such rules, since they refer to objects, must be transcendental. It must show that the possibility of experience depends on the determination of objects by them, and this is what Kant means by a discursive proof. It should also be observed that substances and causes do not admit of construction in the same way as extensive and intensive magnitudes; but as this line of thought is fully developed in the *Analogies* themselves, it is unnecessary to explain it in advance. I shall here consider only the distinction between the subjective and objective time-sequences, which is in fact far less difficult than is sometimes supposed.

Kant is not suggesting that there really are two time-sequences, one in me and one in the physical world. This would be nonsense. All events occur in one and the same time. His problem, which is a real one, can be made clear by an example. Suppose that a choir is singing about 300 yards away from me and that this event is being broadcast. If I turn on the radio I shall hear the actual choir as an echo of the wireless. I might infer from this order of experience that the actual singing was subsequent in time to the broadcast reproduction, but if I did, I should be mistaken. In Kantian terminology the order of apprehension is A–B (broadcast–singing), the order in the object is B–A (singing–broadcast). No physical problem arises out of this discrepancy. It is quite simply explained by the fact that sound travels rather more slowly than light. There is, however, a Kantian problem as to the manner in which we come to know about the physical as distinct from the psychological order of events and it is with this that Kant is concerned in the *Analogies*.

§ 3

Analogies of Experience

Of the three *Analogies* (dealing respectively with permanence, succession, and coexistence) the second is easily the most important and is actually the final answer to the question 'How is pure physics possible?' I shall therefore deal with it at considerable length and give only a brief account of the first and third.

General Principle of the Analogies (B 218–24)

1. B 218–21. Statement of the general line of the argument which is to follow.
2. B 221–3. Distinction between the mathematical and dynamic categories.
3. B 223–4. Reminder that the 'objects' with which the *Analogies* are concerned, although they are reality as contrasted with the data of empirical imagination and sensibility, are nevertheless spatio-temporal and therefore phenomenal.

This introduction suffers, as Kant's introductions usually do, from extreme over-condensation. Some obscurity arises also because it takes for granted much of what follows as well as of what precedes it. What Kant wants to maintain is:

1. The synthetic *a priori* propositions of pure physics which depend on the categories of relation provide rules of procedure for scientific investigation and do not by themselves yield knowledge of the characteristics of objects. They tell us, indeed, that there must be an *x* which stands to A in exactly the same relation as B stands to C. But this information does not enable us to state the nature of *x a priori* in the way in which a similar proportion sum in mathematics does.

2. These rules of procedure are valid only if there are necessary time-relations.
3. Such relations can hold only between objects. Relations between empirical sense-data, it has already been maintained, are themselves merely empirical and are objective only inasmuch as they are recognized as dependent on a transcendental system known *a priori*.
4. The synthetic nature of time is a presupposition of such a system, since it is a necessary condition of the transcendental apperception on which empirical apperception depends.
5. The synthetic nature of time is conceivable only if objects exhibit the three modes of time, since empty time is not an object of possible experience.
6. Therefore objects must provide instances of necessary permanence, succession, and coexistence.

This doctrine is supported by two other lines of argument which Kant sometimes employs. The first approaches the problem from the side of judgement and is as follows:

1. 'The stove is hot' and 'The fire warms the stove' are both judgements of experience, in that they assert necessary relations between things and not merely *de facto* conjunctions of sensa.
2. The significance of such judgements depends on the existence of objects subsumable under the schematized categories of substance and cause.
3. Such objects must exist, since their existence is a necessary condition of the idea of time itself and therefore of all apperception.

The second depends on the doctrine of inner sense, and runs:

1. All my ideas are successive.
2. The possibility of apperception requires that they should be referable to objects.
3. Such objects must themselves be phenomenal, since they provide a basis of necessary synthetic unity, whereas acquaintance with things in themselves, if it were possible at all, must always be empirical only.
4. Hence they must be spatio-temporal and, as such, exhibit the three modes of time.

The argument from judgement is most prominent in *Proleg.*, that from inner sense in the *Second Analogy*.

The essential point is that objective apperception, which the *Deduction* has shown to be a condition of possible experience, depends on the synthetic character of time, which is itself dependent on the existence of objects having necessary temporal relations. The precise character of these relations remains to be demonstrated in the *Analogies* themselves.

First Analogy

The argument here, whether valid or not, is straightforward. It is that the permanence or conservation of *something* in nature is a necessary condition of the idea of time itself. No mere succession of evanescent states could give rise to such an idea unless they were recognized as states of a permanent self. But, Kant maintains, we have no awareness of any such self, and therefore the states must admit of being referred to something else, though we cannot know *a priori* what that something is. Empirical science alone can seek to determine whether it is, e.g., matter, motion, or energy. But as the name substance is usually given to the permanent in reality, we are entitled to maintain *a priori* the truth of the proposition with which the *Analogy* opens.

Second Analogy

The *Second Analogy* has suffered the same fate as the *Deduction* in *A*. It is almost unanimously condemned as a more or less haphazard collection of five or six different proofs of the same proposition hurriedly thrown together for publication. Certainly it is not a happy piece of exposition even by Kantian standards, which in this respect are not very high, but I do not believe that it is as muddled and repetitive in substance as it appears on a first reading to be.

Before we attempt to analyse it there is much to be said for asking what, in the light of the contents of the *First Analogy*, we should expect the *Second Analogy* to contain. For although the form of Kant's exposition is often defective, no one is likely to deny that his belief in the importance of architectonic, that is of orderly and systematic statement, was extremely lively. This leads us to anticipate:

1. An introductory passage added in the second edition.
2. The proof of the principle.

3. Some explanatory remarks on the meaning of the principle in relation to experimental science.

All these are in fact present. The proof is officially given on B 246 and 247[2] (*Der Beweisgrund dieses Satzes . . . einer solchen Erfahrung ist*), though it actually begins rather earlier on B 244 (*Zu aller Erfahrung . . .*). There is an introductory section added in *B* which gives a condensed account of what the proof is to be, and the concluding pages, B 247–56, are occupied with explanation and development. What, then, is the point of the argument from B 234 to B 245? One would expect it to deal with special difficulties in respect of the *Second Analogy* which do not arise in the case of the *First Analogy* and which must be cleared up before the demonstration can be regarded as satisfactory. I believe that this is actually what it sets out to do, though it performs its work in a singularly obscure and clumsy manner.

In order to elucidate the argument we must bear in mind that the nerve of proof in the *Analogies* from Kant's point of view is that necessary temporal relations between things are a condition of the possibility of time itself; that the *First Analogy* has demonstrated the necessity for a permanent in phenomena in contrast to which the succession of their determinations can be apprehended; and that the *Second Analogy* proposes to go beyond this and to prove that the nature of time, and, therefore, the possibility of experience, depend on the validity of the causal axiom, that is, on the subjection of objects to a rule of temporal succession.

Now on Kant's own view this contention raises several difficult problems, since it seems at first sight as if the *First Analogy* has proved rather too much. We might ask:

1. Granted that succession as well as permanence is involved in time, why must that succession be necessary? Since permanence is already established, one might suppose that random succession would be sufficient.
2. What is to be said of the general empiricist argument that causality is inferred from observed regularity in our perceptions?
3. Granted that experience demands succession according to a rule, why must that rule apply to physical objects and not to perceptions as such? For if permanence is provided by

[2] References from the text are given here as the division in paragraphs is unsatisfactory.

the object, the requirements of time could be met by any contrasting succession.

4. Granted that necessary succession in objects is a condition of our empirical awareness of objective sequence, do we still need to prove that it is also a condition of the possibility of time itself?

These at least seem to be the problems with which Kant concerns himself, but the fact that his discussion throughout is dominated by his theory of inner sense and of the successive character of all our perceptual awareness lends colour to the view that he is constantly repeating himself and offering alternative proofs of the same proposition.

If these considerations are sound, the *Analogy* should be analysed as follows:

1. Addition in *B*. The synthesis of imagination determines inner sense only as regards the order of my own activities. It tells me nothing about any objective succession. Furthermore, time itself cannot be perceived, hence some activity of thought is required to provide the necessity which time as an *a priori* form demands. We must in fact conceive the relation between what precedes and what follows in time as necessarily determined, i.e. as irreversible. Thus causal interconnexion between objects is a condition of objective time relations without which apperception is impossible.

This, like the introductory paragraph of the *First Analogy*, is incomplete as it stands. It requires considerable supplementation from what follows, but is probably intended only as an indication of the fuller exposition in the sequel.

2. B 234–6 (*Die Apprehension . . . ist das Objekt*). A general psychological introduction to remind the reader of the position taken up in the *Deductions* and to indicate the application of the view to the present problem. It emphasizes the distinction between ideas and physical objects, but also repeats that the latter are phenomena and not things in themselves. Kant's point is as usual that succession of apprehension does not entail succession in the object. We have therefore to discover what is the criterion by which we are able to satisfy ourselves empirically that such succession really occurs. In his terminology we must ask how the manifold is connected in the phenomenon itself, or what criterion

have we of the empirical truth of the proposition 'A follows B' as distinct from 'I hear A after I hear B'?

3. B 236–40 (*Nun lasst uns . . . was geschieht, möglich*).

Necessary succession. Reflection shows that empirically we assert objective succession only where the order of our perceptions is irreversible (the ship as contrasted with the house). In other words by an objective order we mean and can mean nothing but an order which is determined by a rule, that is, a necessary order.

This passage is concerned not with succession in objects but simply with the distinction between different contents of perception; the contention is that any order (e.g. the succession of night and day) which is regarded as objective is so regarded in virtue of its subordination to the general criterion of irreversibility which entails necessity.

4. B 240–2 (*Zwar scheint es . . . möglich macht*).

Empiricism. The above view is to be contrasted with that of empiricism. We do not, Kant points out, first recognize objective sequence and then discover inductively that some instances of it reveal necessity, though this is what a casual examination of experience suggests. Further investigation proves that all objective sequence is really recognized as necessary and that this recognition must actually be antecedent to the distinction between causal and other sequences of which empiricism claims to give an account.

5. B 242–4 (*Wir haben . . . empirisch erkennen*).

Necessary succession in the object. Kant claims here to prove that just as, in the *Deduction*, it was found that all connexions between sensa presupposed the existence of objects as grounds of synthetic unity, so here the admitted capacity to apprehend some sequences of sensa as objective presupposes the necessary temporal succession of phenomena.

The last paragraph (*Wenn es nun . . .*) is intended to give the transcendental ground of this necessity, namely, that any merely contingent sequence in pure time is unthinkable since the character of time as a form of *a priori* intuition would thereby be destroyed. All succession in phenomena *qua* spatio-temporal must therefore be necessary and not contingent.

6. B 244–7 (*Zu aller Erfahrung . . . Erfahrung ist*).

Proof of the causal principle. I find the detailed argument here extremely difficult to follow, though the general line of Kant's thought is fairly clear. It is that, as time itself is not an object of possible experience, the parts of it cannot be said to determine one another's position. We cannot date particular times with reference to absolute time. But the parts of time must be necessarily determined, because of the *a priori* character of time as a whole. Hence spatio-temporal phenomena must date themselves, i.e. must stand in necessary time relations to one another to make objective sequence thinkable. In other words phenomena must be subject to the schematized category of cause and effect, and therefore the category of ground and consequent is in fact valid in respect of phenomena, which is what the *Second Analogy* sets out to prove.

7. B 247 (*Hier äussert sich . . .*) to end of *Analogy*.

Explanatory remarks. These are mainly important as showing the intimate connexion which Kant recognized as existing between the notions of substance and cause. They make it perfectly clear that Kant was not merely maintaining a simple regularity view of causation, though this is in any case obvious from his previous arguments.

Third Analogy

The *Third Analogy* stands or falls with the *Second Analogy* and requires no special comment. The argument for objective coexistence, by which is meant necessary connexion between physical bodies at a given moment, adds nothing to that in favour of necessary succession. The relation of it to the disjunctive form of judgement is a little obscure, but Kant's idea was presumably that disjunction implies a possibility of choice between alternatives, which is reflected in the reversibility of perception in the case of coexistent realities.

VIII

THE TRANSCENDENTAL ARGUMENT OF THE *ANALYTIC*

THE transcendental argument in the *Analogies*, especially that contained in the *Second Analogy*, is the culmination of Kant's answer to the question 'How is pure physics possible?' It is the nerve of his reply to Hume. Yet it is remarkably difficult to say in detail just what it is that Kant believes himself to have demonstrated. The central point of the difficulty is his extremely casual use of the word 'cause' itself. Certainly 'cause and effect' refers to a relation, and the relation is one of necessary or objective succession; but we cannot really try to elucidate this somewhat obscure form of words without asking what kind of entities are supposed to stand in this relation to one another. At the beginning of the *Analogy* the answer seems clear enough. In the house and ship illustration we are concerned with events, and Kant's argument is that we must know that these have an order of their own which may or may not be identical with the order of our perceptions; for if we did not know this, statements which assert that our perceptual order is sometimes different from the true sequence would have no meaning for us, and then, by the argument of the *Deductions*, there would be no synthetic unity of apperception. Hence the concept of nature as a connected order of happenings of which our private perceptions are projections could never arise. Now this is clearly a forcible argument for Hume to meet. In fact it never occurred to him because of his uncritical use of 'body'. The existence of bodies was for Hume, as it had been to Locke, a datum and not a philosophical puzzle. Kant, however, had come to realize in the *Deduction* that the transcendental object which physics postulates is not in the ordinary sense a thing at all. It is not in itself an object of perception but a 'ground of synthetic unity'. Indeed it is the primitive ancestor of Braithwaite's *Theoretical Concept*.[1] Now if we look at Kant's argument from this point of view, his talk about objective succession anticipates,

[1] *Scientific Explanation*, chap. iii.

though certainly in a confused way, very modern theories indeed, for the whole idea of cause and effect as a kind of metaphysical link connecting things (in the plain man sense) with one another is thus abandoned.

Kant, however, did not give up the old-fashioned view. Like Einstein at a later date, he felt that events were a poor substitute for good solid things.[2] Indeed in the last resort both Kant and Einstein ranged themselves with Dr. Johnson against Bishop Berkeley. Kant covers this up by saying, 'This [account of] causality leads to the concept of action and thus to the concept of force; and so we come to the concept of substance';[3] but he excuses himself from developing this statement.

To put the point very briefly we may say that Kant never made up his mind about what Whitehead called the 'pushiness' of things. The whole weight of his transcendental argument inclines him more and more to saying that this is just an anthropomorphic relic.[4] Human beings push one another about, but it makes no sense to say that physical objects do; all that pure physics is concerned with is rules of synthesis. But Kant could not finally exorcize, any more than Einstein could, his plain man conviction that nothing but a substance could be a *vera causa*. Indeed, I doubt whether in the end he ever quite gave up the idea that things in themselves were what provided the impetus which made the world go round and which somehow eluded scientific explanation. Braithwaite can say: 'The world is not made up of empirical facts with the addition of the laws of nature; what we call the laws of nature are conceptual devices by which we organize our empirical knowledge and predict the future.'[5] Kant meant something very like this, but he never quite said it.

[2] See Max Born's controversy with Einstein. *The Natural Philosophy of Cause and Chance*, chap. x and *Physics in my Generation*, pp. 204–6.

[3] B 249.

[4] Cf. Schlick, *Philosophy of Nature*, p. 90.

[5] Braithwaite, op. cit., p. 339.

IX

KANT'S ACHIEVEMENT

A GOOD way of appraising Kant's achievement in the philosophy of science is to compare the discussion in the first part of the *Critique* with that in the Clarke–Leibniz Correspondence.[1] This was first published in 1717. A German translation appeared in 1720 with a foreword by Wolff, and Kant was certainly familiar with it. Now Leibniz was universally recognized as being in the front rank of European philosophers and Clarke was of comparable standing. He was Newton's accredited representative in metaphysical affairs. Compared with them, Baumgarten, Meier, and Berkeley too, were regarded by those who knew their names, as trivial, and Wolff was at best a second-rater.

Bearing this in mind, it is with something of a shock that we find both Leibniz and Clarke steadily and without a moment's hesitation making use of theological propositions as premisses in a very high-level discussion on scientific philosophy. Indeed the whole thing started with a criticism by Leibniz of Newton's statement that space was *quasi sensorium Dei* and his idea that the planetary system might 'want a reformation' to keep it in good working order.[2]

> Sir Isaac Newton says [retorted Leibniz] that space is an organ, which God makes use of to perceive things by. But, if God stands in need of any organ to perceive things by, it will follow that they do not depend altogether on him, nor were produced by him.
>
> Sir Isaac Newton, and his followers, have also a very odd opinion concerning the work of God. According to their doctrine, God Almighty wants to wind up his watch from time to time; otherwise it would cease to move. He had not, it seems, sufficient foresight to make it a perpetual motion.[3]

Both Leibniz and Clarke took these points and many similar ones which cropped up in the course of their lengthy interchange with perfect seriousness. 'Might God have created the Universe earlier (or later) than in fact He did?' and so on.

[1] Edited by H. G. Alexander, University of Manchester Press, 1956.

[2] Newton, *Optics*, query 31. Alexander, p. 180.

[3] Mr. Leibnitz's First Paper, §§ 3 and 4.

It is not to the point to say that the logic of these difficulties was perfectly respectable and that they can be and have been resurrected in decent, antiseptic costumes. The Principle of the Identity of Indiscernibles still deserves and receives a good deal of philosophical attention. What we find curious is that neither Leibniz nor Clarke saw anything incongruous in the theological costumes. The Principle of Least Action was also thought in the eighteenth century to have important theological significance,[4] and even now attempts are made to extract support from Heisenberg's indeterminacy principle for theological and ethical doctrines.

Kant's first contribution to our thinking about science, to which he righty attached enormous importance, was to show up this kind of talk for the nonsense it is. He removed knowledge to make room for belief. The controversy between Born and Einstein is logically in the same area as that between Clarke and Leibniz, but it is conducted in an entirely different idiom, and the difference is vital to clear thinking about scientific explanation.[5]

This part of Kant's achievement is no longer open to serious controversy; but Kant's view of scientific explanation itself, with which we have been mainly occupied, is in a less secure position. We cannot here be quite sure what he meant because he was not clear himself. Much of the trouble arises from his determined attempt to reconcile his acceptance at its face value of accepted psychological doctrines, especially those of Hume and Tetens, with his increasing awareness of the part played by deductive reasoning in empirical science; and this puzzle was one to which the new way of ideas inexorably led. The distinction between reality and appearance, which is important and simple to use in ordinary language for the purposes of daily life, was converted into a metaphysical fantasy. If we concentrate on this aspect of Kant's view it is not surprising that intelligent critics from Jacobi[6] to Russell have found the whole thing nonsensical. The *Ding an sich* is just a hopeless stumbling-block which Kant can neither justify nor abandon.

I have tried to show that this view of what Kant meant, though

[4] See Max Born, lecture on 'Minimum Principles in Physics', *Physics in my Generation*, pp. 55 ff.

[5] Born, op. cit., pp. 204–6, *Natural Philosophy of Cause and Chance*, chap. x.

[6] Vaihinger, *Commentar*, ii. 36–37.

it can certainly be supported by many quotations from the *Critique*'s, is a misrepresentation. His central contention, however much it is obscured by his unsatisfactory linguistic apparatus, is his reiterated conviction that the distinction between things in themselves and phenomena is not a distinction between two types of entity but a distinction between two alternative ways of talking about the world. The fact that he never got clear what this meant is in a way not very important. What matters is that in his attempts to do so he certainly laid the foundations of the philosophical analyses of scientific method which both philosophers and scientists today find usable as bases for further discussion and development. If we accept as sound Braithwaite's conclusion that 'the business of a philosopher of science is primarily to make clear what is happening in scientific thinking. If this clarification has the secondary effect of encouraging scientists to construct deductive systems and to use theoretical concepts freely, it will, I believe, assist in the progress of science as well as in the better understanding of what science is doing',[7] we can see clearly enough where Kant was successful and where he fell short. As compared with all his predecessors he did bring about a tremendous clarification of what was happening in scientific thinking; he also had more than a glimmering of insight into the conception of deductive systems and theoretical concepts. He failed, understandably enough, because he never considered the possibility that Newton and Aristotle were not the last words to be said on physics and logic; and, even more, because he took it for granted that Locke, Hume, and Tetens had finally cleared up empirical psychology.

[7] Braithwaite, op. cit., p. 358.

INDEX

PRINTED IN
GREAT BRITAIN
AT THE
UNIVERSITY PRESS
OXFORD
BY
CHARLES BATEY
PRINTER
TO THE
UNIVERSITY